The Colonial Compromise

The Colonial Compromise

The Threat of the Gospel to the Indigenous Worldview

Edited by
Miguel A. De La Torre

LEXINGTON BOOKS/FORTRESS ACADEMIC
Lanham • Boulder • New York • London

Published by Lexington Books/Fortress Academic
Lexington Books is an imprint of The Rowman & Littlefield Publishing Group, Inc.
4501 Forbes Boulevard, Suite 200, Lanham, Maryland 20706
www.rowman.com

6 Tinworth Street, London SE11 5AL, United Kingdom

Copyright © 2021 The Rowman & Littlefield Publishing Group, Inc.

All rights reserved. No part of this book may be reproduced in any form or by any electronic or mechanical means, including information storage and retrieval systems, without written permission from the publisher, except by a reviewer who may quote passages in a review.

British Library Cataloguing in Publication Information Available

Library of Congress Cataloging-in-Publication Data

Names: Tinker, George E., honouree. | De La Torre, Miguel A., editor.
Title: The colonial compromise : the threat of the gospel to the indigenous worldview / edited by Miguel A. De La Torre.
Other titles: The threat of the gospel to the indigenous worldview
Description: Lanham : Lexington Books/Fortress Academic, [2020] | "Festschrift for Tink Tinker"—Preface. | Includes bibliographical references and index.
Identifiers: LCCN 2020039745 (print) | LCCN 2020039746 (ebook) | ISBN 9781978703728 (cloth) | ISBN 9781978703735 (electronic) ISBN 9781978703742 (pbk)
Subjects: LCSH: Indians of North America—Missions—History. | Indians of North America—Religion. | Christianity and culture—North America. | Christianity and other religions—North America. | Racism—Religious aspects—Christianity. | Indians, Treatment of—North America—History. | Decolonization.
Classification: LCC E98.M6 C65 2020 (print) | LCC E98.M6 (ebook) | DDC 99.7—dc23
LC record available at https://lccn.loc.gov/2020039745
LC ebook record available at https://lccn.loc.gov/2020039746

*For those who have not
had the privilege
of sitting in a classroom
with Tink*

Contents

Preface		ix
Introduction: A "Real Blanket Indian": A Short Biography of Tink Tinker *Loring Abeyta*		1
1	Christianity, Compromise, and Colonialism as Existential Threats to Indigenous Peoples *Edward P. Antonio*	5
2	Faith and Facts: Dismantling Colonial Constructions *Natsu Taylor Saito*	25
3	"Words Have Meaning": Reflections on a Vector of Tink Tinker's Indigenist Scholarship *Ward Churchill*	41
4	At Cross-Purposes: Conversion, Conscripted Compromise, and the Logic of eurochristian Religious Poetics *Roger K. Green*	55
5	I'm an Indian Too? *Miguel A. De La Torre*	71
6	Niin Naandamo: The Cultural Logics of Kinship and the Theological Detour of Prayer *Mark D. Freeland*	87
7	Impostor God: De-Christianization *Barbara Alice Mann*	103

8	On the Use of the Bible for Mental Colonization *Steven T. Newcomb*	117
9	jesus, the gospel, and Genocide *Tink Tinker*	133

Bibliography	161
Index	175
About the Contributors	183

Preface

FESTSCHRIFT FOR TINK TINKER

Probably no greater honor can be given to a scholar than for their colleagues to compose and contribute articles demonstrating said scholar's influence upon their thinking and writing. A festschrift becomes a collection of essays which investigates and interrogates the scholarship of the academician being celebrated. The chapters which comprises the festschrift demonstrates how the scholar's body of works—over decades—has made a major contribution not just to a select group of academicians, but also to discipline, and more importantly, to the general public. There was never a question that a festschrift honoring the contributions to the field made by George E. Tinker, affectionately known as Tink to his friends, would eventually be written. The only question was when. Coming on the heels of his retirement from the academy, this festschrift becomes our way, as authors of these multiple chapters, of expressing our gratitude for the impact Tink has had on our own intellectual pursuits, as well as our own lives. But the appearance of this book does not indicate Tink has nothing more to contribute. There is still much to learn from him as he feverishly continues writing future articles and manuscripts. We are simply pausing, at this moment in his life, to recognize how much we have been shaped by his academic rigor, his uncompromising commitment to justice, and his activism seeking to create a better world, not just sit on the sidelines composing theses.

I was first introduced to Tink through his piercing writings. While a seminarian at a fundamentalist school, my wife gave me his book *Missionary Conquest*, and insisted it be immediately read. Taking a break from the required readings of Eurocentric scholars (predominately with Germanic names) for my classes was a welcomed interruption. For a Latino only exposed to the Eurocentric theological cannon, reading from a person of color, who rejected all which I was already suspecting to be problematic, was a breath of fresh air. His book ignited a thirst to explore the writings of other scholars of color, specifically those of my community. I made haste to the school's library and checked out every book I could find written by an Indigenous scholar, an African American scholar, an Asian American scholar, and of course, a Latinx scholar. Hence began my true education which took me on a very different trajectory than when I enrolled at Southern Baptist Theological Seminary, a path which began the decolonization of my mind, a task yet to be achieved.

My newfound knowledge meant I would never find a pastorate, so I did what every unemployable graduate student does, I continued my education, obtained a PhD. This lead to a tenured-track position at West Michigan College. Years later I applied to and was hired by the Iliff School of Theology, which has the reputation with the academy of being the social justice school. This was the school where Tink taught as professor of American Indian Cultures and Religious Traditions. There he regularly taught a course which literally blew students' minds, *The History of Christianity and the Modern World*. Tink and I soon began a friendship which lasted years based on many academic discussions and arguments, always pushing each other to sharpen our thoughts. Regularly over drinks, along with our mutual friend Luis Leon (who was writing a chapter for this book but passed away before it could be finished), we participated in much bantering as we maneuvered to see who would get stuck with the check. We also explored the impact the colonization process not only had on our lives, but also on our scholarship. We wrestled with the multiple compromises expect of us as scholars of color. How do we continue our academic pursuits for excellence without first bleeding to death from the multiple micro-aggressive papercuts?

I confess, when Tink announced his retirement (a very Eurocentric concept I keep reminding him) after thirty-two years of service, I was upset. Frankly, Tink presence on the Iliff faculty was one of the main reasons I was attracted to the institution. And while we still on occasion meet for coffee, his retirement is a tremendous lost for Iliff and its students, as well as for me. I did inherit his spacious office, so that space continues to witness the quest for justice. And it is from that same space, which he has occupied for so many years, that this festschrift came together.

I am grateful to the many authors of this book, some who as indigenous scholars work and struggle besides Tink in the quest of justice. Others contributors worked with him as colleagues at Iliff, while still others were his students. All have honored me with the trust of editing their works so that together we can honor Tink. This festschrift is a testimony of our respect and high esteem for Tink's academic contributions and our love for the man.

In a commitment to see the continuation of the work which Tink began, all proceeds of this festschrift go to the Tink Tinker Program Endowment Fund charged with ensuring his educational legacy goes forth, in perpetuity, to future generations. We who are the contributors to this volume humbly hope this text will also be considered as a contribution in recognizing and celebrating Tink's legacy.

—Miguel A. De La Torre

Introduction
A "Real Blanket Indian": A Short Biography of Tink Tinker

Loring Abeyta

In the summer of 1981, Tink Tinker stood with his dad on a hill just west of Gray Horse and Fairfax, Oklahoma overlooking the great bend of the Arkansas River. From that vantage point, his dad could point in several directions and name the land allotments that had been assigned to his father, his ten aunts and uncles, and his granddad after the 1906 Osage Allotment Act. As citizens of the Osage nation, Tink and his dad understood that this knowledge and memory were key to asserting their undiminished sovereignty, no matter the vicissitudes of colonial history. The allotments were 657 acres (surface rights) for each enrolled member. At that time, the older Tinker also remembered the names of every white family that had ended up with ownership of those Osage family allotments, all but one of them alienated from Indian ownership. The one that remained was held not by an Osage relative but by one of his mother's Cherokee cousins. Those days spent with his dad on the Osage Reservation shaped the rest of Tink's life both as an academic and as an American Indian activist.

Earlier that spring, Tink had made his first visit to the Pine Ridge Lakota Reservation on behalf of a national organization that had funded a community development project. Tink had been so struck by the existence of a huge new wooden sign held up by four creosote-soaked telephone poles at the Wounded Knee Massacre Site, announcing that it had been the "battle" of Wounded Knee, that he made the long trip back the next day to take a picture of the sign. Whatever, he asked himself, had become of Oglala Lakota pride? Alas, he arrived too late for the picture. All he found at the Massacre Site were the charred four-hole remnants those poles that had held the sign twenty-four hours before. Oglala pride, indeed! Tink could only think back to the American Indian Movement patriots (including his own relatives) that had been put under siege at the Massacre Site by a U.S. federal military force eight years before—and forever framed falsely by both the government and the press as AIM's "occupation" of Wounded Knee. Pine Ridge is located in what has been persistently the poorest or one of the poorest counties in the United States, so Tink built up his relationships there and frequently took an Iliff class for immersion visits on the rez, immersion in the context of modern colonialism and the Indian struggle to sustain their cultures in the midst of the resulting poverty. Those excursions were never the "oh, let us help you" romance of liberal eurochristians and their churches but were designed as moments of deep learning about a radically marginalized Other.

It was this indigenous cadence of learning and teaching that served as the bedrock of Tink Tinker's thirty-three years at Iliff School of Theology in Denver. At the time of his hire at the school, he had just finished a PhD in Berkeley and had already initiated an American Indian community outreach program in the Bay Area when Iliff recruited him onto their faculty in 1985. Tink taught courses across a wide waterfront, from praxis oriented social justice classes to heavier duty theoretical seminars at the doctoral level.

One mainstay was a doctoral theory seminar titled "Postcolonial Discourse and Other Myths," in which participants discovered that colonialism is very much alive and well, particularly in the persistent abjection of American Indians. I had the pleasure of co-teaching with Tink a theory course on race, gender, and class for twenty-five years in which he consistently and constructively challenged students to think again about their assumptions and biases at these critical intersections of social justice.

Tink retired from Iliff as professor emeritus of American Indian Cultures and Religious Traditions in 2018. Having published a half dozen authored and edited books, Tink also produced nearly a hundred published articles and chapters. Retirement has not slowed him down, to no one's surprise. Tink continues to research, write, and support students and young scholars at a pace that rivals his years of teaching and tending to indigenous community throughout the world.

In tandem with Tink's academic career, he served an important leadership role at Four Winds American Indian Council in downtown Denver for twenty-five years. His work at Four Winds incorporated important community political collaborations and actions, particularly with the American Indian Movement of Colorado. Tink stood on the front lines of many protests during actions in defense of indigenous rights over those years, and on multiple occasions over those years, he contributed testimony in legislative hearings for the effort to abolish Columbus Day in Colorado. This year, 2020, he finally enjoyed the success of the community in this effort.

Looking back, Tink remembers an exchange with a white christian minister after a presentation in which his introduction naturally included the fact of his Osage citizenship. The minister somehow missed this introduction of himself as Osage. Unhappy with Tink's mixed-blood light-skinned appearance, and to question the authenticity of Tink's presentation, she threatened Tink with the ultimate exposure: "Come back to Tulsa with me, and I'll take you up to Pawhuska and show you some *real* blanket Indians." After a long pause, an exasperated Tink finally replied, "Lady, those are Pendleton blankets you're talking about, and they cost a couple hundred each!" He turned the tables on this woman's threat to expose Tink's supposed fraud and asked her if she knew the name of the Osage principal chief, who just happened to be his relative, Sylvester Tinker. Such was the all-too-common experience through Tink's long career of speaking to white eurochristian folk. Yet he was never deterred from his own exposition of historical truth, invader colonialism, and the political realities of Indian country. And he never gave up on educating the eurochristian colonizer class.

In 2019 Tink was given Auburn Seminary's prestigious annual Walter Wink Scholar Activist Award, in recognition of a career lived as both a critical scholar and an Indian community activist. As Auburn's announcement of the award states, Tink's career combined

> efforts both fighting for American Indian justice and challenging eurochristian students and communities to recognize their own history of violence on the continent. His classroom teaching and his publishing is grounded upon the ideal of activist scholarship. His research and publishing have never been satisfied with merely advancing knowledge. Rather, he always tries to rock the boat of the status quo in order to point toward substantive change for justice.

It is impossible to sum up a career as distinguished as Dr. Tink Tinker's even with words as eloquent as those from the Auburn announcement of Tink's Walter Wink award. This award and this honoring of Tink reminds us that his scholarship, activism, community involvement, and especially his commitment to indigenous peoples is exactly the leadership and role model our world needs in these unprecedented and perilous times of the twenty-first century.

Chapter 1

Christianity, Compromise, and Colonialism as Existential Threats to Indigenous Peoples

Edward P. Antonio

I am interested here in the terms of the invitation to write for this book. The theme of the book is *The Colonial Compromise: The Threat of the Gospel to the Indigenous Worldview*. I will discuss the ideas of compromise, threat, gospel, and how they show up in the history of the relationship between colonialism and colonized subjects. I will not engage the theoretical notion of colonialism itself. Instead, I take the historical reality of colonialism as largely understood.[1] My premise is that "compromise" and "threat" are the dialectic through which gospel, construed in this essay as Christianity, and colonialism, operated in the encounter between indigenous peoples and Europeans.

Why address these categories? Does this not, in fact, reify the violence of colonialism against indigenous people beyond history by turning it into a philosophical question? There are several reasons why this is important. First, the everyday practices and discourses which were the substance of colonialism were sustained by many categories. Colonialism did its work through concepts, ideas, beliefs, and categories of thought. Colonial power was often deployed through language and ideology. Second, terms such as "threat," "compromise," and "gospel" carry a moral load, they implicate ethical analysis and evaluation of discursive practices. Indeed threat, gospel, and compromise are themselves such practices. Third, these terms have conceptual dimensions that call for theoretical analysis. Ultimately interrogating how these categories were deployed by colonial subjects and how we ourselves use them today will help us produce better forms of understanding and of "critique of power and ideology."

Did colonialism and the gospel really threaten indigenous worldviews? Was the gospel compromised by colonialism? Were indigenous responses to colonialism complicit in both the work of colonialism and in the work of Christian missionaries?

This essay explores how the categories of "threat," "gospel," and "compromise" work in the colonial experiences of indigenous people in Southern Africa and the colonial experiences of indigenous peoples in the United States. The consistency of these categories across colonial geographies and histories is remarkable. There are striking similarities in their usage which tell us a great deal about the global nature of western colonialism; they categories attest to the use of both similar and different strategies and tactics of colonial subjugation. Although I do not have the space to do it here, it can be argued that the same categories were part of the responses of indigenous peoples which they deployed through resistance, accommodation, the making of treaties and compromise. I will argue that these categories were complex and operated in ways that render the idea that indigenous peoples survived by "conceding" to predatory colonialism highly problematical. The essay argues that what appears to us now as regrettable concessions, compromises, legal treaties, and conciliatory settlements were, in fact, deeply rooted cultural ways of rejecting the logic of the European will to power which propelled the colonial project. The language of "concessions" into which we are beguiled because of the resemblances between treaty-making enforced by colonialism and indigenous democratic practices buys into the logic of power as understood by colonial masters. To "concede" in both Southern African and North American indigenous cultures was a way of refusing to turn one's culture and one's humanity into an absolute principle of relationality. It was an affirmation of openness and cultural solidarity which colonialism violated by its will to power. The fact that indigenous people were thoroughly subjugated is about the brutality of colonialism, not about the failure of their strategies not to "concede." Perhaps "concessions" and "treaties" are evidence for the extent to which indigenous peoples were democratic, welcoming, and inclusive. Colonialism exploited and violated these principles of human generosity. In European colonial thought concessions were extracted not given, they were a sign of weakness and ignorance. In any case, it is important to ask about the discursive context in which indigenous peoples used compromise, responded and reacted to the gospel and engaged and resisted colonialism. Although they are part of the same theoretical grammar, for the purposes of this essay, I will focus on comprise and not concessions.

THE LOCATION OF THE INDIGENOUS SELF

In thinking about Native American and African indigenous responses to colonialism I must first locate myself. I am a Tewe from central Mozambique. The Tewe are a Bantu group of people whose cultures and customs are in many ways like those of the Shona of Zimbabwe. Mozambique was a Portuguese colony. I am also a Shona. My father moved to Zimbabwe when he was young in search of a job and a better future. Zimbabwe, which at the time was called Southern Rhodesia, was a British colony. There he married a Shona woman from the Manyika clan from the eastern highlands of Zimbabwe. The Manyika are part of the Shona. I was born in Zimbabwe. I was born Tewe and Shona. I speak both languages. I also speak, write, or read twelve languages, including English and Portuguese. I grew up speaking Shona, English, and Portuguese. My father's name when he came to Zimbabwe was Phillip Zuzee Antonio. Notice that these names are all colonial names. He came to Zimbabwe with his identity already claimed by colonial systems of nomenclature. At birth I was given the name Edward Phillip Zuzee Antonio. Notice that these names are all colonial. Like my father, I had my identity claimed by colonial systems of naming and identification. Part of what I shall argue in this essay is that the threat to "the indigenous worldview" has always been deeper, more insidious, and thus more real because its structure and claims are supplied by colonial processes of interpellating indigenous identities whose goal is nothing less than to denude indigenous peoples of their very beings. I shall use interpellation in various sense in this essay and I will explain these latter. For now, I use it to designate the modes of dominating and subjugating the other by which colonial logic possess and dispossess colonial subjects by naming and renaming them. Colonial systems of naming and renaming were modes of subjugation, domination and above all owning and possessing the other while at the same time denying the humanity of the other.

I cannot remember my father ever talking about his own indigenous first name. He told us that his real last name was Gatawa, that his mother's name was Zambuko (my daughter's middle name). He also told us that our "totem," our Spirit Animal, the concrete exemplar of our family and clan identity was the Zebra (Mbizi). On my mother's side I am a Buffalo. I am married to a Lion. The Zebra is my clan's natural "doppelgänger," the family double that does its own kind of interpellation, a kind of originary and thus always counter-interpellation. More than a parallel identity, this "double" always demands a return to, a remembrance, and re-inscription of a time before colonialism, a *prior* moment with which all processes of colonial encounter in every situation must reckon. It is a formative phenomenon that lies at the beginning and instantiates and organizes the bond that exists between humans and the natural world. It is this formative reality which missionaries and colonialists desired to extirpate. It is out of this moment that indigenous people have resisted colonial imposition.

The success and failure of colonialism cannot be separated from this *prior* moment. The success and failure of resistance to colonialism, and with even greater reason, cannot be separated from this *prior* moment. In other words, the indigenous is related to colonialism as the determining element:

foundational, formative, and resistive. It is foundational because colonialism is parasitic on this originary reality.

This *prior* moment is repeated overtime and space and manifests itself in many historical guises. I argue that in all their differences and dissimilarities the indigenous peoples of the world embody and share the diversity and variety of expressions of this *prior* event. This essay is concerned with the repetition of indigeneity, its variegated emergence and reinscription overtime and across space in Africa, the Americas, Australia, India, Europe, China, and other places. Indigenous peoples are everywhere. They are the majority of the world's population. To say "indigenous" is not to invoke an abstract category but to name a fundament of human experience. Indeed, every human being has an indigenous home somewhere. Every human being can potentially trace his or her historic (as distinct from historical) identity to a first place, a prior, originary event of being at home in the world. However, many of us have forgotten our indigenous roots. The story of modernity and of colonialism is precisely about the ways in which the indigenous is first marginalized, then banished and finally forgotten. In this essay I want to do some interrogative work. I want to look, in a critical way, at some aspects of how the categories of threat, gospel, compromise and related terms operate in our everyday language, and especially in colonial discourse to perpetrate violence against African and Native American cultures and traditions. I approach the matter in this way not because I wish methodologically and historically to privilege colonialism but because, perhaps in a manner similar to Homi Bhaba in the *Location of Culture*, I want to argue that the terminologies I discuss as part of the context of the encounter between colonialism, Christianity and indigenous worldviews were already part of the traditions and cultures of Africans and Native American; they could identify cultural and existential threats, they knew what compromise was and they understood (not necessarily accepted or accepted without qualification) the message of the gospel as it was being communicated to them. In short, they were not simply duped into accepting colonialism and Christianity. Their responses and reactions were shaped and inflected by how indigenous worldviews themselves provided the basis on which to engage with colonialism and the gospel. More specifically, I contend that indigenous worldviews operated as framing structures of value for these encounters. These framing structures of value consisted of hospitality, generosity, and moral and physical resistance. Indigenous responses to colonial Christianity, law and politics, far from being mere concessions to predatory colonialism were based on fundamental ways of thinking about the other as human. The indigenous concessions which the missionary and the colonizer misunderstood, manipulated, and distorted were part of a whole outlook and worldview.

COMPROMISE

I now turn to the problem of how the colonial compromise and the gospel may or did threaten indigenous worldviews. Again, my intention is not to deny that there was such a thing as the colonial compromise nor to disagree with the assertion that the gospel was a threat to indigenous peoples. In fact, there was not one but many colonial compromises in many regions of the planet unfortunate enough to come under the yoke of European colonialism. There was not one but various kinds of threat posed by the Christian gospel to Africans and Native Americans. All this is openly reflected in the disturbing archive of colonial activity across the various continents.

Now, there are many questions to untangle here. Is the success of colonial Christianity premised on threats and compromises? Are some indigenous thinkers correct in seeing Christianity and colonialism as synonymous with threat, compromise and even violence, symbolic and physical, to indigenous worldviews and peoples? Did both succeed by conquering or by compromising or by both? What does this language of compromise say (Margalit, 2013)? Who were the parties involved in this compromise? How was the compromise achieved? Was the compromise legitimate and to whom? What things were compromised? What was lost and what was gained by the different parties in this compromise? Since this book is about this compromise and the threat of the gospel, we might as well pose yet other questions. What role did the gospel play (de Hueck Doherty, 1995)? Was it part of the compromise or did it function or operate outside of it? Do we concede too much in accepting that the success of colonialism was based on its ability to compromise? Is compromise to be rejected at all times? Are there occasions when compromise can be accepted with integrity? How do we square criticisms of compromise with the popularity of compromise in our democratic practices?

Do we use the notion of compromise to critique indigenous responses to colonialism and to Christianity? In this scenario compromise is seen as failure, as conceding at the expense of certain values and principles. Do we use it to describe the perceived achievements of colonialism or to describe its failure ultimately to vanquish indigenous cultures? I have not said anything about the threat of the gospel. How did the gospel threaten the worldviews of indigenous colonized subjects?

I have asked a large number of questions about both compromise and the gospel because clearly the theme of this book is calling upon its authors to put these ideas to significant use. It turns out that both notions are implicated in complex debates and discussions in a variety of disciplines, such as philosophy, theology, political theory, and business.

With regard to compromise we can identify at least three main approaches: the first thinks of compromise as bad. For example, in current political conversations we are taught that compromise involves betrayal of one's basic values. To compromise is to give up principles and values that are central to one's life. It important to emphasize the importance of values and principles because it is precisely in their name that compromise is deemed bad. It appears that on this view there is something in values and principles that inherently opposes them to compromise. What is it, then, about values and principles that play this role in regard to the nature of compromise itself? It is certainly the case that people see their values and principles as part of their moral and ethical commitments. But, I shall argue that even more fundamental is the manner in which values and principles are seen as the source not just of certain beliefs about what is right and wrong and thus about how to act and behave in the world, they act as the source of one's being and one's identity. Values and principles also actualize what it means to be a human being, they ground our worldview and express our sense of meaning and purpose. Notice the connection I have just made to worldview. This is one important context in which conversations about the "colonial compromise" and the threat of the gospel to indigenous worldviews must be situated. For as we shall see later, what is at stake is how colonialism and Christianity sought to negate indigenous beings and identities, not just their values and principles.

I have so far described only the first of the three approaches to compromise I named above; the idea that compromise is bad. The second approach sees compromise as good. For a start, in this view compromise is a rational way of settling differences and resolving conflicts. It is used in processes such as arbitration, political negotiation and other kinds of legal disputes. On this account there is a sense in which compromise is offered as a value and a principle in its own right. In fact, there are two overlapping meanings of compromise in this approach. One sees it as a substantive moral principle which reason can invoke and use to contain or settle disputes and conflicts. The other sees it as functional, a convenient tool that groups, courts, and arbitration bodies can use for the same purpose. An important distinction between these two meanings is that the parties to negotiation may have opposing ideas of compromise but may still act to affirm it because the alternatives are worse. I call this the instrumentalist understanding of compromise. In either case, compromise functions in the service of harmony, peace, order, and collaboration. There are associations in this view with the psychological phenomena of empathy, understanding, and the capacity to recognize other human beings as human.[2]

A third approach sees compromise as more than just functional, regulative, good or bad. It posits it as a constitutive idea built into how radical and extreme otherness is domesticated by the existence of "a moving or shifting midpoint" in the structure of human encounter. The "midpoint" helps us take cognizance of the relationality of human encounters; it brings to light the fact that as humans we have radically different ways of being in the world and that these ways are also radically similar and overlap with each other. Without such a "midpoint" of recognition, radical difference becomes dominant and deploys whatever powers it may have to annihilate difference.[3] This approach is informed by various philosophical trends: Michele de Certeau's heterology and Emmanuel Levinas' critique of traditional phenomenology are examples of what I mean here (de Certeau's, 1986; Levinas, 2012). Compromise does not lie outside what it means to be a relational being. It is already built into it. The moral principles, values, and functions of compromise derive their justification from this "ontological" or original grounding. Human relationships are always mediated, and their many points of mediation include the requirement to compromise, to be bound by shared expectations or at least to be bound by the deep expectation that they will recognize each other as human. For good or for ill, it is in this reality that indigenous peoples and colonizers encountered each other. It is when the terms of this requirement are not met that compromise functions as threat or danger. Indeed, in this case we can talk about the absence of compromise, the colonization of compromise or the violation of compromise.

Let me follow the suggestion of this last comment about the abuse and failure of compromise by briefly observing that the history of the relationship between colonizers and indigenous peoples is consistently characterized by the way in which compromise turns out to be forced and enforced, it shows up as rotten and as a product of both threat and violence. Compromise in this context was part of a dynamic system of power relations in which material and symbolic goods played an important part in "negotiating" treatises and agreements. Prayer, the bible, the gun, whiskey, papal bulls, and white exoticism were, among other things, the "treasury bills" that served as the coin of investment in the future of colonial adventures both in Africa and in the Americas. If, for example, we seriously take into account the power of the gun and the idea of the "rule of law" on the one hand, and the radical difference between literacy and orality as modes of communication[4] we ought not to be surprised that compromise was often a sham, achieved in a unidirectional, deceptive (ideology at work) and self-serving process of expropriating the other's being, with the gun being the ultimate threat to anyone.

GOSPEL AS THREAT

I have spent some time addressing different ways of thinking about compromise. I now turn to the gospel. Both compromise and gospel are implicated in threatening indigenous worldviews. I shall come later to the idea of worldview. My goal in discussing all these ideas is to establish the ways in which together and separately they belong to a system of historic arrangements that threaten indigenous beliefs and perpetrate violence against them.

In discussing the role of the gospel in these arrangements we must first comment on an important distinction: between the gospel and Christianity. Some take the former to refer to the message of Jesus Christ as contained in the gospels of the Christian Bible.[5] Some have used this distinction to try to preserve what they see as the integrity of the gospel. In fact, this distinction is part of discourse about the place of Jesus Christ in history and culture.[6]

The distinctive feature of the gospel is supposedly that it represents the unfiltered and unadulterated core of Jesus' original preaching and teaching. As we know, Jesus taught peace, love, redemption, and justice. This was what Christians came to call the good news. Christianity on the other hand, is thought of as the reception, interpretation, and appropriation of Jesus' message by his first disciples and by later generations of Christians. These subsequent appropriations are mediated through various cultural, political, and other social meanings in which the original message was changed, corrupted or became ideologically compromised by being coopted to serve interests that did not fit in with the original massage of Jesus. Another view is that Christianity represents both the cooptation of the gospel and its corruption through a process in which it is interpreted through Greco-Roman categories of thought and worldviews which this account sees as incompatible with the "essence" of the gospel. There are several ideas here. The first is that the spread of the gospel in antiquity took place in a context characterized by many competing and "conflicting" cultures and ideas (Bediako, 1999). This means that the communication and the reception of the gospel were always shaped and informed by how the Christian, "gospel" message (whatever it meant then and means now) interacted with the local cultures. Some of the cultures were distinctly the cultures of those in power (e.g., the Roman senators and emperors[7]) and some of the cultures were the cultures of the poor and dispossessed of the ancient world (e.g., the cultures of the Donatists of North Africa over whom St. Augustine presided as bishop of Carthage).

Of particular interest here is the way in which the interaction of gospel and local cultures involved creating cultural interpretive schemas that served as categories of communication and understanding.[8] The apprehension of the new and unfamiliar messages and symbols experienced in this interaction between gospel and culture necessitated the use of the vernacular, local idioms, ways of knowing and categories of thought specific to each context.[9] In other words, understanding the message from the other side required use of local idioms, it required translation using one's own language and cultural frame of reference. This necessarily involved turning the received message, not just the form in which the message was communicated, into one's own language, symbols, and categories. Culture and social context were the determining forces that shaped and informed how a message was both received and communicated. In this process the original message was modified and became mixed up with foreign and extraneous elements from the receiving culture.

Now, this process was repeated countless times over and through many contexts as the "gospel" was transmitted through the many cultures of antiquity, through its entry into Europe, and beyond into the global colonies.

These schemas were necessarily founded on power relationships (relations of power) in which definitions of what counted as legitimate knowledge and subjugated knowledge circulated as ideology. They were ideological because they represented the ruling ideas of the time. Today, we might, following Michel Foucault, think of these interpretative schemas as discursive practices (Foucault, 1994; Marx, 2016).[10]

The second idea is related to the first. As we have just seen, when the gospel became popular in terms of its message or content and in terms of its appeal, it began to spread quickly through the cultures of antiquity and was experienced as a threat of the prevailing religious ideology on which Roman political power and political ideology had relied to justify themselves and to control society. In other words, the widespread appeal of the message of the gospel to the rank and file members of society worried those in power because they saw in it *the threat of the gospel* to their own power and interests.[11] According to this approach, the response of the Roman authorities was to attempt to neutralize the gospel by making it part of the religion of the ruling elite of the Roman Empire. The conversion of Constantine to Christianity in 312CE at precisely the moment when he is facing war with Emperor Maxentius marks the point at which the official cooptation of the gospel by Roman imperial power begins. If we follow the logic of this account, we could argue that it is here that the gospel is first used to create a civil religion, a religion in service of the politics of the city, the state and the country.

Given the focus of our discussion on the threat of the gospel to indigenous worldviews we must now address the seeming problem posed by my claim in the foregoing comments that the gospel was also a threat to those in power. The idea that the gospel posed a threat to indigenous peoples is sometimes taken to portray indigenous people as powerless, marginalized and subjugated. Clearly, the way the gospel threatened Roman power in antiquity was quite different.

I will briefly discuss three ways in which the gospel can be said to have been a threat to those in power. The first is that the universality of the gospel as proclaimed by the Jesus was a threat to the particularism of the national and civic religion of imperial Rome. It represented a different kingdom. The second way in which the gospel threated imperial power and all human political power was in the egalitarian nature of its content. Here was a message that proclaimed the elimination of ethnic, racial, gender, national, and legal differences. In Jesus's message rank, class, and wealth seem not to matter. In this proclamation egalitarian considerations were paired with freedom; freedom from the law and freedom from oppression. We know that all this unnerved the religious and political authorities (both Jewish and Roman) of the day. In the light of these two points we can move to the third aspect of how the gospel functioned as a threat: it required radical change both in human character and social structures. In what can only be understood as a socially destabilizing thrust, the gospel opposed and rejected this world, its cultures and its worldviews. It called for and represented new ways of thinking and a new social order modelled on the impending reign of God. Fourth, the gospel was a threat to indigenous cultures in the same way it was a threat to all cultures. It not only preached the reign of God, it also called for the end of this world, including especially in the hands of colonial missionaries, the end of indigenous worlds.

So far, I have been using the term threat in a very general sense. However, I now shift to discussion of two areas were indigenous peoples experienced both colonialism and the gospel as threat. I want to say something more about the meaning of the term threat.

UNDERSTANDING THREAT

What is threat? What was threatened by the gospel, and why does this matter? In order to understand what we are discussing when we use concepts such as threat, we need to provide some commonly used definitions. The context in which the gospel threatened indigenous peoples is important. It was a colonial context in which indigenous subjects were systematically denuded of their identities, histories, and traditions. The colonial context was characterized by cultural, social, and political conflicts. It matters to understand how the gospel threatened indigenous cultures because it, in fact, did so in a variety of ways. In the context of Jesus's preaching it did so by preaching another world order beyond time and space. It also did so in the hands of missionaries as a tool of colonial domination. Furthermore, we cannot talk about threat without talking about violence, hostility, and power. The theme of this book is the threat of both the colonial compromise and the gospel to the indigenous worldview. While this specific kind of threat is not to be minimized, I believe that to focus on it alone takes away from the deeper problem of violence that indigenous people encountered in their interactions with colonizers.

The future existence of indigenous peoples depended on their ability to successfully resist the threat of violence to their collective being, not just their worldviews. I am invoking here the concept of "existential threat" which I think is both wider and deeper in connecting danger and violence.[12] To be sure, I recognize that "'worldview" as more than just beliefs, outlooks, values, and symbols can be incorporated in a notion of existential threat. My argument is that this move needs to be made explicit because the threat to indigenous peoples was not just a matter of perception or an "idealistic" risk of danger which was never carried out. It was a danger that was realized in Africa and in the Americas.

In other words, I am arguing that given what we know about the violence of colonialism, the language of compromise and threat simply fails to capture the extent to which, again and again, colonial threats against indigenous peoples were realized. It is important not to settle on the idea of threat but to go beyond it, to the goals and aims of threat which were to change indigenous social orders and worldviews by violence. Here we must also wonder about whether or not compromise, threat and "gospel" were not in themselves already predicated on violence. The question is not meant to suggest that violence was inherent to gospel, compromise and threat as such but rather in the ways in which these ideas were utilized and deployed by missionaries and colonialists.

What I want to argue is that the threat of the "gospel" emanated from the ways in which ideology infiltrated the original message of Jesus. This threat was multilayered. I have already suggested that the gospel itself functioned as a threat to all the cultures it encountered.[13] It demanded change, often in ways that respected no culture and no cultural boundaries for it posited itself as the universal Word of God. It demanded doing away with local beliefs and allegiances to indigenous deities.[14] The process of translation and inculturation discussed earlier comprised a second level.

Ideology was the third level at which the threat of Christianity to indigenous worldviews took place. I use "ideology" here knowing full well that this notion is supposed to be "dead" (Laclau, 2007: 201–220). I use it because I think that the belief that ideology is dead is itself the function of ideology. I use the term to describe a system of meanings and power relations which socially functions to conceal domination and oppression by rationalizing, supporting, and justifying the interests of those responsible for prevailing social arrangements. Ideology operates through various tropes: universalizing, rationalizing, naturalizing (appealing to nature) justifying (through religion, philosophy, etc.)

In the encounter between indigenous cultures of Africa and the Americas we come face to face with many different ways in which ideology functioned to defend, explain, rationalize, and justify the colonial project and the need to impose Christianity.

LAW AS THREAT

One of the arenas within which this encounter took place was that of the Law and the "rule of law." It is difficult to overestimate just how this idea was and has been responsible for creating and positing European self-identity as the ground for vanquishing indigenous beings and their ways of thinking. Law was and has always been regarded as a universal figure. It derives from Europe and represents order, and orderliness, peace, and harmony.

The structure of colonial law was also the structure of law as such. Its colonial guises operated fundamentally as a contingency of distance and location mediated by the enunciation and the restatement of law in the voice of the colonial master. This new location and assigned voice of authority were never intended to usurp what law is in itself or to undermine its ultimate source of legitimation, which was always the queen and the king.[15] To speak of law as such is to posit the absence of difference in what law is perceived to be in itself. It is ontologically a self-securing structure of meaning whose deployment across time and spaces does not allow the contingency of distance and location to serve as difference, that which not only represents the other or otherness but also that which might also be a different law. The essential meaning of law is thus universal and this universality rules out difference. As we all know, juridical universality is posited as an inherent property of law. We know, too, that it derives this from a number of sources. The first is the body of the king or the queen. The second is nature. The natural law tradition is a rich source of thought about this aspect of law's universality. The third is Christianity. The history of how Greco-Roman notions of law entered and shaped Christianity was itself already a process grounded in the logic of territorial and colonial expansion. My argument here is essentially that the idea of the "rule of law" has deeper roots than recognized in current conversations about this notion. The roots are also deeply theological. In this theological moment lies hidden a fundamental connection between the ways in which religion provides justification both for the law and for law's commandments.

Theologically this is already a problem for the apostle Paul when he grapples with the relationship between law and gospel. The carryover of this into Christianity and how it impacted the development of major theological traditions (Lutheranism, Calvinism, the natural and canon law traditions in Catholicism) is something we must keep at the forefront of our analysis. This is because this theological moment is consistently deployed together with colonialism as its "ideological" surrogate. The struggles in Luther's theology on the relationship between law and gospel and later in his articulation of the doctrine of the two Kingdoms have not been utilized to think about how theology was both actively involved in the rethinking of the universality and sources of law, and how it always opened up spaces for conflating emerging secularist notions of law with theological ones. We see this in the debates about the humanity of indigenous people in early modern political theory. The humanity of the indigenous was debated ostensibly in political terms which were often framed juridically, and in theological terms. This is why it's so important to pay attention to the topic I am discussing here.

I am arguing that the threat to the indigenous worldview came not just from the gospel but also from the law and that both were part of a developing, yet well-orchestrated structure and process of colonizing indigeneity. The extent to which and the ways in which the idea of law and the rule of law have colonized and radically changed indigenous self-understandings around the globe was informed by how these two ideas relied on intersecting systems of meanings in which law itself was granted the regulative prerogative to mark the parameters of the definition of being human. I want to emphasize here the priority of the regulative ways in which law became constitutive. To place the regulative before the constitutive allows us to see and determine the socially constructed character of the processes by which law comes to play the role it does in dispossessing indigenous peoples of their humanity.[16] The "human" was understood as a legal or juridical entity composed of various kinds of rights whose content was reflexively grounded in the inner demands of the law. All rights, rights of property ownership, basic rights such as the rights to life are created by and founded in legality and are thus both constitutive and regulative. Under law the human is fully present to itself qua human as a function of the law. This is the constitutive function of law.

When colonists claimed that the indigenous had no laws, they also meant that they had no law. But if, on this account, law is constitutive, and what it means to be human is thus naturally or ontologically grounded in law, the colonial denial that indigenous people had no any laws and thus had the law amounts to saying indigenous people are not constituted by law. They stand outside the law. They are not human in the eyes of the law. In this way of thinking the law is not just s a rubric for checking whether or not the rights of certain human entities have been recognized, accepted, and implemented. It is an essential category better understood as originary. It is important to draw out some of the implications for this for what in this volume we are describing as the threat of colonialism to the indigenous worldview. Again, the threat is only partly religious, only partly theological, and only partly metaphysical. The threat is, negatively constitutive. It denies not just the worldview of the indigenous, but indigenous being itself. Law and the rule of law were not autonomous, standalone operations.

But I go further, I also argue that the "rule of law" was always presupposed as a given in this process. Here then we must reckon with the fact that law was an instrument of rule. The phrase "rule of law" must be exegete as a double-edged sword: the one is political (it is about rule, regulation, subjugation, and domination) the other is legal, juridical, and forensic. Together they articulate the limits of subjugation.

But, and this is a major problem, law, for all its ideological self-assertions, was always confronted by the inevitability of the other. The contingency of distance and location was a veritable constraint against which totalizing and universalistic claims had to be revised and the rule of law accommodated to the reality of indigenous ways of existence. In other words, the idea of the rule of law could only work by conceding the humanity of indigenous humans.

ENCOUNTER AS THREAT: INDIGENOUS HUMANITY AS A QUESTION

The encounter with the other could not be denied as a momentous event that required recognition. It was a fact. It was taking place, and in order to succeed colonialism needed to make sense of it. First, then, was recognition that there was something to be engaged. Doubting its cultural value was one thing and doubting its existential presence was existentially impossible. The recognition of this reality was shaped not merely by its presence but rather by its human-*like* presence. I shall call this "anthropological resemblance."[17] The encounter with the indigenous was an encounter with beings that in many ways looked *like* colonial agents themselves. Except in skin color, they resembled humans; they appeared to have language, they seemed to imitate human behavior and to perform the same biological functions of ordinary human beings. For example, they had wives and children, they ate and voided, and battled the elements like other humans. Dealing with intense climatic heat, humidity, or unforgiving rigors of rough winters fall into this category. How to think of these entities? What to call them and how describe them? Were they humans or defective humans? Another species, perhaps? Humans, but lacking some fundamental characteristics of humanity as understood by colonizers? Perhaps Africans and Native Americans were biological or evolutionary atavisms? These human-*like*-figures represented a question mark about creation itself and especially about the heretofore taken-for-granted uniqueness of Homo Europaeus (White, 1978: 150–196). The publication in 1735 of Carl Linnaeus' *Systema Naturae* was an attempt to address and perhaps even settle this question of difference and resemblance which had been in circulation ever since Columbus first set foot in the Americas. In any case, we know that in the Middle Ages and beyond the interrogations of indigenous peoples was often subsumed under the category of the so-called Wild Man.[18]

The reality of the encounter itself shifted the terms on which colonial subjects met and interacted with each other. The threat of the gospel and of colonialism to indigeneity was thus always far from being settled and absolute. The colonial project had no choice but to read itself against the presence of this prior other, this *look-alike* reality, the anthropological resemblance. They are *like* us, but they are not us, but they are *like* us. If they are like us, they must be subjected to the law and be converted to the Christianity by the preaching of the gospel. The strangeness of the human-like figures raised important theological questions about their salvation; it also raised legal questions about the political rights (Padgen, 1987).

DERISION AS THREAT

Apart from law, another strategy used by colonialism and by Christianity was to deploy the logic of what Mudimbe called derision (1988). The role of derision in threatening indigenous existence has not been well understood. It is often mischaracterized as merely polemical. Yet its use runs through many missionary and colonial statements in the service of subverting indigenous lives. Its widespread use is attested in India, Latin America, Africa, Australia, and other places. Derision represents ideologically motivated criticism of the kind of difference seen as residing outside the white, European norm.

This consisted of virulent attacks against indigenous understandings: these were people without civilization, without law, gods, religion, morality, and without any sense of time. Derision is at the heart of the threat to indigenous peoples. It hides as polemic, as ignorance and mere prejudice. When we encounter it, as we do on numerous occasions, in the complex archive of colonial and missionary discourse we are wont to dismiss or even forgive it as merely an expression of ignorant, time-bound insensitivity, idle talk or now, as we might say, locker-room bunter. They did not know any better.[19] However, to think in this way is to ignore the various ways in which derision functioned not just as substantive speech but also as a mode of thinking, a worldview characterized by both psychological projection and other-directed negative filtering which provided the materials around which colonial fantasies about similarities and differences were imagined and constructed. The refusal to see and the denial to recognize the value of *prior others* or the aboriginal and, thus, the priority of indigenous realities was a global colonial strategy. It is at work in Africa, Asia, and the Americas. The goal was to engage in attempts to convert natives to the religion of the master. The logic of derision was the apologetical structure that was used to clear the way for the proselytization and conversion of indigenous peoples.

As strategy to convert, derision consisted of redefining indigenous otherness through the discursive apparatuses of law, education, and commerce. In other words, Christianity was supported in its derisive activities by law, education, and other social processes. It is in these and other strategies that the threat to indigenous beings and their cultures was at work. Emphasizing the gospel as the central threat to indigenous peoples obscures the complexity of the threat and the forces in and out of which it operated. Reducing to law any of the other discursive apparatuses I have named equally obscures the extent and complexity of that threat. Perhaps what sets the gospel apart was the everyday manner in which it was deployed. Those who argued for the "rule of law" did not, ordinarily, run churches, schools, and clinics. They did not preach law in the manner of a missionary on a Sunday morning preaching the necessity to repent to escape hellfire and alienation from the Christian God. The gospel was more immediate, direct, existentially intimate, and demanding. The techniques through which it was communicated and the mechanisms set up for its reception sought to affect every aspect of indigenous life: morality, "religion," bodily movements, language, marriage, childrearing, and traditional medical practices. The intentions of this intimate tutelage were nothing less than to transform the native. Although much of this had a public face and often included whole tribes, clans, and families, transformation was sought first in the individual and secondarily in the social collective.

Derision was a way of drawing the line between normative difference (we are different from them and we are different in acceptable ways because our differences conform to the order of nature and civilization) and aberrant or wayward difference (they are different from us and their difference is marked by a pathological departure from the norms of nature and civilization). In making this claim I am arguing that derision was not simply a matter of disapproving cultural customs. To bring this out I want to briefly discuss the modes of its expression. I will characterize these as a series of dialectically related points. At each point derision participates in the creation of difference. The first point is discursive. Here the marking of difference takes place in speech, in language (without, of course, being reducible to language) and in the general grammar of everyday life. It circulates in the form of words, sermons, gestures, metaphors, direct attacks, scholarly descriptions, moral commentary, and the power relations that are symbolically deployed in the use of language and, are therefore, a central part of what we ordinarily mean by discourse. The second point around which derision marks difference is representation. To deride was to portray indigenous peoples as beings of a certain sort, beings with negative qualities that separated them from normative humanity; they were savages, barbarians, primitive, heathens, and many other negative things. In these terms and descriptions we are offered instances of how representation creates certain kinds of being. Here what seems to be mere words, metaphors, and images turn out to be constitutive of the being of indigeneity. It is remarkable just how much these terms and description are recycled in and through many colonial and missionary registers across the world.

The third point at which derision functions as a marker of difference through the symbolic means by which it operates to achieve its goals is performance. Derision was performative. We can approach this from a philosophical angle following J. L. Austin's *How to Do Things with Words*. On the basis of Austin's argument, we could then say that the language of derision is meant to actually accomplish certain things. What I am arguing is that colonists and missionaries had a serious purpose in deploying the strategy of derision: to change the world, not merely to interpret it.[20] This would be accomplished by civilizing and converting indigenous peoples. There is I think a connection here between performance and representation. At one level derision functions as a symbolic mirror in which the indigenous people must see their own ugliness, their lack of manners, lack of time, religion, and civilization. Having thus seen themselves they must now reject their ways, convert to Christianity, embrace the rule of law and adopt modes of being that place them on the proper evolutionary journey to civility. These changes demonstrate the performative nature of derision. In other words, conversion and becoming civilized as response to derision show how derision actually acts in the world, on peoples and cultures.

NOTES

1. See William Howitt, *Colonization and Christianity: A Popular History of the Treatment of the Natives by the Europeans in all their Colonies*, Vols. I and II (London, UK: Longman, Orme Brown, Green & Longman, 1838). I cite this old work because it brings into view in one place the European treatment of indigenous peoples from various parts of the globe. Howitt was writing at a time when European colonialism was thriving. He is something of an insider.

2. It is arguable that indigenous humanity is deeply characterized by something like this approach. Certainly in Africa, Ubuntu is based, at least in part, on this way of thinking about human interactions.

3. The difference between "radical difference" (we are the absolute reality; and "difference" (those others whose otherness owes itself to our reality) is crucial here.

4. The use of literacy as a way of understanding agreements in cultures predominantly shaped by communicative orality was a disingenuous way of engaging in negotiation.

5. For example, Albert Nolan's book, *Jesus before Christianity* (Maryknoll, NY: Orbis Books, 1992).

6. A classic discussion relating to some of the issue in the relationships between gospel and culture see Marianne P. Bond, *The Gospel of Rome versus the Gospel of Jesus Christ: Two New Testament Responses to the Churches Founded by Paul*, https://www.pbs.org/wgbh/pages/frontline/shows/religion/symposium/gospel.html.

7. Ibid.

8. The idea of interpretative schemas gestures toward the function of hermeneutics in acts of translation. I maintain that any single translation orbits realms of choices from among which the translator must settle upon a particular translation. The choice he or she makes is never neutral. It is always an act of interpretation. As such this interpretation is loaded with biases, ideologies, beliefs, and perspectives that the translators bring into the work of translation.

9. See for example, Graydon F. Snyder, *Inculturation of the Jesus Tradition: The Impact of Jesus on Jewish and Roman Cultures* (Harrisburg, PA: Trinity Press International, 1999).

10. The juxtaposition of Marx and Foucault here is meant to provoke interest in the question of the relationship between power and ideology and how power and knowledge operating through accepted cultural and social practices are always operate ideologically.

11. I do not have the space to fully explore this rather significant point. What is clear here is that the idea of the threat of the gospel can, in fact, operate at many levels. In this case it is the traditions of a powerful Roman elite, a powerful imperial religion and the dominant forces of subjection and subjugation which all this represented which are threatened by the gospel (Larry W. Hurtado, *Destroyer of the Gods: Early Christian Distinctiveness in the Roman World* (Waco, TX: Baylor University Press, 2016). Arguably, then, the threat of the gospel cuts in different ways. If this is correct, we may ask: What is it about the gospel that makes it work in this way?

12. See Gilad Hirschberger, Tsachi Ein-Dor, Bernhard Leidner, and Tama Saguy, *How is Existential Threat Related to Intergroup Conflict?: Introducing the Multidimensional Existential Threat (MET) Model*, doi:10.3389/fpsyg.2016.01877.

13. This is clearly the message of books such as, Rodney Stark, *The Triumph of Christianity: How the Jesus Movement Became the Largest World Religion* (San Francisco, CA: HarperOne, 2011); Bart D. Ehrman, *The Triumph of Christianity: How a Forbidden Religion Swept the World* (New York, NY: Simon and Schuster, 2018). The triumphalist tone is clear as is the clear acknowledgments of conquest.

14. Wayne A. Meeks, *The Collision with Paganism: Conspicuous by their Absence at the Great Roman Civic Festivals, Early Christians were Often Viewed with Suspicion and Mistrust*, https://www.pbs.org/wgbh/pages/frontline/shows/religion/first/paganism.html; again, see also Hurtado, *Destroyer of the Gods*.

15. See Anthony Padgen's old, but still important essay "Dispossessing the Barbarian: The Language of Spanish Thomism and the Debate over the Property Rights of the American Indian," in *The Languages of Political Theory in Early Modern Europe*, ed. Anthony Padgen (Cambridge, UK: Cambridge University Press, 1987).

16. Yet, it is precisely this which in its "ideological" manifestations the law contradicts. Its totalizing, universalistic, and absolutist structure serve as the basis for this contradiction.

17. I want to use this idea of "anthropological resemblance" to assert that the route to the recognition of indigenous peoples as humans was not direct but involved inferences and suppositions that depended on certain observable characteristics of

human anatomy and culture. Lest the reader thinks this is far-fetched, I point to the fact that two disciplines that played a key role in the classification and European colonization of peoples across world emerged to interrogate this anatomical and cultural resemblance. The first was Physical Anthropology and the second was Cultural Anthropology. Carl Linnaeus's *Systema Naturae* of 1735 must be counted among the founding works of at least one branch of Physical Anthropology. The pseud-science that was practiced in the name of these disciplines and how these disciplines them came to be implicated in racist thinking will not detain me here.

18. See Richard Bernheimer, *Wild Man in the Middle Ages* (Cambridge, MA: Harvard University Press, 1952); and Edward Dudley and Maximillian E. Novak, eds., *The Wild Man Within: An Image in Western Thought from the Renaissance to Romanticism* (Pittsburg, PA: University of Pittsburgh Press, 1972).

19. Remarkably, and by and large, they still do not know any better today.

20. Or as Karl Marx stated: "Philosophers have only interpreted the world . . . the point is to change it" (1888: 101).

Chapter 2

Faith and Facts
Dismantling Colonial Constructions
Natsu Taylor Saito

> [T]he most important gift we have to give back to our colonizer may be the foundational discursive modalities of the intellectual tradition of the oppressed. We have a different way of seeing the world and engaging in critical analysis of the world that is transformative and liberating.
>
> —Tink Tinker, *American Indian Liberation*

INTRODUCTION

Stories matter.[1] As Ben Okri observes, "One way or another we are living the stories planted in us early or along the way, or we are also living the stories we planted—knowingly or unknowingly—in ourselves." These stories give direction and meaning to our lives, and if we are willing to "change the stories we live by, quite possibly we change our lives" (1997: 46). Professor George "Tink" Tinker gives us stories, new stories, the types of stories that open us up to ways of being that can change our lives and the futures we leave to our children and grandchildren.

When I first began reading Tink Tinker's work, I expected it to elucidate threats posed to indigenous peoples and worldviews by the colonial imposition of Christian ideology. Titles like *Missionary Conquest: The Gospel and Native American Cultural Genocide* were a clue. And, in fact, he explains how Christian missionaries helped consolidate the United States' control over indigenous peoples and their lands. How they enabled the enslavement and exploitation of indigenous labor, the eradication of economic self-sufficiency, and the establishment of reservations that were, in reality, sites of mass and indefinite incarceration. These representatives of the Christian church leveraged their influence to have indigenous ceremonies and spiritual practices outlawed (1993: 6–7). They stole American Indian children; abused and traumatized them in boarding schools; and did all they could to undermine "the extended kinship system upon which an Indian nation and individuals depend for their identity" (Ibid.: 8; 2004c). In other words, as Tinker states straightforwardly, missionaries working among American Indian nations have been "partners in genocide" (1993: 4).

What I did not know to expect, initially, was how Tinker moves beyond the damage that has been and continues to be done to indigenous individuals, communities and nations, to provide deeply thoughtful genealogies that trace genocidal conduct of this sort to its roots in the Western colonial worldview that undergirds Christian proselytizing. And while this constitutes an invaluable contribution to the literature, Tinker does not stop there. Had he done so, he would have left much of his audience—conservative, liberal, or "progressive"—feeling comfortably smug about the fact that they rely on science and rationality rather than religion in choosing what to believe and how to act on those beliefs.

Writing in 1925 the philosopher Alfred North Whitehead pronounced as a "great fact" that "there has always been a conflict between religion and science" (1925), and the dominant narrative of Euroamerican settler society continues to portray religion and science as competing worldviews. We are often told that we need to choose between faith and facts, as illustrated by debates over evolution and climate change. Tinker urges us to probe a bit deeper, helping us see that the construction of a binary opposition between Christianity and science simply deflects attention from their colonial commonalities.

Tinker refuses to be constrained by these options and is as critical of scientific materialism as he is of Christian ideology.

> I must confess that I am not yet a believer in the 'fact' of evolution. I do not believe that we Osages evolved from monkeys. However, should it someday be actually proven . . . I would be deeply honored to share such a respectable lineage—even though the only monkeys in North America arrived with the colonial occupation. (2004b: 108)

As this illustrates, he always assesses the "knowledge" of the colonizers from an indigenous perspective, refusing to disregard historical, material or spiritual realities.

Tinker is very clear that consciousness—spirit, if you will—permeates everything. The rocks are our grandparents; the plants talk to each other, and to humans when we pay attention (Ibid.: 114). *Mitakuye oyasin*, the Lakota phrase often translated as "for all my relations," is to be taken literally to incorporate not only other humans or even that to which we generally attribute life, but "all the above me and below me and around me things" (2008: 48–49). Moreover, spirit crosses barriers of time and space. Tinker shares two experiences from visits to the site of the 1864 Sand Creek Massacre. He reports being joined in prayer at sunrise by an Indian woman who disappeared leaving no footprints and, later, being "quietly stunned by the sounds of a large and busy village coming from the cottonwoods" where the old village had been (Ibid.: 126–127). Western science cannot adequately account for these experiences and, therefore, it cannot allow them to be real.

Ultimately, "rationality" plays a role as significant as the colonizers' religion in attempting to crush indigenous perspectives. Twenty-first century American settler colonialism allows for some recognition of religious difference but has little tolerance for those who reject modern science (Pinker, 2013). Nonetheless, as Tinker points out so powerfully, the substitution of "scientific facts" for religious ideology does nothing to change the political, historical, and cultural dynamics of colonization. Western science is an outgrowth of Christian ideology, with its hierarchical, universalizing, linear, and anthropocentric framing of relationships. Science—like colonial armies—rode in with the missionaries, and it has fueled (quite literally) the colonial domination of those deemed Other. Ultimately, the scientific "progress" the dominant narrative takes such pride in has brought the planet to the brink of destruction.

Tink Tinker's observations about the colonial presumptions that undergird both Western science and religion are discussed in the following part. The next section moves beyond the confines of a colonial worldview to some of his insights into cultures and understandings that have been kept alive by indigenous peoples despite the colonial onslaught. The next section summarize a few of the conclusions Tinker reaches that I find most helpful in considering how we can imagine a world in which all of our relations can thrive.

COLONIAL PRESUMPTIONS

The United States is the world's most powerful settler colonial state. Its exploitation of indigenous nations, lands, and resources is ongoing and, like all forms of euroderivative colonialism we have seen over the past several centuries, it claims a "civilizing mission" to justify both the devastation it causes and the profits it reaps (Anghie, 2005: 3–6; Saito, 2019). From a colonial perspective, "[s]ettlement in a new, unknown, uncultivated country is equivalent to an act of Creation" because it signifies "the transformation of chaos into cosmos" (Fitzpatrick, 1992: 47; quoting Eliade, 1965: 10–11). And to "civilize" is "to bring out of a state of barbarism; to instruct in the arts of life, and thus elevate in the scale of humanity" (*Oxford English Dictionary*, 1971: 448).

Science and religion, as constructed in the Euroamerican master narrative, both presume "civilization" to be humanity's common objective and measure progress toward this universal goal in terms of "control" over nature. Both assess all of human history in terms of a linear progression toward some version of salvation, in that process collapsing the multiplicity of human experience into one teleological narrative (Smith, 1999: 29–32). This "universal" narrative entrenches colonial rule by placing euroderivative colonizers at the forefront of human progress and development, and indigenous peoples trailing in their wake (Wolf, 1982: 5). In contesting this framework, we quickly find that the most deeply embedded presumptions are the most difficult to expose. For this reason, one of the most important gifts of Tinker's scholarship is his deconstruction of the presumptions undergirding what is all too often considered "common sense."

Worldviews are multidimensional, overlapping, and capable of encompassing what appear to be contradictory premises. As a result, they do not readily lend themselves to a compartmentalized analysis. Nonetheless, doing my best to comport with what Barbara Alice Mann so trenchantly describes as "the Western demand for Categorically Demarcated Linearity with Conclusions" (2016b: 1), this section considers Tink Tinker's insights into five conceptual underpinnings common to both colonial religion and science: (1) that there is *a* universe and it is hierarchically structured; (2) that human-ness is defined by the exploitation and control of nature; (3) that truth is found by breaking things down into their smallest component parts; (4) that the temporal takes priority over the spatial; and (5) that progress is not only inevitable but linear and unidirectional.

Hierarchy

In the worldview common to Western civilization, there is one reality: a singular universe, organized in a hierarchical manner that places humans above nature, second only to something generally described as God or (scientific) Truth. "Euro-Westerners have come to divide the world into a clear hierarchy of the divine, the human, and nature—from greatest to least, in that order" (Tinker, 2004b: 118). "Human-ness" is defined by distinction from the world of nature. People have linguistic and conceptual abilities that animals do not, allowing the development of art and literature; we cultivate the earth, which provides the material basis for our highly organized societies, distinguished particularly by cities; we have scientific understandings that allow us to produce goods, provide sophisticated services, and control our environment. Each of these achievements is evidence of humanity's superiority to nature.

Once one conceives of the world as hierarchically ordered, all relationships can be ranked in terms of status and power; everyone and everything is defined in terms of superiority or inferiority to someone or something else. Even in the Christian spirit realm, not only are some humans closer to God than others but there are, apparently, hierarchies of angels and demons as well. In secular society, specialists or experts are superior to "regular" people and "[a]nthropologists talk about specialization as a process of social evolution that moves away from the primitive toward the modern and more complex societies of the Euro-West" (Ibid.: 117).

In a world where any given individual or people is necessarily better or worse than others, it is not surprising that human beings would be racialized, gendered, and assigned identities intended to keep them "in their place," literally and figuratively. Thus, we see that the colonial subjugation of indigenous peoples was explained initially in terms of their distance from God—or even their lack of a "soul." However, as these "inferior" peoples began converting to Christianity, "science" stepped in to explain their dispossession in terms of their smaller cranial capacity, their lower IQs, or their genetic proclivity to violence (Gould, 1996).

Dominion

The Judeo-Christian tradition tells us that, from "the Beginning," humanity's purpose and well-being was to be measured by its control of nature. Witness its creator's initial instructions:

> So God created man in his *own* image, . . . male and female created he them. And God blessed them, and God said unto them, Be fruitful, and multiply, and replenish the earth, and subdue it: and have dominion over the fish of the sea, and over the fowl of the air, and over every living thing that moveth upon the earth. (KJV Gen 1:27–28)

The messages conveyed by this directive include, first, that people are separate from and have an essentially antagonistic relationship to nature; second, that God, the creator and ultimate authority, has assigned humans the task of subjugating the earth; and third, that "living things," at least those of significance, are the ones that move. In light of this origin story, it is not surprising that euroderivative societies have been characterized by "the theological, philosophical, scientific, and economic struggle for control over the world, its environment, and its 'resources'" (Tinker, 2004b: 118).

Once it is presumed that people are defined by their distinction from nature, it follows that human progress or development is rightfully measured by the extent of our conquest of nature. This is implicit in the association of civilization with cities, but reaches much further with the bifurcation of mind and body and the status given to "reason," which is defined as a distinctly human attribute. Rationality, in turn, furthers human conquest and control of the earth through scientific and technological advances. As Tinker notes, quoting Vandana Shiva, "'Nature' was transformed in the European mind from a self-organizing, living system to a mere raw material for human exploitation, needing management and control" (Ibid.: 11; Shiva, 1997: 104).

Science and technology, of course, give humans the ability to enrich themselves by harnessing or converting nature and thus are cast as foundational to Western civilization. The exploitation of natural resources is known in colonial-speak as rendering the earth "productive." In turn, the ability to do this is what justifies control over those resources and undergirds Western conceptions of property ownership (Williams, 1990: 246–248). Both science and religion emphasize that this isn't just one of many possible paths; it is *the* path to fulfilling human purpose.

Individuation

"[T]he very first missionary to enter any Indian community effectively initiated a political division of that community that proved genocidal," Tinker tells us. And this is because it forced members of a community to choose between participating in the culture of that community or "participation *as an individual*" in the colonizer's religious tradition (2008: 6–7, emphasis added). His characterization of this process as genocidal is neither rhetorical nor hyperbolic. As article II of the UN Convention on the Prevention and Punishment of the Crime of Genocide states, genocidal acts are "committed with intent to destroy, in whole or in part, a national, ethnical, racial or religious group, as such." The destruction of indigenous peoples *as such* was exactly the intent of the missionaries, and of the settler state more generally (Churchill, 1997).

This notion that salvation can be attained at—and *only* at—an individual level, with no concern for how the transformation might affect the survival and wellbeing of the community, permeates Angloamerican society. Tinker points out that "the 'development' of the West has resulted in an accelerating process of individuation," which leaves each person "on her own to care for her own survival." By contrast, he emphasizes, in traditional Osage societies it was recognized that "every person was critical to the functioning of the whole people" (2004b: 117).

In Western culture, individuals are not woven into a communal fabric of relationships, but atomized, disconnected from what once might have been regarded, quite literally, as their "roots." Ultimately, they are rendered fungible. "[T]he Western habit of identifying things one at a time, as discrete isolates, standing alone and operating independently," Mann notes, "misrepresents the community required not only of humans but of all spirits" (2016b: 242). This reductionism is endemic to Western science and its "social sciences" as well, where "knowledge" is equated to the ability to break something down into its smallest component parts, with little if any regard for the relationships between wholes that might actually help us understand phenomena (Gallagher, 1999: 79).

Temporality

Tinker emphasizes that "[w]hether in its capitalist or socialist (marxist?) guise, history and temporality reign supreme in the euro-west, where time is money and 'development,' or progress, is the goal" (2008: 7). The late Vine Deloria, Jr. considered the most fundamental ideological difference between American Indian and Western European immigrant cultures to be their respective orientations to space and time. "American Indians," he said, "hold their lands—places—as having the highest possible meaning, and all their statements are made with this reference point in mind" (2003: 75).[2]

Deloria contrasts this with the observation that "[i]mmigrants review the movement of their ancestors across the continent as a steady progression of basically good events and experiences, thereby placing history—time—in the best possible light" (Ibid.: 75–76). Tinker explains that "[s]pace as it has been understood by the children of Europe in America has tended to mean room to expand, to grow, or to move around in: these are temporal processes. As such, then, 'Manifest Destiny' is quintessentially a temporal doctrine even as it consumed the space of this continent" (1986: 70). Spatiality, as understood by indigenous peoples, is not the same as territoriality; it is, rather, "a spiritual, not a geopolitical, issue" (Mann, 2016b: 54).

Mann explains that "[t]he interactions and relationships formed among things residing in any space—say, in the desert southwest or on the moon—create a specific spiritual consciousness that is simply not transportable or transferable to any other locale" (2016b: 55). This is very different to the Judeo-Christian faith, with its "solitary, male and—most stunningly—*portable* god" (Ibid.: 39). Both Western science and religion view knowledge as discrete, universal and transferrable across space. Their adherents believe themselves to be constructing a "body" of knowledge—the aptly named "canon"—that makes advances over time, and they regard those most familiar with this canon to be at the forefront of human civilization (Tinker, 2008: 7).

The combination of a religious mandate to dominate the earth and the assessment of the worth of any given human endeavor in terms of scientific "progress" has brought us to a place in which ecological devastation threatens our very survival. Ironically, we are simultaneously assured that science will save us. Thus, for example, in his 2009 inaugural address President Barack Obama promised to "restore science to its rightful place, and wield technology's wonders" to improve the quality and cost of healthcare, to "harness" nature to "fuel our cars and run our factories," and to "roll back the spectre of a warming planet" (Coghlan, 2009).

Progress

Each of these premises common to the colonial master('s) narrative—the hierarchy that places humans above nature and measures their worth by its exploitation, the atomization that isolates individuals from their communities and transforms relational knowledge into bits and bytes, the privileging of the temporal over the spatial—contributes to the construction of a worldview, or perhaps a cosmology, in which human history and, indeed, all of life, inevitably proceeds along a path that is not only linear but unidirectional.

The "classic" story of European colonization has been described as somewhat circular, "an *Odyssey* consisting of an outward movement followed by interaction with exotic and colonized Others in foreign surroundings, and by a final return to an original locale" (Veracini, 2010: 96). By contrast, settler colonists intend to remain in the colonized territory, and bring with them a purported sovereign prerogative to establish a new state on someone else's land, a state over which they will exercise permanent control. There is no turning back, no endpoint to their vision beyond the permanent normalization of settler hegemony; it is a totalizing narrative within which "the discontinuation of a settler colonial circumstance remains unthinkable" (Ibid.: 104).

Similarly, both Christian and secular Western ideologies are constructed upon a narrative of continual progress, generally measured in terms of growth and consumption. This framework precludes the need for redress or reparations, for the restoration of balance, when grave injustices have occurred. Rather, those who have been exploited or dispossessed can simply be uplifted by the always expanding material benefits of a world in which science and technology allow humans to consume the natural world at an ever-increasing pace. The most significant feature of human societies, in this paradigm, is whether they are already "developed" or still "developing"; there are no other options (UNDP, 2017; Saito, 2010). As summarized by Tinker, "the ethos of development strategies, including sustainable development, is that human beings have unlimited potential, which it is somehow *un*ethical *not* to utilize and/or exploit" (2004a: 20).

As he points out, however, the "development" paradigm presumes continuous expansion, thus making "sustainable development" an oxymoron (Ibid.: 9; also Asara et al., 2015). Actual sustainability requires reciprocity, which can be understood as "maintaining a balance and tempering the negative effects of basic human survival techniques" (Tinker, 2004a: 20). The insistence upon development, "sustainable" or not, he concludes, "requires a capitulation to genocide on the part of indigenous peoples" and "stands to cost the world community a set of lived cultural values that may be the key to world survival" (Ibid.: 21).

In all of these ways and many more, Tinker explains how the Western colonial paradigm, whether expressed in religious or secular terms, is life-threatening to indigenous peoples and, more generally, to life on this planet. In this process, he goes beyond critique to provide glimpses into alternative ways of organizing human societies and of understanding our relationships to each other and to all that exists. These are always, it seems, firmly grounded in reality, in sharp contrast to the colonial constructions that always seem to be rooted in denial. The following section considers a few key aspects of the indigenous perspectives Tinker presents as an alternative to the "progress" and "development" that are killing us.

GROUNDED PERSPECTIVES

John Mohawk told the story of Hopi traditionalist Thomas Banyacya's visit to Niagara Falls, where he stopped to take in the seemingly endless maze of transformers, towers, and cables that transport electricity from the generating plant out into the world. Banyacya reflected that in Hopi teachings, Spider Woman comes back to "weave her web across the landscape. Everywhere you will see her web. That's how we will know that we are coming to the end of this world, when we see her web everywhere. I believe I have just seen her web" (2010: 91). Tink Tinker's scholarship lets us see that Christianity, as imposed by the European and Euroamerican colonizers, and Western science or secular rationality are not only built on the same foundations but also lead us to the same place, to Spider Woman's web.

The choices presented to us within the Euroamerican settler paradigm—religious or secular, liberal or conservative, White nationalist or "multicultural"—are not real choices between fundamentally different approaches. Instead, they all reinforce the web. We do have options, he insists, but to see them we have to be willing to step outside the totalizing belief system of the contemporary Western world. We have to stop trying to force a diverse range of realities into narrow understandings of time, space and consciousness; to accept that perhaps we live not in *the* universe but in a "pluriverse" of perspectives and realities (Esteva and Prakash, 2014: 41).

In *Grassroots Post-modernism* Gustavo Esteva and Madhu Suri Prakash credit Yvonne Dion-Buffalo and John Mohawk with the observation that colonized peoples can "become *good subjects*, accepting the premises of the modern West without much question; become *bad subjects*, always revolting against the parameters of the colonizing world; or become *non-subjects*, acting and thinking in ways far removed from those of the modern West" (Ibid.: 145). To truly escape the colonial paradigm we must become non-subjects and this, in Irene Watson's words, requires us to "think about the condition of dispossession outside the 'logic of possession (as a hallmark of modernity, liberalism, and humanism)'" (Watson, 2015: 149, internal citation omitted).

In *American Indian Liberation*, Tinker suggests that we begin to think outside the logic of possession by acknowledging four "fundamental, deep structure cultural differences" between European and indigenous ways of relating to the world (2008: 7–9). First, it is essential to appreciate the "distinction between a culture that builds its worldview out of a notion of space and one that builds its worldview out of a notion of time" (Ibid.: 70–74; 1986: 69). As Barbara Mann explains, because "geographical place of origin is an essential aspect of genuine Indigenous knowledge . . . a tradition or ceremony developed in one place makes no sense, or worse, makes lethal sense, in another place" (2016b: 12).

This nexus between place-based relations and consciousness brings us to Tinker's second fundamental difference, that American Indian cultures are communitarian, and that spiritual involvement is for the people—the people as a whole—not for "individual salvation or personal spiritual empowerment" (2008: 8). The goal is not "progress" or "salvation" but the maintenance (or reestablishment) of balance and harmony among the people and all of their relations.

Tinker's third point of distinction is that indigenous ways of being recognize and depend upon the interrelatedness of everything that exists—everything that is part of the natural world, as well as that which results from human activity. The larger community at issue is "not the modern state but rather consists of animals (four-leggeds), birds, and all the living, moving things (including rocks, hills, trees, rivers, etc.), along with all the other sorts of two-leggeds (e.g., bears, humans of different colors) in the world" (Ibid.: 9; also 2004a: 92). This is why Tinker can reject the notion of a linear evolution of the species, while presuming that monkeys are among his relatives.

There are no inanimate objects in this understanding of the world (2008: 10). Rocks not only have consciousness, but they are our grandparents, our oldest living relatives who, because they have so much more experience, are also our wisest relations (Tinker, 2004b: 108). This brings us to Tinker's fourth point of cultural identification. If we are related, very literally, to the natural world, it follows that our primary attachment would be to particular lands, to specific geographic spaces. We are related to all trees or rocks or rivers just as we are related to all of humanity but, beyond that, we have longstanding ties to the particular beings that have nurtured and cared for us over time. Viewed from this perspective, it becomes clear why our relationship to specific locations would be primarily understood not in terms of ownership but of mutual responsibility (2008: 9).

Having illustrated that there are ways of understanding, ways of *being*, that do not require us to remain within the narrow range of options—all ultimately destructive—proffered by the dominant euroderivative narrative, Tinker goes on to identify some priorities equally relevant to indigenous and non-indigenous peoples. We now turn to some of these.

PATHS

The colonizers' paradigm, reflected in their religious ideology, their scientific "truths," their technology and their "progress," has brought the world to the point of ecological collapse. We see Spider Woman's web everywhere and it may be that we are coming to the end of this world. But there remains the possibility that if we change the stories we live by, we can change not only our lives but those of *all* our relations. In this endeavor, Tink Tinker says, "the people we have hurt the most with our incessant modality of progress, development, and globalized economic system of exploitation are the very ones who may be able to help us understand and reimagine our fragile human place in the world" (2004b: 122).

Like other critical scholars of color, Tinker thus urges us to employ a "methodology that speaks 'from the underside of history'" (Tinker, 2008: 35; also Matsuda, 1987). Doing so in his own work, he reaches conclusions that, not surprisingly, may take us well beyond our comfort zones. Here, I focus on Tinker's conclusions with respect to three topics I find particularly significant: race and poverty, indigenous sovereignty, and the restoration of balance.

Racism and Poverty

Tinker's work is refreshingly clear about the fact that the problems faced by indigenous peoples cannot be reduced to racism and poverty. There is no doubt that American Indians have been racially subjugated throughout U.S. history and are consistently found to be "the economically poorest identifiable group in America" (Capriccioso, 2012). All too often, their poverty is presumed to be attributable to racism. This leads scholars, activists and policy makers of the dominant society, whether on the right or the left, to advocate on their behalf for equal treatment and economic develop programs. Tinker, however, is adamant that to thus relegate American Indians to "the poor" as a primary social classification "presumes a racially non-Indian world of social hierarchy, socioeconomic organization, and social class structure" (2008: 136).

In other words, racism and poverty are not the cause of indigenous dispossession but manifestations of the ongoing colonization of indigenous peoples. "Our oppression and the resulting poverty . . . are rooted in the economic need of the colonizer to quiet our claims to the land and to mute our moral judgment" on the settler state's "long history of violence and conquest" (Ibid.: 23). At its heart, the issue is not material wellbeing or subordination within settler society—that is, not a problem of race *or* class—but the right of indigenous peoples to their own identities and cultures. What is being denied is the right to self-determination, a right vested not in states or governments but, collectively, in the people (Watson, 2015: 90–91).

Tinker recognizes that racism and poverty are functions of colonial occupation. This is a foundational principle that has tremendous implications for all people of color, indeed, for everyone, in American settler colonial society. As long as the settlers are intent on occupying indigenous territories and rendering them profitable, poverty will be inevitable and none of us will be free from racism (Saito, 2020). In other words, Tinker's analysis goes beyond American Indian liberation to propose a decolonization that would benefit us all.

State Formations

Because Tink Tinker is a strong proponent of traditional indigenous ways, some may be surprised by his declaration in *Spirit and Resistance* that "the recovery of religious traditions is not our first need today" (2004a: 4). Rather, he says, the priority is sovereignty, and sovereignty "must include the international recognition of a people qua people" and their ability to move from "development"—including "sustainable development"—to "sustainable stasis" (Ibid.: 6). For many in the Western world, the concept of sovereignty necessarily implicates statehood. But for Tinker "the very emergence and eventual dominance of the modern state and the concomitant degradation of indigenous national entities contribute significantly to our situation of ecological injustice and devastation" (Tinker, 1996: 169).

States, Tinker concludes, "*must necessarily* oppress indigenous peoples, must destroy our self-identity, our cultures, and our religious and spiritual traditions" (2008: 25). The emancipatory potential of this position cannot be overstated. The contemporary international legal order is composed of state actors, and to many of us it seems "natural" for lands and peoples to come under the exclusive jurisdiction of a particular state. But history tells us otherwise. The current state-centric system is generally traced to 1648 and the

Peace of Westphalia, but it took an additional three centuries before the world was divided up almost exclusively between state actors.

Human societies had been organized in different ways for millennia before states were imposed upon them, and "substate" forms of governance continue to be as influential, in many respects, as state governments. "Possession of sovereignty is the result of force threatened and applied," and "[s]tates are the results of wars fought and won, rather than of some sort of natural truth about the community," Paul Kahn observes (2004: 263). Rosa Ehrenreich Brooks suggests that "if we stop fetishizing the state, perhaps many phenomena that now often appear . . . as problems . . . would instead appear as virtues or opportunities" (2005: 1181–1182), and this is exactly what Tinker does.

He urges us to recognize the state for what it is—a European political construct—and to turn our attention from reforming the state to (re)building the "small, local, autonomous communities" that flourished around the world prior to 1492 (Tinker, 2004a: 21–22). This, he emphasizes, would allow actual indigenous sovereignty and self-determination to flourish. Again, this is a path that could prove liberatory to us all. State formations have not contributed in any significant way to human wellbeing, and history tells us that nations and peoples can be organized in multiple and overlapping ways. Territories have long been shared between peoples, and individuals have often identified themselves within networks of relationships rather than as subjects of a particular state sovereign. We would all do well to heed Tinker's advice and begin thinking beyond states.

Reciprocal Completion

Because the ideological justifications of Euroamerican colonialism rest on the presumed superiority of Western civilization, the colonial project has denigrated and attempted to eradicate the identity and knowledge base of the colonized. As summarized by Albert Memmi, those who have been colonized have been "removed from history," stripped of a role in "every decision contributing to [their] destiny and that of the world, and all cultural and social responsibility" (1965: 91). If we want to move beyond the constraints of a European colonial world order that has given us genocide, enslavement, gendered and racial oppression, and ecological devastation, we cannot accept its foundational premises. If we wish to restore a world in which harmony and balance are given primacy, we will have to develop—or reclaim—decolonized approaches to thought and language.

Ngũgĩ wa Thiong'o tells us that colonial rule is consolidated not only with brute force but also by what he calls the "cultural bomb"; one that "annihilate[s] a people's belief in their names, in their languages, in their environment, in their heritage of struggle, in their unity, in their capacities and ultimately in themselves," thereby eventually "mak[ing] them want to identify with that which is furthest removed from themselves" (1986: 3). For Tinker, defusing this cultural bomb turns on an understanding of the sacred "as a duality of reciprocal completion, as the Sacred Above and the Sacred Below, as male and female, as Sky and Earth" (2008: 18).

This manifestation of duality is reciprocal because it rests on the premise that both parts are required for wholeness or completion; it should not be confused with "the euro-western concept of duality as a *binary opposition*" (Ibid.: 28; Tinker, 1996: 164). As noted earlier, Barbara Mann emphasizes that the Western construction of binary opposites and its "habit of identifying things one at a time, as discrete isolates, standing alone and operating independently, misrepresents the community required not only of humans but of all spirits" (2016b: 242).

Not surprisingly, indigenous peoples have understood reciprocal dualities not as theoretical abstractions but as tangible realities rooted in land and spatiality. Thus, Tinker reports that among the Osage

> every detail of social structure—even the geographic orientation of the old villages—reflected a reciprocal duality of all that is necessary for sustaining life. Thus, the *hu"ka*, or earth moiety, situated to the south of the village, and the *tzisho*, or sky moiety, situated to the north, represented female and male, matter and spirit, war and peace; but they only functioned fully because they were together, and together represented wholeness. (2008: 72)

Again, these are insights that may well be critical to our common wellbeing. "It is the task of all sentient things—and everything is sentient—to recognize and maintain the smooth balance of the halves in the gestalt of the whole" because "[w]hen the Twinship stops, the Cosmos crumbles" (Mann, 2016b: 242–243).

Concluding Thoughts

Tink Tinker's foreword to Deloria's *God is Red* describes it as "a forceful challenge to the presumed inherent hegemony of the western intellectual tradition" (2003: xii). The same can easily be said about Tinker's body of work. It critiques not only Christianity, or Western theologies, but also the belief in science and materialism that pervades settler colonial societies and may well be more insidious than religious indoctrination. Tinker lets us see that the substitution of "scientific facts" for religious ideology does nothing to change the underlying political, historical, or cultural dynamics, and that the entire colonial paradigm must be challenged.

"The contemporary crisis calls for imagining new stories that can generate life and not conquest" (Tinker, 1996: 173). Sometimes this means turning our assumptions on their heads. Thus, for example, Tinker tells us not only that rocks are our relatives, but also that because they have been around the longest, they have accumulated the most wisdom. This, in turn, explains why "[i]f there is a hierarchy of beings in the Indian experience of the world, humans are found at the bottom rather than at the top, being the youngest and least wise of all living things" (2004b: 108).

With insights like these, Tinker encourages us "to ask ourselves what is lost, or simply missing, from the Western scientific record and what is gained by exploring indigenous avenues of philosophy and research" (Ibid.: 113). The answers, it seems, are of critical importance to indigenous and non-indigenous peoples alike. As we come to understand that our collective survival may well depend on perspectives that originate beyond the confines of a colonial worldview, that embrace a pluriverse of cultures and understandings that have been kept alive by indigenous peoples despite the colonial onslaught, we can see that the survival of indigenous peoples, as such, is essential to our collective survival and our liberation.

NOTES

1. © 2019. Distinguished University professor and professor of Law, Georgia State University College of Law. Many thanks to Miguel De La Torre for organizing this *Festschrift*, and to Ward Churchill, Barbara Alice Mann, Glenn Morris, Sharon Venne, Irene Watson, Robert A. Williams, Jr., and Michael Yellowbird for insights that have allowed me to fully appreciate the significance of Tink Tinker's scholarship. As for Tink, I cannot find words adequate to the gifts of your work, wisdom, and support.

2. This prioritization of space is vividly illustrated in Lera Boroditsky's observation that in the Kuuk Thaayorre language spoken in northern Australia, cardinal directions identify all spatial relations—the fork, for example, being to the east of the knife (2011: 64).

Chapter 3

"Words Have Meaning"

Reflections on a Vector of Tink Tinker's Indigenist Scholarship

Ward Churchill

Words have meaning. And their meaning doesn't change.

—Antonin Scalia (Senior, 2013)

It may seem more than slightly perverse that I've elected to begin this appreciation of my longtime friend and coconspirator George Tinker—or Tink, as he prefers—by quoting so wretched a eurosupremacist reactionary as the late supreme court justice Tony Scalia. Be it noted, then, that the juxtaposition entails precisely the sort of revealing irony that Tink has in my experience always been wont to enjoy. He'd be the first to acknowledge the truth embodied in Scalia's two brief sentences and, were the phrase "as a matter of mere expediency or convenience" added at the end of the second, the observation might well have been one offered by Tink himself. The difference is that while even a cursory review of Scalia's record exposes the duplicitous posturing with which his lofty utterance was imbued, scrutiny of Tink's, no matter how exacting, produces a diametrically opposing result. Indeed, as much as anyone with whom I've been privileged to engage over the past half-century, and far more than most, Tink has consistently applied this principle.

There are myriad ways in which this might be illustrated, but of particular importance in my estimation is Tink's unswerving adherence to the meaning assigned to the word "genocide" by Raphaël Lemkin, the Polish-Jewish jurist *cum* refugee from the nazis who coined the term toward the end of World War II. To glimpse anything approximating the range of implications attending Tink's integrity in this regard—not least the manner in which it has informed and shaped his broader scholarly practice of "calling things by their right names" irrespective of whatever discomfort might be thus induced or the degree of risk incurred in doing so, a stance firmly grounded in American Indian traditions of knowledge formation and transmission, especially those of his Osage people—it seems necessary to trace the brief but illuminating career of the now woefully misunderstood word "genocide."

A CASE STUDY IN THE SUBVERSION OF MEANING

In an August 1941 radio address to the British people, Prime Minister Winston Churchill observed that the nazis were demonstrably committing what at that point remained "a crime without a name" (1941: 6474). Three years later, in his magisterial study of nazism's colonial policies, *Axis Rule in Occupied Europe*, Lemkin remedied the situation remarked upon by Churchill by devising a neologism combining "the ancient Greek word *genos* (race, tribe) and the Latin *cide* (killing)" to describe "the destruction of a nation or of an ethnic group," categories he often merged as "national groups," explaining in a footnote that "[a]nother term could be used for the same idea, namely *ethnocide*, consisting of the Greek 'ethnos'—nation—and the Latin 'cide'" (1944: 79).

Lemkin was clear from the outset that, far from describing a freshly minted phenomenon, and less still a crime unique to the nazis—as Churchill's comment might be taken to imply—his new term "denote[d] an old practice in its modern development" (Ibid.). Moreover, recognizing the potential for misimpressions arising from its third syllable, he was at pains to emphasize that the word genocide should *not* be construed as a synonym for mass murder. Rather, it was meant to encompass *any* systematic effort by one country or society to bring about the dissolution and eventual disappearance of another. As he explained the core concept:

> Genocide has two phases: one, destruction of the national pattern of the oppressed group; the other, the imposition of the national pattern of the oppressor. This imposition, in turn, may be made upon the oppressed population which is allowed to remain, or upon the territory alone, after removal of the population and the colonization of the area by the oppressor's own nationals. Denationalization was the word used in the past to describe the destruction of a national pattern [but] is inadequate [because] it does not connote the imposition of the national pattern of the oppressor. (Ibid.: 79–80)

Lemkin's foundational elaboration was thus antithetical to the notion that extermination of the "oppressed population" constituted the sole, or even primary, criterion by which the nature of its oppression might be "properly" assessed as genocidal; were it otherwise, there would be no population upon whom "the national pattern of the oppressor" could be imposed. This is not to suggest that he somehow failed to grasp that genocide could be, had been, and was in fact being accomplished through the physical liquidation of targeted groups; to the contrary, his seminal chapter summarized methods employed to that end by the nazis against European Jews, Poles, and other Slavic peoples (Ibid.: 87–89). Rather, Lemkin's point was that such an approach was and remained the exception, not the rule (Ibid.: 79). Most commonly, he observed, genocide has been perpetrated through "a coordinated plan of different actions aiming at the essential foundations of the life of national groups . . . the objectives [being] disintegration of [their] political and social institutions, of culture, language, national feelings, and economic existence" so that the group loses viability and dissolves (Ibid.).

Initially, Lemkin divided "the techniques of genocide" into eight categories: Political, Social, Cultural, Economic, Biological, Physical, Religious, and Moral (Ibid.: 82–90). In 1947, as its first priority in fulfilling its mandate to pursue "the progressive codification of international law," the newly formed United Nations enlisted Lemkin—along with two others who seem to have contributed little—to draft a convention defining "the crime of genocide" and prescribing appropriate punishments for those guilty of engaging in it (Cooper, 2008: 88–100). In this effort, Lemkin reorganized and condensed the original eight categories into a three-part typology—Physical, Biological, and Cultural:

- *Physical genocide* included not only direct killing, but the imposition of such "slow death measures" as denial of an "adequate means of livelihood" to the targeted population through expropriation of their land and other property; denying them adequate nutrients, medical care, and shelter; and subjection of members of the group to certain types of "medical" and "scientific" experimentation.
- *Biological genocide* devolved upon "the systematic restriction of births" through involuntary sterilization, compulsory abortion, and/or segregation of the sexes.
- *Cultural genocide* encompassed a range of actions, from prohibition or criminalization of the targeted people's language, to the forced exile of their political, intellectual, and religious leadership, systematic "destruction or diversion to alien uses" of their "historical and religious monuments," destruction or "dispersion" of documents or objects of historical, artistic, or religious value, and the "forced transfer"—that is, removal—of their children, "forcing upon the [latter] from an early and impressionable and receptive age a culture and mentality different from their parents" (Lemkin, 1947a: 232–236).

Here again the greatest weight was placed on "the destruction of the national pattern of the oppressed group" and "imposition of the national pattern of the oppressor" through a "coordinated plan of different actions," albeit with the "actions" subsumed under the single heading of "cultural genocide." In sum, the draft convention retained definitional consistency with Lemkin's original concept, that is, that genocide(s) might be hypothetically consummated without the death of a single member of the group(s) targeted for elimination (Davis and Zannis, 1973: 18, 20; Jones, 2006: 13). To be sure, he recognized that such would never be true in "the real world" since the modalities of genocide are overlapping, interactive, and inevitably combine to some extent in any given context (Lemkin, 1947b: 147), but embraced this very complexity as confirming his position. As illustration, he launched a massive historical survey of genocidal processes, including three chapters devoted to genocides impacting American Indians, but it remained unfinished when he died in 1959 (McDonnell and Moses, 2005; Jacobs, 2012: 379–401).

It has become somewhat fashionable to dismiss Lemkin's founding definition of genocide as it never saw concrete application in criminal proceedings. Even "the Nazis tried at Nuremberg were not specifically accused of 'genocide,'" or so it is said. Actually, in the International Military Tribunal's June 1945 indictment of the two-dozen top-ranked surviving nazi officials tried at Nuremberg, the defendants were accused of participating in "deliberate and systematic genocide" (International Military Tribunal [IMT], 1947: I: 43–44). The indictment was drawn up by U.S. Supreme Court Justice Robert H. Jackson, temporarily serving as his country's chief prosecutor, and while his phrase was unattributed in the indictment, in the ensuing trial both Britain's chief prosecutor and his deputy cited the definition of the crime posited "in Professor Lemkin's well-known book" (IMT, 1947: XVII: 61; XIX: 494–519). The word genocide did not appear in the tribunal's verdicts, but neither was anything said to indicate a dismissal of the charge or the exoneration of any of the defendants to whom it applied (Schabas, 2000: 44).

The United States conducted an additional twelve "thematic trials" of lesser nazis at Nuremberg between 1946 and 1949 and each case was framed in a manner incorporating the charge of genocide as Lemkin defined it. On December 11, 1946, before verdicts were reached in any of these trials, the UN General Assembly passed Resolution 96(I), "affirm[ing] that genocide [again, as Lemkin had defined it] is a crime under international law which the civilized world condemns" (Abtahi and Webb, 2008: I: 34). This nullified claims that "the crime of genocide was not part of international law" (Stiller, 2012: 114), and was cited to rebut the defense of *nulla poena sine lege* (there can be no penalty without law) in the "Jurists' Trial" of 1947 (Nuernberg Military Tribunals [NMT], 1950: III: 983).

In July 1945, Justice Jackson famously declared that, "If certain acts ... are crimes, they are crimes whether the United States does them or whether Germany does them, and we are not prepared to lay down a rule of criminal conduct against others which we would not be willing to have invoked against us" (1949: 330). This is worth bearing in mind when considering that in the so-called RuSHA case of 1947–1948, the offenses charged fell almost entirely under the headings of biological and cultural genocide as framed in Lemkin's draft convention (NMT, 1950: IV: 609, 622–626, 631–632, 636–639, 642, 639–666, 674–689, 701–702, 713–893, 989–1072, 1075, 1100–1111, 1118–1120). Unquestionably, Lemkin's conception of genocide *did* have legal force, however transiently, and it *was* applied in criminal proceedings.

That it did not prove more durable resulted from the gulf separating Jackson's noble rhetoric from the harsh reality that not one of the four powers represented on the international tribunal at Nuremberg—least of all the United States—was willing to be held to "the rule of criminal conduct ... laid down against" the nazi defendants. The great about-face commenced the moment they began to seriously assess the ramifications of the draft convention through the lens of their own policies. This triggered a complex series of maneuvers by major UN member-states to protect themselves by narrowing the scope of the crime so as to omit practices of which they were not only guilty but in which they fully intended to continue to engage (Schabas, 2000: 64–90).

The resulting "compromise" all but eliminated cultural genocide as a form of the crime, thereby not so much inverting Lemkin's concept as truncating it beyond recognition (Davis and Zannis, 1973: 21). Thus, under Article II of the 1948 Convention on Prevention and Punishment of the Crime of Genocide, the term refers to "any of the following acts undertaken with intent to destroy, in whole or in part, a national, ethnical, racial or religious group, as such":

(a) Killing members of the group;
(b) Causing serious bodily or mental harm to members of the group;
(c) Deliberately inflicting on the group conditions of life calculated to bring about its physical destruction in whole or in part;
(d) Imposing measures intended to prevent births within the group;
(e) Forcibly transferring children of the group to another group.

The United States, alone among the major powers and despite its key role in engineering this glaring definitional subversion, has refused to be bound by even these meager constraints. Declining to ratify the convention for forty years, it did so in 1988 only after attaching a "sovereignty package" claiming a "right" to exempt itself from compliance at its own discretion (LeBlanc, 1991: 253–254). Accordingly, Tony Scalia studiously evaded employment of the word genocide in his opinions, either, as in *Employment Division v. Smith* (1990), by (re)framing issues in a manner allowing him to simply ignore the concept or, as in *Brown v. Entertainment Merchants Association* (2011), by dismissively using "alternate terminology."

While the U.S. posture is anomalous and has thus attained little resonance among scholars, Canada's is another matter entirely. Although it ratified the Convention in 1952, it did so with the proviso that for domestic purposes "the definition [of genocide] should be drawn somewhat more narrowly than in the International Convention so as to include only killing and its substantial equivalents" (Davis and Zannis, 1973: 23). Canadian courts have since enforced this "narrowly drawn definition" by ruling, as in *Daishawa v. Friends of the Lubicon* (1996), that it is libelous for anyone—including victims—to accuse perpetrators of genocide on any other grounds (Churchill, 2003: 254–255), and Canada's definitional stance has been so widely imitated within the burgeoning academic enterprise known as "genocide studies" as to be virtually hegemonic.

By 1960, an increasingly well-populated segment of the "Free World" intelligentsia had begun to cohere around the objective of casting a patina of validation over official distortions à la Canada's. They have done so by concocting and continuously rehearsing a "sociological definition" of genocide wherein the phenomenon is invariably portrayed as consisting *exclusively* of the physical liquidation of targeted groups through direct killing and/or the imposition of "slow death measures" (e.g., Drost, 1959: II: 125; Horowitz, 1976: 19–20; Harff and Gurr, 1988: 360–361; Chalk and Jonassohn, 1990: 23–24; Charny, 1997: 75–76), or, at most, a combination of physical extermination and systematic prevention of births (Fein, 1990: 24). Such inconvenient matters as the infliction of serious mental harm and forced transfer of children, although both are posited as "genocidal acts" in the Convention—have simply been absent from mainstream scholarly discourse.

Meanwhile, as ably surveyed by Bartolomé Clavero, an overlapping cast of characters was proceeding along a parallel track to relegate the entire cultural component of genocide to the status of a separate, presumptively lesser, and still uncodified offense they dubbed "ethnocide" (Clavero, 2006). Their subterfuge is readily revealed by the misrepresentation of the word itself by a pair of its leading proponents as having been "coined by the French after [World War II] to cover the destruction of a culture without the killing of its bearers" (Chalk and Jonassohn, 1990: 9). It is immaterial whether the authors, both "acknowledged experts," were unaware of Lemkin's coinage of the term ethnocide—suggesting they'd never read him—or were deliberately falsifying its origin in order to conceal the fact that it is a synonym for genocide, not a word invented to describe some other process.

From there, "scholarly" efforts to further pare down the definitional parameters of genocide have moved into genuinely bizarre realms of restrictive criteria that would, if accepted as valid, likely leave the concept void of any remaining legal or analytical utility. Even in contexts involving the infliction of mass death, the abovementioned pair of "experts," rejecting the Genocide Convention's reference to group destruction "in whole or in part," have asserted that only cases where the perpetrators' demonstrable intent was/is to exterminate a target group in its entirety should qualify (Ibid.: 23). They and others have argued as well that only where the target group does not attempt to physically defend itself should its destruction be deemed genocidal (Ibid.: 22–23). As historian David Stannard has observed, the list of hurdles conjured up also includes the scale of killing, proportion of the target population destroyed, rate of extermination, means by which the killing was/is perpetrated, and on, and on (1996: 169–180).

In the main, such arguments—polemics, really—have been advanced by two distinct camps, both highly politicized. The more prolific has been composed primarily of Jewish scholars bent upon arriving at a definition of "true" genocide "confirming" that it "has happened [only] once, to the Jews under Nazism" (Bauer, 1978: 38), that their experience is therefore "phenomenologically unique" (Katz, 1994: 3, 51–62), and that they—or more accurately, Israel—are/is entitled to monopolize the "moral capital" inhering in such "incomparable" suffering (Alexander, 1980: 47). Their counterparts in the second camp corroborate these contentions, either directly or implicitly, insofar as doing so absolves their own societies of guilt (e.g., Friedberg, 2000).

A MASSIVE DOSE OF DENIAL

Susan Griffin, writing from a self-consciously euroamerican standpoint, once aptly mused that "[t]here are whole disciplines, institutions, rubrics in our culture that serve as categories of denial" (Griffin, 1992: 162). Nowhere is this more obviously manifest than in the refusal, ubiquitous among Griffin's sociocultural cohort, to acknowledge any aspect of U.S. history that might dispel their triumphalist fantasies of its "exceptionalism" and "innocence" (Saito, 2010), least of all the ongoing genocide(s) of the continent's indigenous peoples upon which the United States' very existence has always been contingent. Corresponding with Griffin's insight, a voluminous literature, together with a couple-thousand Hollywood movies, a much larger number of television programs, myriad documentary films, and a vast panorama of other degrading/dehumanizing imagery, have been devoted to buttressing the matrix of collective denial.

Not surprisingly, an appreciable segment of the material explicitly denying the genocide of American Indians has been produced by those like Steven T. Katz, whose singular purpose has been to "prove" the uniqueness of nazi judeocide (1994: 18n40, 87–91). Others pursue multiple agendas, as illustrated by the notorious Guenter Lewy, who attained disrepute during the 1970s as a leading academic apologist for the U.S. slaughter in Southeast Asia before going on to make a career of never meeting a genocide other than the Sho'ah—as the judeocide is known in Hebrew—that he *didn't* deny (e.g., Chomsky, 1982; Hancock, 2002: 60–61). Suffice it to say that Lewy's 2004 screed, "Were American Indians the Victims of Genocide?" is entirely compatible with the rest.

Prominent recent examples from what was characterized above as a "second camp" of deniers include Peter Cozzens' *The Earth is Weeping* (2016), an "entertaining version of the Indian wars" kicked off with the bald assertion that whites "never intended to exterminate the Indians," as evidenced by the "fact" that "no real attempt [was made] to destroy the tribes on a larger scale" than the systematic obliteration of numerous peoples recounted in the rest of the book (d'Errico, 2017). Cozzens' recipe, shared by S. C. Gwynne in his more narrowly focused *Empire of the Summer Moon* (2010), is old hat, essentially a canoodling of the absolutionist canards with which mainstream "American Indianist" historiography has been larded for decades (Ostler, 2015).

More innovative approaches have also emerged of late. The most insidious surfaced in Gary Clayton Anderson's *The Conquest of Texas*, where he announced that the state's frankly exterminatory drive to become an Indian-free zone "never rose to the level of genocide," and that his interpretation of that ugly history was intended to "create a new paradigm…utilizing the more moderate and well-understood process of ethnic cleansing" (2005: 7, 14–15). Gratified by the reception accorded his initial foray, Anderson followed up with *Ethnic Cleansing and the Indian*, explicitly intended to demonstrate that "[g]enocide did not occur in America, primarily because moral restraints prevented it" (2014: 13). What Anderson revealed instead was the extent of his ignorance of his subject matter.

Professing it "presumptuous to use modern terms [like genocide] to describe past historical realities [*sic*]" (Ibid.: 8), Anderson seems oblivious to the fact that the term "ethnic cleansing" first appeared in the translation of a 1991 Serbian policy directive quoted by journalist Blaine Hardin. In striking contrast to his purported objections to applying "modern terms" in historical analysis, Anderson situates his "new paradigm" in still more recent developments, that is, "new definitions called the Rome Statutes [*sic*] . . . crafted between 1998 and 2002" (2014: 5). In actuality, there are no "Rome

Statutes." There is a single Rome Statute of the International Criminal Court (ICC) whose Articles 6–8, upon which Anderson dwells, offer no "new definitions" of genocide, crimes against humanity, and war crimes but instead rely on the terminology of the Genocide Convention, Geneva Conventions, and Nuremberg Charter (Ibid.: 5–8; Roberts and Guelff, 1982: 157–338).

Anderson further "explains" that, "as defined by the United Nations in 1948 [and] more importantly by the reformed definitions utilized by the ICC today," genocide is an "act to destroy an entire ethnic group" (2014: 9). This elides the inconvenient phrase "in whole or *in part* [emphasis added]" found in Article II of the Genocide Convention and reiterated, verbatim, in the Rome Statute. Similarly, he offers no hint that in 1992 the UN General Assembly addressed the issue of ethnic cleansing for the first time, declaring it to be "a form of genocide" (Shaw, 2015: 68), that in 1993 the World Court (ICJ) issued an opinion holding that "it is difficult to regard the Serbian acts [of ethnic cleansing] as other than genocide" (Ibid.: 69), or that the International Criminal Tribunal for the Former Yugoslavia—a transient ICC prototype—has "recognized 'cleansing' as genocide in several [additional] cases" (Ibid.).

The balance of *Ethnic Cleansing and the Indian* follows the same pattern of, to borrow a phrase from Tony Scalia's dissent in *King v. Burwell* (2015), "interpretive jiggery-pokery," as Anderson systematically distorts and/or invents "facts" to support his case-by-case assertions that "it may have been a crime, but it was not genocide." Such is the state of "responsible scholarship" in the United States that his squalid performance received generally favorable and sometimes glowing reviews in several mainline academic journals, prompting a growing infiltration of the "'cleansing' euphemism" into not just scholarly but official and popular discourses as well (Shaw, 2015: 66). This, in turn, reveals that euroamerica's overall state of denial regarding its genocide(s) of American Indians has reached such a depth that it's actually *eager* to embrace a terminological evasion that leaves it guilty "only" of wholesale and sustained engagement in crimes against humanity.

RESTORING THE MEANING OF A WORD

The implications of Tink's *Missionary Conquest* (1993), signified by his use of the term "cultural genocide" in the subtitle, must be assessed against this tortuous backdrop of definitional subversion and the scale of euroamerica's psychointellectual investment in denying responsibility for even the most amputated characterization of genocide. Until *Missionary Conquest*, references to the genocide of American Indians had been mostly restricted to radical oratory, notably that of "black militants" like Malcolm X, Stokely

Carmichael—even Martin Luther King joined in—and, with far greater emphasis, John Trudell and other American Indian Movement (AIM) spokespeople. With the exceptions of Nakota legal scholar/theologian Vine Deloria, Jr., who occasionally employed it in his books during the early seventies (Deloria, 1969: 97; Deloria, 1973: 127, 173, 194; Deloria, 1974: 164–165, 231–247), and its more concerted usage in books by Renapé/Lenape historian Jack Forbes and euroamerican revisionist Richard Drinnon toward the end of the decade (Forbes, 1979; Drinnon, 1980), genocide was sometimes implied, but the word itself was conspicuously missing from writing by and about American Indians.

This began to change during the run-up to the Columbian Quincentenary (e.g., Todorov, 1984; Thornton, 1987; Sale, 1990), a trend culminating most notably with the 1992 release of David Stannard's *American Holocaust* and Forbes' *Columbus and Other Cannibals*. While forcefully injecting the forbidden term into the conversation, the focus of both books was on physical genocide and, in this sense, they're representative of others during the period. It should be noted that, although I discussed Lemkin's conceptualization at considerable length therein, much the same holds true for my *A Little Matter of Genocide*, published five years after Stannard's and Forbes' benchmarks. As a consequence, while our material breached the wall of silence marking euroamerica's denial of genocide, it did so in a manner more consistent with Canada's abridgment of the term than the meaning Lemkin originally assigned it.

Before *Missionary Conquest*, the only book I'm aware of that squarely addressed the cultural genocide of North America's indigenous peoples—as such, not by employing "ethnocide" as a euphemism—was *The Genocide Machine in Canada*, an awkwardly titled but groundbreaking 1973 study by eurocanadian researchers Robert Davis and Mark Zannis that found little traction in the United States. *Missionary Conquest* was thus foundational in terms of restoring the core of Lemkin's concept to its rightful station. Indeed, Tink's explanation of cultural genocide might well have been written by Lemkin himself.

> Cultural genocide can be defined as the effective destruction of a people by systematically or systemically (intentionally or unintentionally in order to achieve other goals) destroying, eroding, or undermining the integrity of the culture and system of values that defines a people and gives them life. First of all, it involves the destruction of those cultural structures of existence that give a people a sense of holistic and communal integrity. It does this by limiting a people's freedom to practice their culture and to live out their lives in culturally appropriate patterns (Tinker, 1993: 6).

After emphasizing that the process is aimed in no small part at destroying "the spiritual foundations of a people's unity [and] relationship to the Sacred

Other," he observes that "the social aspects of cultural genocide involve a wide variety of changes . . . imposed on Indian nations, [including] the nuclear family ideal and displac[ement of] the extended kinship system upon which an Indian nation and individuals depend for their identity . . . fostering a dysfunctional co-dependent relationship between an alienated remnant of the [targeted] people" and those seeking to eliminate it (Ibid.: 6, 7–8). Unmistakably, his depiction is that of Lemkin's deliberate and relentless "destruction of the national pattern of the oppressed group [and] imposition of the national pattern of the oppressor."

Tink's straightforward use of the term cultural genocide in his historical analyses of the means by which traditional American Indian spiritual/epistemological systems have been forcibly supplanted by Christianity has exerted a profound influence on subsequent indigenous intellectuality. So, too, his framing of genocide as an inherent dimension of colonialism—another term he insists upon using correctly—in keeping with Lemkin's 1944 observation that the form in which the crime is perpetrated is contingent upon whether the perpetrators' goal is to "colonize the oppressed population [or] the land alone," as well as Sartre's clarification a quarter-century later that "colonization is not a matter of mere conquest."

> [I]t is by its very nature an act of cultural genocide. Colonization cannot take place without systematically liquidating all the characteristics of the native society . . . . For the subject people this inevitably means the extinction of their national character, culture, customs, sometimes even their language. (Sartre, 1968: 615)

Tink was by no means the first to explicitly characterize U.S. Indian policy as colonialism. Cherokee anthropologist Robert K. Thomas had done so as early as 1966, as did Jack Forbes, among others—including the U.S. Commission on Civil Rights—during the seventies (Thomas, 1966–1967; Forbes, 1974; U.S. Commission on Civil Rights, 1975). The link between colonialism and genocide, while sometimes implied, was not brought out in these articulations, however. I began doing so during the mid-eighties, in an article on the culturally genocidal effects of policies such as the forced relocation/dispersal of the Big Mountain Diné (1985), following up with others addressing a range of other matters (e.g., 1993, 1994), and, in *A Little Matter of Genocide*, I stressed that Lemkin assigned no hierarchy to the crime's physical, biological, and cultural forms (1997: 70, 388 n, 433). Still, it wasn't until 2004 that I mustered an entire book—*"Kill the Indian, Save the Man"*—centering upon the cultural genocide of American Indians as a concomitant of colonial subjugation. Fittingly, Tink contributed the preface to that study.

This last, I think, bespeaks the more or less continuous interaction he and I have enjoyed from the late eighties onward, not only professionally, but personally, socially, spiritually/ceremonially, and, as with our repeatedly being arrested together while confronting the "celebrations of colonialism and genocide" embodied in Denver's annual Columbus Day parades, politically. While we found ourselves to be philosophically congruent in many respects from the beginning, what has transpired over the years has been a sort of "cross-pollination" of ideas and sensibilities reflected in my 2004 effort as well as Tink's *Spirit and Resistance*, released the same year, and in his *American Indian Liberation* four years later (2004a: 41, 73–74, 79, 137n23; 2008:7n10, 57, 80n31, 82, 126–127n1, 149). It's not that we've ended up saying the same thing—we haven't—but that the complementarity of our thinking has led us along parallel paths. The result is that our "work products" are mutually reinforcing and, more importantly, mutually completing.

A good illustration of how key elements of our analyses have synchronously evolved can be found in our understandings of colonialism. During the early 1980s, as a means of distinguishing the mode of colonization evident in contemporary North America from the "classic" overseas variety, I was heavily reliant upon the Gramscian concept of "internal colonialism," especially as adapted to the U.S. context by Bob Thomas, Stokely Carmichael, Rodolfo Acuña, and others during the "long sixties" (see Churchill, 1985). The same may safely be said of Tink, as he quoted Thomas and cited my principal articulation of the premise, to support his own position in *Missionary Conquest* (Tinker, 1993: 116, 165 n13). By the mid-nineties, influenced by Fanon, Maxime Rodinson, and, in particular, Cherokee activist/conceptual artist/cultural theorist Jimmie Durham, I was finding the concept of "settler state colonialism" to be of far greater utility in describing the subjugation of American Indians (e.g., Churchill, 1997: 84, 421–422). During the first decade of the new millennium, although Tink initially opted to describe the United States as an "immigrant colonial state" (2004a: 8), we each became ever firmer in embracing the settler colonial paradigm (e.g., Churchill, 2003: 1–2, 64n90, 158; Tinker, 2004a: esp. 8, 66; Tinker, 2008: 11–15, 49, 113, 149; Churchill, 2010: esp. 40–42).

The routes we've taken on the basis of such conceptual commonalities have remained inseparably related yet readily distinguishable. One rather clear indicator of the distinction(s) at issue can be extracted from our "records of citation." While the weight I've placed on physical extermination has coincided with the biases of most analysts and thus led to my work being more frequently referenced in the recent swell of scholarship purportedly seeking to expand understandings of genocide (e.g., Stoett, 2004: 35, 48–49; Short, 2016: 6, 18, 198–199; Huseman, 2016: 160–161, 172–173), Tink has clearly evinced greater heft with respect to "the missing piece." He was, for instance, the *only* scholar quoted and discussed with regard to cultural genocide in Elazar Barzan's early effort to introduce the "topic" of indigenous peoples to a mainstream survey of genocidal phenomena (2003: 124–126). Similarly, he was the sole Indian quoted/cited in the chapter on American Indians in Laurence Davidson's *Cultural Genocide*, the first book length effort to restore the excised component of Lemkin's typology to the field of genocide studies (2012: 41–43).

Over the past decade, Tink and I have occasionally found ourselves cited in conjunction with one another in the literature of that and cognate fields, at least by those prone to acknowledging both indigenous peoples and the crime's cultural dimensions (e.g., Pine and Stearn, 2018: 16). It has been even more encouraging to see the same conjuncture make its appearance in the next generation's theses and dissertations, and, most of all, to find the young Nehiyaw (Cree) legal scholar Tamara Starblanket skillfully interweaving quotes from both of us with others garnered from Sartre, Césaire, and Agamben in *Suffer the Little Children*, her interdisciplinary study of the cultural genocide wrought by more than a century of Canada's forced transfer of successive generations of indigenous youngsters for indoctrination in church-run residential schools (Starblanket, 2018: 173–176).

As Israel Charny observed nearly twenty years ago, "slowly but surely, a broad ecumenical group of scholars of all cases of genocide is emerging" (2002: 470). Undeniably, a growing number of American Indians can be counted as members of that group and, like Starblanket, are consciously employing the term in a manner consistent with its original meaning (e.g., Mann, 2005; Smith, 2005). Indeed, among Native North America's newest generation of scholars, many are by now so accustomed to such usage that they no longer feel a need to explain it, less still to argue the point with deniers (e.g., Estes, 2019). The same can be said for a few of the settler society's more honest historians (e.g., Kakel, 2011; Lindsay, 2012; Ostler, 2015). It's not that the "rubrics of denial" under which the settler colonizers' ongoing genocide(s) of American Indians were so long and insistently buried have been relegated to history's dung heap—far from it—but it's fair to say that counterhegemonic understandings are steadily gaining both force and momentum.

One can easily imagine the wraith of Raphaël Lemkin beaming with belated gratification at this turn of events, while that of Tony Scalia gnashes its teeth as his dictum is held to its literal meaning in this connection, absent any ability on his part to dissemble, obfuscate, or evade the implications. As Oglala Lakota elder Mathew King once explained to me, to know your location at any point in a journey across the plains, it's necessary to look back toward the place from whence you've come, and only by knowing where you are can you set the course you must take to arrive at your intended destination. By this, he meant that understanding your present circumstance requires an accurate knowledge of history, and only by clearly apprehending the current situation can you undertake the actions necessary to attain a desirable future, not only for yourself but for coming generations. In such an endeavor, I was instructed by Muskogee elder Philip Deere, it is imperative that things be called by their right names.

This is especially true when, as with American Indians, both past and present involve the endurance of genocide. To call it anything other than what it was and will always remain is to preclude genuine understandings of both the past and present, thereby foreclosing upon the realization of a future free of genocidal subjugation. The alternative is oblivion, a reality with which indigenous scholars, activists, and allies alike are increasingly coming to grips, and which is defining the terms and forms of their resistance to perpetuation of the settler colonial status quo. The "war against oblivion," as a leading chronicler of the Maya liberation struggle in the Yucatan has described it, is far from won, but the signs are propitious (Ross, 2000). Hence, as we enter the twilight of our respective journeys, it seems to me that Tink and I can each glean satisfaction from knowing that, both individually and collaboratively, we've consistently done our parts to steer the process in the right direction.

Chapter 4

At Cross-Purposes

Conversion, Conscripted Compromise, and the Logic of eurochristian Religious Poetics

Roger K. Green

Tink Tinker asked the contributors of this book to deal with the theme of native compromise. Etymology of the word "compromise" invokes a notion of mutuality, but we know that compromises between eurochristian colonizers and indigenous peoples have been asymmetrical. I therefore want to qualify my contribution here by emphasizing the notion of *conscripted* compromise for indigenous American peoples, a term I pull from David Scott's *Conscripts of Modernity*. My use of "Indigenous American Peoples" includes indigenous peoples of Turtle Island and *Abya Yala*—both continents known as "the Americas"—who have together faced conscripted compromises as they became unwitting and often unwilling participants in eurochristian religious poetics of sacrifice. These poetics evidence what Scott has called a "problem space" drawing our attention to persistent patterns of destruction occurring today throughout both contents, where indigenous lives are "spiritualized" through process of mnemonic erasure, policies of "termination," and outright violence. Where indigenous Americans, their remaining lands, resources and even cultural practices are broadly regarded as able to be expropriated, extracted, assimilated. Where such lives are treated as "expendable." As Scott says, a problem-space signals a place for intervention. It "is an ensemble of questions and answers around which a horizon of identifiable stakes (conceptual as well as ideological-political stakes) hang" (2004: 4). In this chapter, I draw on the theme of conscripted compromise to highlight Idealized Cognitive Models (ICMs) at work in eurochristian religious poetics, following the work of Tink Tinker (Wazhazhe, Osage) and Steven Newcomb (Shawnee/Lenape). I also employ the work of Luis León and Barbara Alice Mann (Seneca), emphasizing *processual* accounts of such poetics trans-generationally, as they perpetuate genocidal thoughts and actions against indigenous peoples today. Drawing from eurochristian poetics of sacrifice across two continents, I argue that current iterations of violence against indigenous peoples, and women in particular, display centuries-long logics of indigenous erasure. An analysis of the poetics of sacrifice tied to work on ICMs offers an instance for intervention and decolonization, although what decolonization will mean for indigenous peoples will necessarily differ from the processes that eurochristian must undergo to become aware of their continued complicity in violence toward indigenous peoples.

Conscripted to a european phantasy structure of sacrifice, indigenous American worldviews were compromised early on to entirely androcentric "humanist" religious and legal poetics. This is reflected in the *Requerimiento*, which to a certain degree acknowledged the rational agency of indigenous Americans under the notion of "natural law." In 1510, the Council of Castile wrote the *Requerimiento*, which was to be read to all Indians upon contact. Despite its humanist attempt to avoid slavery by asking indigenous people to willfully submit to their new eurochristian authorities and *convert* to christianity, the final warning in its last paragraph clearly echoes the languages of the earlier papal bulls of Christian Discovery, conscripting indigenous Americans once again to poetics of sacrifice in earlier documents for the expansion of christenDOMination:

> But, if you do not do this, and maliciously make delay in it, I certify to you that, with the help of God, we shall powerfully enter into your country, and shall make war against you in all ways and manners that we can, and shall subject you to the yoke and obedience of the Church and of their Highnesses; we shall take you and your wives and your children, and shall make slaves of them, and as such shall sell and dispose of them as their Highnesses may command; and we shall take away your goods, and shall do you all the mischief and damage that we can, as to vassals who do not obey, and refuse to receive their lord, and resist and contradict him; and we protest that the deaths and losses which shall accrue from this are your fault, and not that of their Highnesses, or ours, nor of these cavaliers who come with us.[1]

Refusing the *Requerimiento* was in itself grounds for an Augustinian "just war" against the refusers.

That the language of the *Requerimiento* was that of provocation was not lost on those sent to deliver its message. As Robert J. Miller *et al.* write:

> Many conquistadores must have worried that this preposterous document would actually convince Indigenous peoples to change religions and accept Spanish rule and prevent the explorers from gaining conquests and riches because they

took to reading the document aloud in the night to the trees or they read it to the land from their ships. They considered this adequate notice to the natives of the points in the *Requerimiento*. So much for legal formalism and the free will and natural law rights of New World Indigenous peoples. (2010: 15)

Miller *et al.*'s bitter last sentence is understandable, but perhaps that bitterness also reflects too much optimism for the very category of "natural rights," which itself develops within a eurochristian poetic frame. Miller *et al.* note that, in Francisco Vitoria's lectures in the 1530s, Vitoria strengthened Spain's claims to empire by declaring that indigenous Americans "possessed natural rights as free and rational subjects" and moved away from legitimacy based on the papal bulls of donation while at the same time grounding a theory of international law based on 'natural rights' and 'universal obligations of a eurocentrically constructed natural law'" (Ibid.: 14). This further conscription enfolded humanist, "rights-based" language within earlier claims to christian princes' "right" to rule.

The result for indigenous Americans was essentially the same as with the poetics of the *Requerimiento*: resisting infidels would in turn require Spain to "protect the faith" by waging "just war." As Stephen Greenblatt notes:

A strange blend of ritual, cynicism, legal fiction, and perverse idealism, the *Requerimiento* contains at its core the conviction that there is no serious language barrier between the Indians and the Europeans. And to a thoughtful and informed observer like [Bartolomé de] Las Casas, the dangerous absurdity of this conviction was fully apparent: Las Casas writes that he doesn't know "whether to laugh or cry" at the *Requerimiento*. (1991: 98)

In the historical context of a rather recently conceived notion of universal "natural rights," which understood humans as having a certain capacity for reason, the absurdity makes a bit more sense; but as Las Casas and others *knew* at the time, the *Requerimiento* was merely a ritualized instance of expropriative possession. The "requirement's" conscription and its cowardly delivery highlights the asymmetrical conditions of the compromise forced upon indigenous peoples across two continents.

Such a conscription resulted in shared forms of resistance across diverse groups of people indigenous to the invaded lands, conscripted to the term "Indian." It has become standard practice in Native American scholarship to focus on cultural-determination and continuity, as well as material contributions by indigenous peoples in the world economy in recent years. Here I am thinking of works such as Jace Weaver's (Cherokee) *The Red Atlantic* and Marcy Norton's *Sacred Gifts, Profane Pleasures: A History of Tobacco and Chocolate in the Atlantic World*. Such works importantly contest narratives that would merely assign victim status to indigenous Americans, but historical accounts alone do not signal the continued indigenous critical thinking articulated writers such as Leanne Betasamosake Simpson (Michi Saagiig Nishnaabeg) in *As We Have Always Done* and Nick Estes (Lower Brule Sioux) in *Our History is the Future*. These writers perform what Gerald Vizenor (Anishinaabe) has termed "survivance." Vizenor writes, "Survivance is an active resistance and repudiation of dominance, obtrusive themes of tragedy, nihilism, and victimry" (2008: 11). He specifically contrasts this with monotheism, which "takes the risk out of nature and natural reason and promotes absence, dominance, sacrifice, and victimry." Indigenous writers who perform survivance evidence ICMs of distinct indigenous peoples.

Tink Tinker and Steven T. Newcomb have addressed this issue in terms of deeply framed ICMs, emphasizing the transgenerational transfer of comportment and worldview. They insist, against pedantry around the term "essentialism," on an account of indigenous worldviews. Mark Freeland (Sault St. Marie Anishinabek) defines "worldview":

> as an interrelated set of cultural logics that fundamentally orient us to space (land), time, the rest of life and provides a prescriptive methodology for how to relate to that life. This definition is designed to provide a corrective to the lack of consistent use of the term. Worldview as a concept is often used but rarely defined. This lack of precision undermines the ability of the term to communicate cultural difference at a deep level. Since there is so much misinformation and misunderstanding to Indigenous relationships to land, I privilege a definition of worldview that can communicate those fundamental relationships to time and space. (2021: 10)

Barbara Alice Mann (Seneca) has detailed twinned concepts that persist with local variations across the two continents against the European colonizers' religious frames. She writes:

> Now that no one's being gunned down *en masse*, at least not on this continent, for talking back to the gatekeepers of Western culture, I expect that this trickle of Turtle Island voices will sweep into a tsunami. Maybe it will even become obvious to the old guard of academe that in refusing, refuting, and otherwise disputing Christian hegemony, Indians are not "weakening" their arguments by "essentializing" Indigenous tradition but are decentering Euro-Christianity as the all-inclusive norm. (2016b: 40)

Taking these indigenous voices in concert, I suggest that "survivance"—beyond being an aesthetic ("of the senses")—signals also an indigenous ICM.

Newcomb and Tinker have explored ICMs to articulate the worldview of eurochristians. Following them with a longer history of eurochristenDOMination in mind is necessary to understand conscripted compromises. The DOM here refers to Steven Newcomb's *Pagans in the Promised Land*, where he analyzes linguistic frames such as the vertical notion of the Latin notion of "the dominate":

> A key point here is that the categories and concepts of federal Indian law, including such concepts as discovery, dominion, domestic dependent nation, tribe, and so forth, are cultural and cognitive products of the dominating society. These terms are evidence of the various ways that the society of the United States has employed the human imagination to interact with the original indigenous peoples of this hemisphere in a dominating and subjugating manner. (2008: 18)

Newcomb articulates the hierarchical presence specifically in the Conqueror ICM and the Chosen-People-Promised Land ICM. The vertical scheme of power plays out in several ways. Newcomb writes:

> The ICM of the Conqueror posits a central figure, such as a king, monarch, or pope, who is considered to come from or be derived from a divine source. The presumption of the conqueror's divinity leads to the additional presumption that the conqueror has "divine right" to exert control or force, which is understood as being UP, as reflected in the metaphor POWER IS UP. Conversely, those peoples whom the conqueror has subjected to his control are conceptualized as being DOWN in relation to the conqueror, as reflected in the metaphor LACK OF CONTROL IS DOWN. Furthermore, the conqueror is presumed to have the divine right not just to rule, but also to spread or expand his reign or domination outward by expanding his rule to "new" lands by means of war or force of arms. This conception is found in the term *imperium*, or "a dominium, state, or sovereignty that would expand in population and territory, and increase in strength and power." In order to find or "discover" additional lands that the conqueror can subdue, he must send representatives forth to search out, discover, and find *new* lands to conquer and subdue. (Ibid.: 24)

Conscripted compromise is not merely subjugation to "law"; it is conscription to a particular religious poetics of sacrifice.

Echoing Newcomb's analysis, Tinker explicitly addresses the "up-down image schema" imposed upon indigenous peoples through colonization—the same up-down schema that Newcomb attributes to the Doctrine of Discovery. As Tinker writes:

> Here, I am not simply objecting to the language of god and creator as language embedded in a european worldview or christian ideology. It is much more crucial to notice that imposing these religious metaphors of a hierarchical divine as an overlay on Indian cultures irredeemably distorts Native culture and destroys

the intricacies and the beauty, that is, the coherence of the Native worldview. An up-down linguistic cognitive image schema functions to structure the social whole around vertical hierarchies of power and authority. (2013: 169)

In contrast to such religious poetics, as Tinker argues, indigenous worldviews are relational, emphasizing locality and balance:

By local and cosmic we mean to say that Indian folk experience their own place at the center of a cosmic whole, but that their experience of the cosmos is not an experience they would be in any way tempted to impose on other peoples who experience the cosmos in other local places. To that extent, Indian communities were never evangelical or proselytizing. (2015: 207)

Important to ICM analyses is that fact that cognitive models, while metaphorical, are also *physical*, as George Lakoff's work on ICMs has attested. Beyond cognitive science alone, however, Tinker and Newcomb focus on *intergenerational* transfers that go far beyond normative uses of "ideology." It is not that native people do not at times become nominally Christians; nor is it that a eurochristian like myself cannot intellectually understand that in stories of Sky Woman Falling, for example, natives see their existence as dependent on animals and plants as elder siblings, as *relatives*.

In the eurochristian worldview by contrast, humans are the pinnacle of creation, charged with superior "stewardship" over animals and nature (*Genesis* 1:28; 2:15). Thus, even if I can intellectualize how attitudes toward environmental balance for indigenous peoples might play out differently than those temporally orientated toward a de-territorializing *Parousia*, where Jesus is a "new" Adam; regarding animals and plants as my relatives is not part of my eurochristian deep framing. In the conscripted compromises of indigenous peoples to eurochristian religious poetics, "survivance" adheres to transgenerational indigenous ICMs. With these nuanced descriptions of worldview in mind, let me now turn again to compromises in the southern continent.

As Juan Carlos Garavaglia notes, the importation of the encomienda system to the southern continent necessarily built upon and corrupted two local indigenous concepts of reciprocity. The first category of the encomienda system was *mitayas*. *Mit'a* is Quechua word for "turn," meaning that certain people would take their turn doing service work for the larger community. In the colonial context, Spanish and Portuguese colonizers reframed the concept according to a eurochristian hierarchical model where subjects of a king pay "tribute" and "taxes": "*Mitayos* were to keep living in their own villages while serving in rotation on the Spaniard's lands or doing other tasks. Sometimes the products of their service were also called *mita*" (1999: 10).

This was partly because the Spanish needed a ready supply of Indian labor to get their colonies started.

The second version of the *encomienda* system was the *yanacona* or *originario*. These terms applied to Indians who were separated from their communities permanently to serve the Spanish. Again, with the Quechua word *yanacona* there was a pre-Spanish context for leaving one's home to go work somewhere else. As Garavaglia explains, it had to do with "high-status specialists" who were needed in different places," but under the Spanish hierarchical model the term came to mean something like "bondage," and this was a form of slavery. Even in the passage from *The Cambridge History of the Native Peoples of the Americas* that I am citing here, the term "high-status specialists" rings as something like "free masons" in feudal Europe, who were "free" from local servitude because they were specialized enough to participate in grand projects such as the building of massive cathedrals. Such conceptions distorted and transformed indigenous forms of reciprocity through a particular process of subduing.

Within the first fifty years of contact, Garavaglia notes a shift from *mitayo* to *yanacona* system. This was "a process by which people legally entitled to stay in their home villages were taken under so-called protection by the Spaniards when they went to Asuncíon [now the capitol of Paraguay] to 'pay' *mita*, and in time were enslaved by out-and-out purchase" (Ibid.: 11). The pattern of "becoming" *yanacona* and the need for "protection" was part of a eurochristian process of converting both the land and the peoples there into "Christendom" or eurochristianDOMination. It also conscripted natives to new foreign forms of social organization unthought of in initial compromised alliances between some indigenous groups and the newcomers.

There were practical reasons for the process. At first, the Spanish could not control everyone. They needed local alliances. But as they gradually gained a hold on territory, there was no longer need for *mitayos*. The early colonizers in this way prepared the way for the homogenizing descent of the *Basileia* or "kingdom" of Christ through the uprooting de-territorialization of the Conqueror ICM. This made way for the Franciscans, who sought more explicitly to "civilize" Indians by converting them using *reducciones* after 1574, a prelude to reservations in the north (Ibid.: 17). Although converting Indians had been a tool for invasion since the beginning, the rapid decline in population from violence, disease, and cruel working conditions had the colonizers worried that the Indians would not reproduce enough children to carry on multiple generations of forced labor. On top of that, a new generation of *mestizos* had grown up. This of course increased the reliance on imported slaves from Africa.

The trafficking of women was another tool of colonization used from the outset, though not separate from the religious poetics of sacrifice. Spanish men generally did not bring women with them, and so through both rape and marriage alliances early on, eurochristian sought establish dominance. As Garavaglia notes, indigenous peoples of the region already intermarried between local groups to maintain political balances. The result of intermarrying created elaborate kinship systems that the colonizers could hardly understand. One result in indigenous contexts was that a man's family was in service to another group if a woman from his family partnered with that group. The lack of gender balance among the colonizers as they arrived speaks not only to their inherent masculinist patriarchy, it also speaks to a fundamental way that they would never reciprocate in the social patterns of indigenous peoples. It would have been inconceivable for a Spanish man to serve Indians because his sister married one.

In the form of class divisions, complex racial distinctions based "blood quantum," and steadily consistent violence against indigenous women on both continents, eurochristian colonization persists today. It is important to see such violence against women not merely as "secular" violence but within the Conqueror ICM. Attention to gender in this context also ought to be complimented with attention to the Survivance ICM to articulate crucial distinctions between indigenous gendering and progressive liberal ones reading women's rights into de-territorialized eurochristian notions of "freedom."

As with the conscripted compromises that morphed *mit'a* and *yanacona* concepts into "reduced Indians," discourse on "conversion" to "religion" is also one of compromise. With respect to southern contexts, Eduardo Viveiros de Castro notes with suspicion the "secularized" use of "culture," which acted as a reoccupation of earlier theological structures:

> For we, moderns and anthropologists, tend to conceive of culture in a theological mode, as a "system of beliefs" to which individuals adhere, so to speak, religiously. The anthropological reduction of Christianity, such a decisive enterprise for the constitution of our discipline, could not help but impregnate the culture concept with the values it hoped to grasp. "Religion as a cultural system" presupposes an idea of culture as a religious system. (2011: 12)

He notes that the "bad habits" the Jesuits saw in the Tupinambá in terms of culture: "The Jesuits saw 'culture' as the hard core of the elusive indigenous being."

The stereotype of the "backsliding," converted "irrational savage" (who was incapable of maintaining converted status) persisted across both continents. Eduardo Viveiros de Castro writes that, for eurochristian, the "defining feature of the [sixteenth century] Amerindian character" in South America was based on a stereotype of inconstancy: "the half-converted Indian who, at the first opportunity sends God, the hoe, and clothing to the devil, happily returning to the jungle, prisoner of an incurable atavism" (Ibid.: 5). Viveiros de Castro believes much of the stereotype stems from the Tupian people of Brazil and cites a Jesuit of the period (Nóbrega) complaining:

> These heathens are not like the heathens surrounding the early Church, who would either quickly mistreat of kill anyone who preached against their idols, or believe in the Gospel, thereby preparing themselves to die for Christ. For since these heathens have no idols for which they die, they believe everything that is said to them. The only difficulty lies in taking away all of their bad habits . . . which requires extended stay among them . . . and that we live with them and raise their children, from the time they are small, in doctrine and good habits. (Ibid.: 8)

The openness to "believe everything that is said to them" speaks to an element of compromise on the part of natives, but the Jesuit conscripts it to the eurochristian frame of the irrational, "gullible," or "half rational" savage. He also notes the absence of impulses to "sacrifice" themselves. In the Jesuit's model, "true" conversion was predicated on a prior civilizing and the fact that Indians were only "half-converted" reaffirmed their "inconstant" status and lack of full rationality. More than the fact that the passage reveals a clear genocidal intent to indoctrinate children and erase "bad habits," there is a marked commitment early on to a multigenerational process of extirpating indigenous ways. Conversions were to be ritually repeated over and over.

As Kenneth Mills details in his review of colonial Inquisition records regarding extirpation (genocide) of Andean practices in the seventeenth and eighteenth centuries, indigenous resistance is remarkably dynamic amid the most horrible of conditions:

> One cannot explain satisfactorily Andean religious endurance simply by invoking such things as the Andean people's remarkable determination or the strength of their reciprocal relationships with their ancestors, as important as such things were. Recognizably Andean religious patterns retained their significance because they changed. In many parts of the mid-colonial Archdiocese of Lima, Andean religious survival was as much about a dynamic. (1997: 5)

Survivance ICMs are not static; yet the colonizers commented frequently on the "backsliding" among indigenous peoples, generation after generation, while still holding to a very clear intention of installing a european religious hierarchy.

Backsliding into "pagan ways" was used to further justify brutal subjugation over generations, yet the colonizers were also capable of a slow change over time. For example, in seventeenth-century Peru:

> In the Archdiocese of Lima, the Indian who was viewed as a pagan or an idolator, and whose errors derived from complete ignorance of the Christian truth, had for the most part become a distant figure of an early colonial past. This Indian's replacement, both in reality and especially in the minds of many Spanish Christians, was a "new Christian"—an American *converso*—a baptized and at least superficially instructed convert of whom certain things could now be expected. (Ibid.: 24)

Early accounts record no "idolatry," but the persistence of a eurochristian worldview concerning ChristenDOM informed the civilizing desire in an increasingly "evolutionary" trajectory. As Anthony Pagden has summarized: "In time, Indians and all other 'barbarians' will become 'civilised' beings, just as the Europeans climbed up from barbarous beginnings via Greece and Rome until finally they reached the condition of the Christian *homo renatus*" (1982: 106): the "reborn" human. This historical trajectory and "evolution" conceive an expropriated and de-territorialized *ascension* resituated through a *rebirth*. The "converso" here enacts a subalternate mimesis of *Homo renatus*.

As indigenous Americans lost the status of sylvan innocence, their punishments for revealing persistent "pagan idolatry" become harsher: "Witchcraft, along with demonology, had become something of a science in its own right, and thus offered Hispanic churchmen plenty of convenient points of reference and authority" (Mills, 1997: 95). "Devil-worshiping" sorcerers were blamed for the persistence of "pagan idolatry" particularly in rural areas because Spanish colonizing techniques had focused initial on the "upper class" leaders among Inkas, assuming in true eurochristian fashion that conversion among "leaders" would "trickle down" to the masses. So, in multiple evangelical waves, often following revivals or "awakenings," eurochristian went off again to spread gospel to "heathens."

In the south, during the sixteenth and seventeenth centuries, we see a period where *caciques* or native leaders were left in control of *mita* "payments" in a transitioning economy where natives gave tribute to a sovereign they would never see. This disruption of the preceding economy caused profound changes, eventually leading some *caciques* in the late seventeenth century to be investigated for their own harsh treatment of Indians. During the period, *caciques* had gone through a process of conscripted "rebirth," gradually replacing oral memory and *khipus* with European writing systems less dependent on collective memory. These were "new *caciques*." As Thierry

Saignes writes, this was in many ways a reversal of pre-contact economic relationships:

> Perhaps the losers lost out because of excessive respect for "moral economy" and the duty to redistribute wealth among their subjects. As for the success of the new contenders, it was above all due to their expertise in commercial accumulation. The mercantile reorientation of the *ayllus* [kinship networks], in a setting of endemic fiscal corruption, afforded brilliant opportunities for "social climbing." When the "new men" of the seventeenth century took over from the old lineages, they knew more than their predecessors about the strategies of financial and judicial manipulation and about forming alliances with local and regional government agencies. (1999: 71)

Still, by the eighteenth century, these "once-powerful lineages suffered economic impoverishment, arbitrary dismissal, or replacement" by crown-appointed governors, and throughout the entire region, "Inka domains deteriorated into more or less predatory arms of Spanish commerce and taxation." As with marriage "alliances," the conversion from *mita* to *yanacona* to "reduced Indian" is a process of expropriation and de-territorialization that finds its internal reflection in the "reborn" *cacique* whose upward mobility is entirely tenuous awaiting later waves of civilization. This kind of missionary work continues on a global scale today.

Moving north, in Luis D. León's analysis of *difrasismo* tendencies among Aztecs, he stresses the processual nature of "religious poetics." Noting the constant in-betweenness in Nahual conceptions of *neplanta* and the duality of dissonance that produces *difrasismo*, which can be "described [as] the philosophical quest for explanation, religious poetics, but was used also as a metaphor for poetry or poem" (*flor y canto*) (30). *Difrasismo* names a process of metaphorical formation between different words to form a metaphorical unit common to Mesoamerican cultures. While already imbricated within the necropolitics of nation-state dominance, León sees "religious poetics" as a "viable method not only to study and understand the way people attempt to make sense of themselves, others, and religion, but also to do, make and achieve religion itself" (2004: 17). I read León's work alongside Vizenor's "survivance" ICM, finding his processual emphasis useful. In addition, Barbara Mann has advanced a "fractal view of genocide" through analogies of tsunami's "wave train" by focusing on (1) the duration of event, (2) the level of government acquiescence, and (3) the level of populism "naturalized" through repetition and ignoring of injustices involved. Mann's work significantly attends to the overlapping ideological affordances glossed over by seeing violence against indigenous peoples as isolated events. When we combine these emphases on process with Tinker and Newcomb's stress on ICMs, we get something more nuanced than the charge of genocide as a crime. We get a glimpse that the attempted erasure of indigenous peoples across both continents is endemic to a eurochristian religious poetics of sacrifice.

The poetics of sacrifice begin with the baptismal erasure of indigenous lands through the importation of the Doctrine of Christian Discovery. Absent a christian sovereign, under international law, the land was deemed *terra nullius*, or "nobody's land." Part of this was outwardly affirmed by eurochristian through the literal death of indigenous inhabitants. In the north, *The Charter of New England, 1620* again evidences the conscripted compromise:

> And also for that We have been further given certainly to knowe, that within these late Yeares there hath by God's Visitation reigned a wonderfull Plague, together with many horrible Slaugthers, and Murthers, committed amoungst the Sauages and brutish People there, heertofore inhabiting, in a Manner to the utter Destruction, Deuastacion, and Depopulacion of that whole Territorye, so that there is not left for many Leagues together in a Manner, any that doe claime or challenge any Kind of Interests therein, nor any other Superiour Lord or Souveraigne to make Claime "hereunto, whereby We in our Judgment are persuaded and satisfied that the appointed Time is come in which Almighty God in his great Goodness and Bountie towards Us and our People, hath thought fitt and determined, that those large and goodly Territoryes, deserted as it were by their naturall Inhabitants, should be possessed and enjoyed by such of our Subjects and People as heertofore have and hereafter shall by his Mercie and Favour, and by his Powerfull Arme, be directed and conducted thither. (Thorpe, 1909)

People who want to minimize the genocide of indigenous peoples frequently claim that disease did much of the killing, as if that somehow counterbalances the atrocities of direct, physical violence and enslavement to de-territorialize and depopulate lands occupied by indigenous peoples. In this passage we see that, building on the claims to territories unclaimed by a christian sovereign, the colonizers imagined, in a foreshadowing of Manifest Destiny, that God was intentionally clearing the path for colonization by wreaking a plague upon the "savages." Emily Conroy-Krutz's history of nineteenth-century U.S. Protestant foreign missionary societies notes that a "hierarchy of civilization" was essential to christian imperialism: "It was precisely because this hierarchy existed and because it was possible to move up toward civilization and Christianity that the mission movement existed" (2015: 50).

In the early English colonies, Indian practices deemed "religious" were to be punished by death, following an anti-blasphemy law passed in 1644 after Indians heckled and laughed at Eliot's attempts to evangelize them, as Tinker notes in *Missionary Conquest* (1993: 29). Jace Weaver explains that Matoaka ("Pocahontas") was christened "Lady Rebecca" as a public display of England's "civilizing" influence. She also attended a showing of *The Tempest*, which was partly based on a shipwreck involving her husband which had become popular news in England. Apparently, James I was even angry at her husband, John Rolfe, for marrying a "princess" above his station, fearing "Rolfe might assert some future claim on his Virginia Colony for having married royalty" (2014: 149). That English royalty were capable of seeing the political alliance with a native "princess" is clear, but very real diplomatic alliances such as this did little to curb the eurochristian poetic phantasy with respect to the "savage Indian" because the intention of the religious separatists was to establish their own colonial government. Francis Jennings notes that the word "savage" went through linguistic pejoration among English colonizers in particular, who "never adopted the conception of the Noble Savage": "The word *savage* thus underwent considerable alteration of meaning as different colonists pursued their varied ends. One aspect of the term remained constant, however: the savage was always inferior to civilized men" (1975: 59). The fictional aspects of poetic conscription are evident.

Articulating the power of deep and surface structures, Tinker writes in *Missionary Conquest*:

> even as the initial deep structures of the native peoples began to be transformed by the new missionary surface structure, no one should be so naïve today as to assume that the transformation resulted so quickly in the adoption of Puritan English deep structure, either at the linguistic or psychological level. (1993: 34)

Indeed, even if we were to ask just how long a deep structure lasts against an all-out assault on one's relatives, surely the more significant overwriting deep structure would be the experience of trauma itself. As Tinker writes, "it was problematic because the English structured reality in ways that made it difficult for the missionaries to have any clarity at all about the Indian conceptual world and finally made it difficult for them to contemplate genuinely across barriers so severe" (Ibid.: 39). The result was genocidal, even if missionaries were well-intentioned.

Mimetic importations of eurochristian religious poetics were also incorporated into ideas of Indian "savagery" to reenact the Christianization of pagan peoples of Europe through rituals of "playing Indian." With respect to "New England," Philip Deloria has articulated the politics of indigenous-identity-appropriation. May-Day carnivals brought performances of class reversals to Turtle Island, where "white [settler] Indians" came to signify their "natural" Americanness by forming "St. Tammany" societies, supposedly in reverence to "Tammenend, a Delaware person who had granted William Penn access to the river and woods" (1998: 13). On May Day, "King Tamany" was burned by white colonizers dressed as Indians: "The rituals worked in countervailing ways. Tammany's death was a metaphor for the 'disappearance' of Indian people from the land, the destruction of the old cycle, the dawning of another era in which successor Americans would enjoy their new world" (Ibid.: 18). The romance of the dying or "extinct" Indian today must be constantly rejected by indigenous peoples against centuries of "playing Indian" and entitled cultural appropriation presented as "tribute." Sacrificial poetics are undeniable here, though forming marital alliances with natives upset the attempts of Puritan officials who wanted to maintain a starker distinction between colonizer and "savage" to perpetuate "just wars" whenever it suited them.

Richard Drinnon has followed the trials of English lawyer and colonizer, Thomas Morton, with respect to his tensions among Puritans in "New England." The title of Morton's *New English Canaan* (1637) appropriately evidences Steven Newcomb's emphases on the eurochristian religious poetics in *Pagans in the Promised Land*. Drinnon exposes the ambivalences between land and citizenship at work in Morton's book:

> Who were the real "uild people"? The Indians? They were at home in the land, treated Morton and other planters hospitably, shared what they had (as in "Platoes Commonwealth"), danced as a form of communal art, and derived other innocent delights from living in their bodies. Or the Saints? They hated the land, had already massacred some of the inhabitants, defaced their graves and otherwise abused their hospitality, clutched avariciously at property and things, forbade dancing, and generally denied the pleasure of their bodies. Even the careless reader could not miss Morton's answer: "I have found the Massachusetts Indian[s] more full of humanity then [sic] the Christians; and haue had much better quarter with them; yet I observed not their humors, but they mine." He perceived at its inception the stereotype of the treacherous savage and rejected it out of hand. (1980: 19)

Morton's efforts at establishing the colony of Merry Mount have been recounted in literary retellings from Nathaniel Hawthorne to Robert Lowell, which emphasize May Day celebrations imported from his part of England. The dances encouraged marriage-alliances between English men and native women—the same colonizing tactic used in the south.

At issue was the role of land and rights to it. Native women were the political leaders, and alliances with them granted some local currency, even if the Crown and later American government would claim under the importation of the Doctrine of Discovery that Indians could not hold title to land or sell it to colonizers. The baptism of the land had already christened it in the name of the "Father." Suffice it to say that it was and is less easy for Indians to become Christians, even after multiple waves of missionary conquests, than it is for eurochristian to "play Indian" so as to grant themselves an idea of their natural right to the soil and native spirituality. Morton, in his Anglicanism, like the Franciscan Bartolomé de las Casas, was perhaps more "humanitarian" than the Puritans; yet both were eurochristian civilizers nonetheless. They were working with emergent humanist notions already enfolded within conscriptions of Discovery Doctrine.

With respect to the "Great Awakening" almost a century later, Linford Fisher writes: "Despite an emerging culture of Indian Separatism in many Native communities after 1750, colonial ministers and missionaries were convinced the Awakening had failed and attempted to continue in their efforts to evangelize the same Native groups" (2012: 10). Echoing Tinker's essay on the irrelevance of European concepts of religion with respect to Native Americans, Fisher writes:

> At the most basic level, Native Americans did not separate out something called "religion," nor did they have ideas about the world that might resemble a creed or systematized belief system—or any other religious convention like written scriptures that contemporaries might have identified with European religions. Native religions were virtually synonymous with culture. (Ibid.: 16)

While I generally agree with this statement, I refer back to Tinker and Viveiros de Castro's account of Jesuits to highlight that merely replacing "religion" with "culture" does not really work. "Culture" and "cultivation" play into the same up-down image schema that Tinker and Newcomb point out.

In addition to Drinnon's account of Thomas Morton and the Merry Mount colony in New England recent work on gender alliances in northern contexts note instances of matriarchal alliances and survivance. Barbara Alice Mann's *Iroquoian Women* analyzes the process of "Euro-forming, in which 'universalist' and 'archetypal' notions create facile readings based on analogy" (2000: 62). Susan Sleeper-Smith's *Indian Women and French Men* emphasizes women's role in maintaining indigenous political structures within political and religious contexts (2001: 5). Such works importantly point to the persistence of indigenous deep framing among *conversos*. But again, we should see the asymmetry of eurochristian religious poetics as a strategic shadow text informing marital alliances. It will take multiple waves, what Mann calls a "tsunami" of indigenous voices to articulate in more detail the indigenous ICMs of survivance.

CONCLUSION

In this chapter, I have briefly covered instances of conscripted compromises during the first few centuries of contact between european colonizers and indigenous peoples. Building on analyses of ICMs in Tinker and Newcomb, I have employed Luis León's concept or religious poetics along with Barbara Mann's articulation of fractal genocide to further emphasize the transgenerational *process* of eurochristian poetics of sacrifice. I have contrasted those poetics by linking Vizenor's description of survivance to analyses of ICMs. Focusing on intergenerational attempts at indigenous conversions by eurochristian, I have articulated processual patterns across two continents, in both Catholic and Protestant contexts.

Conscripted compromises in the *Requerimiento* and *The New England Charter* were enfolded into earlier versions of the Doctrine of Christian Discovery, as were humanist conceptions that would increasingly "grant" rational agency to "backsliding" natives. As the centuries unfolded, "reduced status" of indigenous peoples through concentrated *reducciones* and reservations decreased the necessity for political alliances, even though marriages were still used to gain access to native land as it was increasingly converted into "property."

Within this analysis, ongoing violence toward native women ought to be read with an eye toward eurochristian religious poetics of sacrifice. According to the National Congress of American Indians, murder and sexual violence against native women occur at rates that exceed other populations, and the perpetrators are most often non-native.[2] An analysis of conscripted compromise allows us to contextualize the problem space of such violence within the processual ICM of eurochristian religious poetics of sacrifice. Violence against native women in particular ought to be tied to a centuries-long de-territorializing process that uproots indigenous lives through a hierarchical spiritualizing move toward transcendence. Attention to such poetics is therefore no mere literary analysis of textual conscription; rather, it points toward a necessary place of intervention.

NOTES

1. Council of Castile, "Requerimiento 1510," *nationalhumanitiescenter.org*, Accessed February 23, 2020, https://nationalhumanitiescenter.org/pds/amerbegin/contact/text7/requirement.pdf.

2. National Congress of American Indians, *Statistics on Violence against Native Women*, February 7, 2013, Accessed March 26, 2020, http://www.ncai.org/attachments/PolicyPaper_tWAjznFslemhAffZgNGzHUqIWMRPkCDjpFtxeKEUVKjubxfpGYK_Policy%20Insights%20Brief_VAWA_020613.pdf.

Chapter 5

I'm an Indian Too?

Miguel A. De La Torre

In his groundbreaking book, *Missionary Conquest*, Osage scholar George (Tink) Tinker argued that "the Christian missionaries—of all denominations working among American Indian nations were partners in genocide. Unwittingly no doubt, and always with the best of intentions, nevertheless the missionaries were guilty of complicity in the destruction of Indian cultures and tribe social structures—complicity in the devastating impoverishment and death of the people to whom they preached." Christian missionaries, regardless as to how holy they may have been, regardless of their best intentions in defending Indians from decimation, contributed to and was complicit with the dehumanization of Indians, constructing them "sometimes as savage and sometimes as innocent but childish, yet always as culturally (and, hence, spiritually) less than the European-Christian norm" (1993: 4). Tinker provides scholars with a ruler by which to measure not only heroes of the faith responsible and complicit with the Eurocentric settlement of the Western Hemisphere, but those who were intellectual heroes. For me, one such hero is my intellectual mentor José Martí. This chapter explores how he would measure up against Tinker's ruler.

José Martí was not a missionary. He instead was an "enlightened" freethinker of the late nineteenth century who held a very low opinion of Christianity when used as a means of maintaining ignorance. He was cognizant of the historical connection between colonialism and Christianity, writing: "the product of empire of the Caesars is Christianity!" (*OC* 22: 96).[1] Wedged between the declining power of colonial Spain and the emerging imperial expansion of the United States, he is recognized as an intellectual whose writings were well known throughout *latinoamérica*; being the main conduit through which the U.S. political and cultural ethos came to be known from the villages of Patagonia to the border towns of northern Mexico. His journalistic articles found in daily newspapers throughout *latinoamérica* read more as literary essays geared to raise consciousness about oppressive structures than reports on actual events. Yet ironically, even though he spent the last fifteen years of his life writing from New York City, even though a six-ton bronze statue of him on horseback depicting the instant he was mortally wounded while riding into battle sits at the Artists' Gate entrance to New York City's Central Park (located on 59th Street where 6th Avenue dead ends) between the other *latinoamérico* heroes—Simón Bolívar and José de San Martín (a trinity of revolutionaries)—few North Americans know anything about Martí.

José Martí was the organizational founder of the Cuban revolutionary movement of 1895 which sought independence from Spain. Professionally, he was a recognized professor of philosophy and linguistics, a translator and multilinguist, a first-class propagandist and storyteller, an art critic, journalist, ethnographer, scholar-activist, revolutionary strategist, diplomat representing Argentina, Uruguay, and Paraguay, and through his works *Ismaelillo* (1882) and *Versos secillos* (1891), an established international poet and founder of the literary genre *modernismo*. His writings touch on the subjects of history, anthropology, art, economics, philosophy, politics, science, sociology, and of course, religion. He lived a sacrificial life of poverty, raising consciousness on how *latinoaméricano/as* can incorporate a different type of modernity, a way of thinking different from Eurocentric thought. José Martí, I have argued elsewhere, was a precursor to what would come to be known, some seventy years after his martyrdom seeking Cuba's independence, as Liberation Theology.

Martí was an enlightened thinker, decades before his time. Probably no other *latinoaméricana/o* of his time was as progressive. He envisioned a new political reality free of racism and rooted in the incorporation and celebration of the contributions made to *latinoamérica* by Indians. His *nurestra América*, our America—as oppose to *la otra América* (the other America of the Anglos)—was the first Eurocentric postcolonial project of the Western Hemisphere. No doubt, during an era when the norm was the continuous use, misuse, and abuse of Indians, Martí has been celebrated for being the first non-indigenous person to recognize the interconnectedness of Indian oppression with the normalization and legitimization of oppressive structures throughout *latinoamérica*, and the importance of including native populations as equals in the construction of any future América. "American intelligence is an indigenous plume," Martí wrote (OC 8: 336). He was very outspoken and clear as to who was to blame for the oppression of indigenous populations. In his play written to commemorate Guatemala's independence, "*Drama Indio*," he impugns the church and the colonial government for their cruelty toward Indians (OC 18: 131–51). Yes, he sought to defend and save the Indian from oppression, seeking to make them co-laborers in the construction of a new *latinoamericano/a* identity. No doubt, his best intentions for Indians were sincere and heartfelt. Still, if we take Tinker's scholarship seriously, his vision for *nuestra América* was no less genocidal to Indian identity and culture.

L'HOMME SAUVAGE

Martí held no romanticized illusion concerning Cristóbal Colón, referring to him as "El Inglorious Columbus" (*OC* 21: 377). Elsewhere, he called him a "pirate, thief, and cowardly counterfeiter" (*OC* 5: 204). Neither does he mince words concerning the atrocities committed by the Spanish conquistadores: "The conquistadores have stolen a page from the Universe" (*OC* 8: 335). He vexes poetically against those responsible for the genocidal atrocities visited upon the Indians; yet, he remains complicit in their cultural genocide by agreeing with Colón's assessment about the original occupants of the island. Early in Colón's encounter with the Taínos, he described them as "very simple-minded and handsomely-formed people" (1492: 114). Colón's initial comments concerning the Taínos would contribute to what would come to be known as the noble savage, a concept philosophically expanded by scholars, who like Jean-Jacques Rousseau, portrayed "primitive" man as noble existing within his state of nature. The image of a noble savage was useful as long as Indians remained placid; but, if they ever were to rebel against European oppression, then the savage was emphasized.

The Taínos became a construct of the imagination of *conquistadores* and colonial administrators. The *l'homme sauvage*—the savage man who could be either noble or debased—was a social product which bore little resemblance to reality. This newly "discovered" Indian resonated with the popular figure of medieval times who symbolized the negation of Christianity, a folk version of the Antichrist, and a grotesque imitation of man for he was a creature of the devil (Dickason, 1980: 71, 74). The European imaginary space of unknown worlds was inhabited by cannibals, women with three breasts, cities of gold, cities solely occupied by women warriors, giants, and a Fountain of Youth. When Europeans came in contact with an unknown continent full of unclassified flora, fauna and humans, they imposed upon this land and those who occupied the land the images of their imagination. This debased humanity of medieval fancy reinforced by Colón's diary entries, was projected upon the Taínos.

Thus, the Taínos were seen and perceived as wild men, nymphs, satyrs and pygmies; a soulless humanity descended from a different "Adam." Because they were "savages," there existed no moral impediment from economically benefitting from them for they were not members of humanity; and as such, had no claim to property rights. While conservatives relegated Indians outside the human family, progressive provided a kinder, gentler assessment. While progressive thinkers accepted the humanity of Indians, they nonetheless continue to argue they were savages, not because they were outside the human family, but rather, because they were stuck at a lower evolutionary stage. If indeed their primitiveness was due to a lack of civilization and Christianization, then their cure, their salvation, can be achieved through consciousness raising, through assimilation to the so-called superior Eurocentric culture, and through their embrace of a Eurocentric world view. So, for those who lean more conservatively, the Indians were like beast of the field which as an asset could prove to be profitable; for liberals like Martí, Indians can rise above their station through education. For the Indian, both perspectives proved damning.

The construction of Indians, as beast or primitive, justified disenfranchisement throughout *latinoamérica* for centuries, an oppression still present during the time Martí lived in Mexico and Guatemala, where he witnessed their marginalization first hand. Yet, in spite of the misery witnessed concerning their relegation to the underside of society; he nonetheless appreciated their importance in constructing a new ethos and more just society throughout the Américas. He chastises his fellow *latinoaméricano/as* for expressing shamed for possessing indigenous roots: "Those born in the Américas, who are ashamed because they wear the Indian loincloth of the mother who raised them; whom they disown. Rascals! For leaving the ill mother alone in her sickbed" (*OC* 6: 16). His support for Indians went so far as to insist they had no obligation to support or belong to White civilization: "The Indian in his people's reservation, who barely has meat to eat or something to wear, has reason to resist paying the public burdens of a citizenship he does not enjoy, and laws written in a language he does not understand" (*OC* 10: 374). Martí recognized that the continuous abusive treatment Indians faced hindered the creation of any future *patria* rooted in justice: "How can we walk forward, with history before us, with this crime behind us, with this impediment" (*OC* 10: 273).

Yes, Martí was—like Bartolomé de las Casas before him—a sincere defender of the Indians. But like de la Casas, as Tinker argues, Martí remained complicit with the cultural genocide of the Indians because any attempt to bring justice to Indians for the betterment of the Américas, was brought about through paternalistic lens requiring their assimilation to the dominant Spanish culture. Even when defending Indians or praising their culture, Martí still described them in cartoonish caricatures. They remained in his mind primitive and savage—*l'homme sauvage*. Yes, Martí's recognized the sufferings and hardships Indians faced at the hands of whites; however, he continued to perpetuate Jacques Rousseau "enlightened" myth of the noble savage, writing: "The indigenous people of América were a noble race!" (*OC* 10: 88). Elsewhere he wrote: "The Indian is discreet, imaginative, intelligent, predisposed by nature to elegance and culture. Of all primitive men, he is the most beautiful and least repugnant. No savage people exist that are in such a hurry to beautify themselves, nor do they do so with such grace, correction and abundance of colors" (*OC* 8: 329).

But even though the Indian was noble and beautiful, they still lacked the necessary fortitude to rise from the evolutionary stage in which they were stuck: "In that country of birds and fruits, men were beautiful and kind; but they were not powerful. They had blue thoughts like the sky, and as clear as the stream, but they did not know how to kill" (*OC* 18: 442). Their character is romantically described by Martí as "a noble and impatient race, like men who begin to read books from the back. They do not know the small things but are ready to tackle the big. They always love the dowry adornments of the children of the Américas, and for them they show off, and for them their movable character sins, the premature politics and the leafy literature of countries in the Américas" (*OC* 8: 334). And while the white Spaniard's burden is to assist in the civilization of Indians, if they were not careful, the Indian could stunt progress: "The Spanish-American character today is in all ways superior [to Saxon America], in spite of its confusion and fatigue, to what it was when it began to emerge from the disorganized mass of grasping clergy, unskilled ideologists and ignorant or savage Indians" (1894: 176).

Regardless of Martí's best intentions, regardless as to how sincere and sympathetic he was concerning the plight of the Indians, he contributed nonetheless to their whitening process by succumbing to the paternalistic characterization of indigenous people: "The indigenous race, accustomed, by unforgivable and barbaric teachings, to laziness and selfish possession, neither sow, nor let sow. And the energetic and patriotic [Guatemalan] Government obligates them to sow or obtains permission to sow. And what they, who are lazy, do not use, the [Government], anxious about the life of the *patria*, breakdown into lots and gives them away. Because to only do good, force is just. For this alone, I have always thought" (*OC* 7: 134). Unquestioningly accepting the stereotypes of his day, Indians, absent of intelligence or any vision for a future, remained pitifully tied to the land. He writes: "Savings is useless for those who do not know the pleasures produced by capital—smart, honest and accumulated savings. [The Indian] has nothing because he wants nothing. He does not work for his wellbeing because he does not want a more loving home, a softer bed, a more valuable outfit, a better stock table than he already has. The intelligent man is asleep at the foundation of another beastly man. The [Indian] race sees no further than today. He works for what he needs, he produces what he thinks he will consume. His intelligence is narrow, for narrow is everything he conceives and does. The imbecile race, for here is our opinion explaining this miserable race" (*OC* 6: 281). True, he places the blame of their laziness on the centuries of oppression endured and the teachings received; nevertheless, in his eyes, the Indian remains lazy. True, the countries of *latinoamérica* have a moral obligation to rectify the situation; nevertheless, the Indian remains ignorant. Indian hope and salvation can only come about through Spanish education. Defining Indians through the use of Eurocentric concepts concerning the commodification of land, and capitalist paradigms of ensuring land yields profits; Martí advocates that they be forced to be employed by the government and to cultivate land for the common good and the enrichment of landowners.

THE U.S. INDIAN

Martí spent the last fifteen years of his life living in New York City. And while to the best of our knowledge, he never came in contact with North American Indians, he nonetheless wrote about them and their treatment at the hands of Anglos. He had no qualms holding the United States responsible for the crudity employed to steal the land of its original inhabitants: "This government has just compelled a miserable tribe of Indians to abandon forever their auspicious villages, leafy forests and joyful valleys" (*OC* 9: 37). He recognized the horrific conditions faced by Indians sent to reservations: "But in these reservations, there is only misery. There are agents, who like the lions of Phaedrus' fable, are in charge of distributing the assets of the Indians, who instead take a greater portion for themselves" (*OC* 9: 297). Indians faced all types of abuses from those overseeing their interests. These agents "maintain [the Indians] as beasts. They hate them and rejoice debasing them to later claim they are vile" (*OC* 10: 287).

Martí riled against the U.S. government for their mistreatment of Indians, specifically the reservation system which he saw as fatal to indigenous people: "The Indian is dead because of this vile [reservation] system which extinguishes his personality. Man grows through his own physical activity. Likewise, grinding grows because of the speed of the wheel, which when not active, like the wheel, rusts and rots" (*OC* 10: 323). Besides pitying the conditions under which North American Indians were forced to suffer, Martí recognized and confessed complicity with their situation. He blames vices like alcohol abuse, gambling, and indolence on the consequences of reservation life which distorts the true noble nature of "300 savages" (*OC* 10: 323). Quoting a prominent author and advocate of his time, Erastus Brooks, Martí writes: "There is no [Indian] vice for which we are not responsible! There is no Indian bestiality of which it is not our fault! Indian agents are liable in keeping them brutalized under his rule!" (*OC* 10: 325).

While Indians faced abuse at the hand of Anglos, Martí nonetheless, lifts up some members of the dominant culture with the best of intentions who tirelessly worked on behalf of indigenous people. In 1882, Martí praised General Nelson Miles efforts for attempting to civilize the Cheyenne. General Miles served during the Civil War and played a major role in almost every campaign during the American Indian Wars in the Great Plains. Once the Indians were pacified, Miles, according to Martí, was good to them (*OC* 9: 297). Specifically, Martí admired how Miles sold the war horses of the Cheyenne and replaced them with workhorses that could plow and farm the land. Additionally, instructors were provided to instruct Indians on agricultural techniques. Such action eliminated the Cheyenne's temptation to wage war. A happy ending to Martí's narrative is provided as he claimed once the first corn crop was harvest, the Cheyenne were transformed into successful farmers (*OC* 9: 298). Unfortunately, absent from his glowing analysis was any mention of the disruption to Cheyenne's lives, society, and worldviews as they were now forced to follow Eurocentric models of civilization. Nevertheless, Martí praised what General Miles accomplished, a blueprint for future cooperation between Indians and Anglos.

Domesticating and pacifying Indians occurs through their erasure. Martí's limited awareness of the consequences of conquest within the United States' context, especially in the "frontier," led him to a problematic solution when discussing the U.S. "Indian Question." The answer to the question becomes assimilation through education and hard work so that the Indian can ascend the evolutionary scale and enjoy the benefits of participating in a market economy and a superior political social order: "From those copper faces will come a new light. Education will reveal them to themselves. We will not be ashamed when an Indian comes to kiss our hand. He will give us pride to come close and give it to us" (*OC* 6: 352–53). Ignoring the separation of Indian children from parents, Martí praised the work of Indian Schools, specifically those established for the Cherokees. He measured the success of Indian Schools by those few graduates who went on to Ivy League Universities like Yale (*OC* 10: 273).

Telling is an 1885 essay written by Martí titled "Indians in the United States." In this essay he described the third annual meeting held by white "friends of the Indians" beside the picturesque retreat at Lake Mohonk to "calmly seek how to attract [Indians] to an intelligent pacific life" (*OC* 10: 319). The solution to the "Indian Question" for Martí was to increase federal efforts in integrating them into the economic and cultural structures of the United States—that is Eurocentric economics structures and white culture. Assimilation and integration were beneficial for Indians because they were "deprived of civil joys and social aspirations of white people, they [would] view with indifference the public school system available to them, as will not detach from the savage existence of the tribe . . . the Indian is not like that in nature, instead he has become that through an imposed system of idleness and debasement for the last hundred years . . . those same noble conditions of personal arrogance and attachment to territory stirs him like a wild beast" (*OC* 10: 322–23). Martiana scholar Anne Fountain raises two obvious disturbing questions concerning the Mohonk Convention worth repeating: (1) Why would Indians trust whites on land deals concerning lands originally stolen from them? and (2) Why were there no Indians present during these discussions concerning their welfare and future? (2014: 85).

Salvation for the Indian, according to both Martí and the Mohonk Convention, was the absorption of the Indian into the same government responsible for their historical and current oppression. Specifically, Martí calls for the abolishment of the "corrupt and unjust" reservation system which perpetuated violence, even though in his mind the original looting of Indian land was, "rational and necessary." Slowly, national lands had to again be made available to Indians, "fusing them with the white population." Yearly stipends to tribes must be abolished because it only "encourages begging and vagrancy," thus moving the Indian from a communal worldview toward a Eurocentric individual identity. Working common land had to cease so that they could be divided into plots and distributed among individual families for a period of twenty-five years. Lands not apportioned was to be sold by the government for "colonization." As guardians of the Indians, the U.S. government was to use the proceeds from the land sales for the "industrial education and betterment" of all Indians. Indian schools are to be improved, moving away from "verbiage or finer points," and instead focused on how to "raise animals and plant fields." If Indians resisted these initiatives designed for their well-being, then they must be "compelled" to work so they could "return to their pure souls" and obtain U.S. citizenship—even though citizenship meant renouncing war, forfeiting lands held, and rejecting indigenous identity (*OC* 10: 326–27).

INDIOS BLANCOS

Martí writings concerning the incorporation of Indians to any *latinoaméricano/a* future can be defined as a thesis calling for liberty, equality, and fraternity (à la the French Revolution) between Indians and Spaniards, poetically imaging a unity as "epaulets and doctoral robes, in countries that entered the world with hemp sandals on their feet and headbands on their head" (*OC* 6: 20). He avoids a simplistic definition for the struggle for unity as one between "the civilized and the barbarous." All humans are essentially the same. Although Martí rejects the popular classifications of superior and inferior races as proposed by positivist thinkers of the time like Herbert Spenser; he nevertheless attributed certain intrinsic characteristics to different racial and ethnic people. Inferiority was not innate, but it was taught and learned. Thus, only education can restore the natural harmony among equals. In Martí's mind, the Indians, as a "natural man is good, who complies and values superior intelligence." But when those with superior intelligence mistreated the natural man, then "the natural man does not forgive, ready to recover respect by force." Thus, those holding superior intelligence, those who are cultured, for the sake of achieving unity, must include "uncultured elements" in their respective nature, least society digresses into violence and chaos. For Martí, "The uncultivated masses are lazy, and timid in the ways of intelligence, and wants to be well governed; but if the government hurts them, they would shake it off and govern themselves" (*OC* 6: 17).

Martí argues that "The [Latin] American intelligence is an indigenous headdress. Can you not see how the same blow which paralyzed the Indian, paralyzed América? And not until the Indian walks, América will not begin to walk well" (*OC* 8: 336–37). Jeffrey Belnap, a scholar of fine arts, takes issue with this passage. He proposes that Martí, "goes so far as to equate this act of affective cross-identification with the forging of a fiction of kinship, an act of cross-identification in which the intelligentsia learns to don an 'Indian headdress' and imagine itself as descended from Native American peoples 'by blood'" (1998: 194). The pure Indian, as well as the pure Black, the pure Spaniard (whatever the word "pure" connotes) must all be erase in order for Martí to create a liberative *patria* based on his ideals, a Cuba which nevertheless essentially remains Eurocentric in culture, ethos, power and tradition while appropriating the cultural "headdress" of all who fall short of whiteness. For the sake of constructing nationhood, whites of the Américas, like Martí, engage in identity cross-dressing, becoming Indian when beneficial.

Predating José Vasconcelos's influential book *La raza cósmica*, Martí questions *mestizaje*, the genetic mixture of races, specifically Indian and Spaniard. Vasconcelos (1882–1959) was a Mexican philosopher and statesman credited with creating a way of combating the prevalent positivism of his time by reimagining and celebrating a *mestizo* Mexican culture to combat the belief of the evolutionary superiority of Anglos. In his early writings Martí had some concerns with the utopian concept of *mestizaje* believing that *lationamérica* heritage would be denigrated by the passive resignation of Indians and the absence of a work ethic among Spaniards. This view evolved into a somewhat positive stereotype where *latinoamérica* would benefit from the Spaniard's courage and determination and the Indian patience and generosity (Abel, 1986: 144). Still, even this more evolved positive view of *mestizaje* still essentially remained paternalistic and stereotypical. The Indian, as symbol, is to be affirmed and incorporated into what it means to be a Cuban;

however, a return to the original Indian had to be avoided at all cost. This symbol representing flesh and bone indigenous bodies must remain invisible. Upon this *mestizaje* trope a new nationalism for the Américas is created. For Martí, his call for a nation rooted in *mestizaje* becomes a call for racelessness, an attempt to create a race neutral nation.

Erasing the Indian was not that difficult to accomplish in Cuba. According to Martí's understanding of the Indian presence on the island, none existed because they all were genocide during the conquest. Elsewhere throughout the Américas they are a "constant factor" to which the colonizers owe a debt; while in North America, they were "drowned under a formidable white pressure or diluted in the race invasion" (*OC* 8: 329). But in Cuba, there are two reasons why an Indian problem cannot exist. First, there cannot be an Indian problem because there were no Indians left, for all were completely decimated by the mid-sixteenth century. The complete genocide of the island's indigenous people was a belief held by Martí who wrote: "For in ten years [since European arrival] there was no living Indians left of the three million!" (*OC* 18: 440). However, Martí's assertion is inaccurate. By 1514 the colonization of Cuba may have been complete; but, contrary to popular Cuban historical imagination, Indians were not annihilated. By 1570, in spite of the massive destruction of Taíno life, three towns (Los Caneyas, Trinidad and Guanabacoa) were entirely inhabited by Indians, two towns (Sabana de Vasco Porcallo and Sancti Spíritus) had Indians representing over half the population, and only two towns (Santiago and La Habana) were entirely Spanish. Spanish control of the island was restricted to small scattered settlements of mainly non-Spanish populations. Rather than total and complete genocide, a large portion of Taínos assimilated (through rape and/or marriage) into the Spanish dominant culture ceasing instead of being culturally indigenous (Knight, 1978: 42–43). The usage of the word genocide to describe the final solution of the Taíno people lacks nuance. A more accurate term would be ethnocide. While the indigenous ethos was nearly extinct, Taíno ancestry survived, evident through the transmission of biological, cultural, and linguistic traits. And contrary to Martí's assertions concerning Cuban Indians total annihilation, he knew this to be false. In his wartime diaries, he records staying at the hut of an Indian hostess, Domitila (*OC* 19: 217). Although he knew Indians survived the Spaniard conquest; still it was important for him to keep Indians in the grave so that he, along with all Cubans, could be born-again as a natural descendant of the anti-imperialist Indian.

Literary scholar Susan Gillman explains, "Just as Martí's rhetorical invocation of the Indian elides the role of the African in 'our *mestizo* America,' so too, more broadly, does *mestizaje* assimilates by whitening the people of America; so too does *indigenismo* celebrate a mythic Indianness while destroying actual Indians and displacing black Africans"

(1998: 96). *Blanqueamiento*—whitening—became a prerequisite for nationalistic advancement. *Blanqueamiento*, in short, was a home-grown Cuban eugenic-based strategy which went beyond the Indian to also encompass the African. The establishment of *patria*, along with the institution of racial reforms was based on whitening Indians and Africans. This concept was best articulated by José Elías Entralgo, Dean of the Faculty of Humanities at the University of la Habana after Castro's revolution, proponent of a Cuban version of eugenics, and chairperson of the 1959 *Movimiento de Orientación e Integración National*—Movement of National Orientation and Integration. Entralgo argued for a cause and effect relationship between "mulattoization" and national integration, thus applauding the rape of the women of color by Spaniards as the necessary means by which to uplift less evolved people. In *La liberación étnica cubana*, published in 1953, he wrote: "The day ... when a white slave master first had intercourse with a slave Negress in the bush or in the *barracoon* was the most luminous for mankind ... A vivifying transfusion took place that engendered a fertile and plastic symbiosis. From such miscegenation was to emerge new physical attributes and ascending psychic and oral virtues" (Moore, 1988: 47). By erasing races through whitening, Martí eradicates their subjectivity while silencing their voices.

MAS QUE INDIO

Cuban identity and *patria* are built on several different national symbols. Upon one particular and potent symbol crucial in the construction of Cubanness is the Indian named Hatuey. As the original inhabitants of the island were being brutally massacred, a *cacique* named Hatuey, arose in the land as an indigenous liberator of his people. He created a loose confederation of some four hundred Taíno men, women, and children on the eastern part of the island to resist the invading *conquistadores*, engaging in a guerrilla style war of resistance for several months. Becoming a threat to Spain's colonial designs, Cuba's first Spanish governor, Diego Velázquez, led a 1511 expedition to capture the renegade chieftain and pacify the island. Apprehended, Hatuey was sentenced to death. He was condemned to be burned at the stake. Before the fires were lit, a Franciscan friar sought his conversion to the Christian faith, promising heaven for believers and threating hell for heathens.

Hatuey is reported to have asked if he would find Spaniards if he went to heaven. When the friar answered affirmatively, Hatuey requested that the fire be lit for he never wanted to go to a place where he would find such cruel people. Such demonstration of *machismo* in the face of death endeared Hatuey to all Cubans, making him a modern symbol for Cuban resistance, specifically as a warrior against foreign powers such as Spain during the colonial period, and later the United States. But for Hatuey to be a symbol for all Cubans, he first had to die at the stake so he could then be born-again as a patriot of a new white Cuba. The living Indian Hatuey died so that a mystical whiter Indian of past imagination can be transfigured into an internationalist warrior. All Cuban symbols must be born-again as white. And hence the second reason why Cuban cannot have an Indian problem, because all Cubans are now Indian.

Among the leaders who organized the annual conferences at Lake Mohonk was Richard Henry Pratt, (Ellinghaus, 2006: 96) a leader and plenary speaker of the 1893 and 1895 conferences (Maddox, 2005: 111). In an 1879 speech given by Captain Pratt concerning the education of Native Americans within the U.S. borders through boarding schools, he pragmatically stated: "Kill the Indian in him and save the man" (Katanski, 2005: 3). This cultural genocidal methodology of "kill the Indian in him" would resonate with Martí, even though he sought a different outcome. More important than "save the man," Martí was concern with constructing a new "man" which would incorporate all Cubans. The reason predominately white Cubans can embrace the *cacique* Hatuey, who fought against Spanish invasion and genocide, as the island's most potent symbol is because Martí provided a methodology by which to resurrect all indigenous people as ontological white Cubans. But before one can have resurrection, there must be crucifixion. Hatuey—along with all Indians—must first die so they can be resurrected as the patriot of a new Cuba where they are celebrated for their *machismo*, not his *indigenismo*. Hatuey undergoes a transfiguration which turns him into an internationalist warrior like el Ché. In short, to become a Cuban symbol for all, he must first be whiten.

With the disappearance of the Indian (and the African for that matter), all Cubans become Indian (and Black). For Martí, to be Cuban meant "*más que blanco, más que mulato, más que negro*"—"more than being white, more than being a mulatto, more than being black" (*OC* 2: 299). Although he did not write it, no doubt Martí would totally agree with adding, "*más que indio*." An Indian problem cannot exist because first, as already mentioned, there are no physical Indians left, all being genocide from the island since the mid-sixteenth century; and second, if a colorblind society is achieved where there is no *más blanco, mulato, o negro*, [*o indio*] then Indians would also be guilty of the sin of genocide. All Cubans, regardless of DNA tests, are white, black, mulatto, and Indian. Indians, for whites, have always been more useful dead, gone, and invisible; so that the dream of a more just and inclusive society, which fondly (re)members them, can be constructed. A desire might exist to include the Indian in Cuban thought; nevertheless, it is important the Indian to remain invisible. "Dead," according to Law professor Larry Catá Backer, "the Indian could be transformed, generalized, denatured, and repackage for the benefit of emerging elites . . . indigenous people supplied the foundations for a trope, both literary and political, which is essential for the construction of cultural, ethnic, racial, and political identities distinct from traditional colonial masters of emerging Latin American states, as well as from that great power to the north" (2008/09: 203–204). Indians only work for the colonized European descendants if they are reduced to symbols, not as flesh-and-blood entities; because Indians as symbols, allow colonized whites to inherit Europe's former possessions without the responsibility of dealing with their complicity with Indian genocide.

Yes, Martí wrote numerous essays to celebrate and honor Indians throughout *latinoamérica*, a position few, if any other white *latinoaméricano/as* took during his time; nevertheless, his lofty rhetoric lacked substance. Because there were no races—only Cubans—he remained silent on what exactly society or government could do to create a more racially just *patria*. Rather than praxis, he relied on an overabundance of hope and political optimism. Racism would come to an end because of human good nature, specifically white humans. Martí's colorblindness blinded him to depths of white's hatred for all which fall short of the white ideal. By denying the existence of racial and ethnic groups, Martí preserved Cuba's racial hegemony by advancing a new repackaged Cuban white supremacy which effectively masked structural inequalities and injustices under the rubrics that we were *más que blanco, más que mulato, más que negro*. In spite of the omnipresence of white supremacy in every aspect of Cuban life—then and now—on the island and in the exile—the white dominant culture was able to insist on a rhetoric which absolved them of culpability. The implementation of Martí's colorblindness moved the discourse from addressing deep held Cuban institutionalized oppression to creating a political correctness expunging collective complicity with genocide.

Racial injury, when it did exist, was thus reduced to the individual and not structural, rationalized as an expected outcome of individuals competing as equals. Racial reconciliation under the guise of *más que blanco, más que mulato, más que negro* [*más que indio*] created an anti-racist national philosophy which miserably failed in fundamentally transforming the social structures which historically maintained and sustained Cuban white supremacy. Marti's raceless nationality allowed white Cubans to insist on the end of white supremacy even while those negatively impacted continue to suffer under oppression. Historian Alejandro de la Fuente documents how Black intellectuals of the Republic ridiculed white rhetoric concerning a Cuba with all and for all; used as a cantilena by politicians for votes. The Republic may have been made by all, but it benefited the few (2001: 33).

But what if those who are descendants of the Taínos refuse to disappear? What if they refuse to be influenced by the white Spanish roots of our culture? Then that Indian remains primitive. Indians are more useful for Cuban identity to be dead and/or invisible; so, the dream of a more just and inclusive Cuban society can be constructed. The inclusion of the Indian in Cuban thought is important as long as the Indian remains invisible so that all Cubans, especially the descendants of those who fed the indigenous Taínos to the dogs, can now claim to be descendants of Hatuey. No doubt Martí had the best of intentions; nevertheless, he undermined his own work. As noble as his lifelong work to combat racism and seek the fraternity of humanity; he still planted the seeds which would define how Cuban white supremacy would be manifested throughout the twentieth century.

MARTÍ *EL INDIO*

Because the Indian is born-again as white, a symbol for all Cubans, then Martí too can claim to be Indian, finding stronger kinship ties with those who hail from the same geographical location than blood ties. He writes: "What does it matter if we descend from parents with black blood and white skin? The spirit of men floats on the land in where they lived and still is drawn in with the air they breathe. It comes from fathers from Valencia and mothers from the Canary Islands, but in our veins flow the enraged blood of Tamanaco and Paracamon and claiming as its own . . . the heroic and naked Caracas warriors!" (*OC* 8: 336). Critical theorist Jeffrey Belnap argues that for Martí geography trumps biology. His father may have been born in Valencia and his mother in the Canary Islands, but his identity is formed by his social location finding kinship not with the Spaniard colonizers, but the indigenous warriors who fought them (1998: 205). With the Indian gone, assimilated into whiteness, Martí can now claim his *indigenismo*, even adopting the Indian name "Anáhuac" (Nahuatl for "close to water") for his membership to the Masons and for some of his revolutionary writings. If the Indian can be erased, then a new one can be constructed to which Martí, and all other non-indigenous Cubans can claim affinity. The consequences of Martí's disconnecting the Indian from *indigenismo* continue to be manifested in Cuba today. Hatuey, along with all Indians ceases to be symbols of resistance against white Europeans; becoming instead symbols for the descendants of white Europeans who at first resisted Spain, then the United States. All Cubans are now Indian; regardless as to how white their skin pigmentation might be. Because there is no Indian, only Cubans; Fidel Castro, a white man, is also able to be Indian and speak as an Indian. He said: "In this [Eastern Cuban] region, *our* people began the struggle, at first against the *conquistadors* . . . and a name figures in our history as the first fighter for our country, that of the Indian Hatuey . . . he was the first fighter, the first chief, the first martyr of our country (1985: 1, italics added). Castro, following Martí's philosophical lead, claims those who fought against the *conquistadors* as "our" people. Catá Backer said it best "in a Cuba without Indians, but where the memory of the Indian is revered, Cuba can seek to assert the rights of indigenous peoples everywhere without having to confront the issue of its own Indians" (2008/09: 202). Because of Martí, reinforced by today's political leaders, I, a predominately white Cuban, can say "I'm an Indian too." Or can I? Let us hope not.

NOTE

1. All of Martí's quotes—unless otherwise noted—have been translated from the original Spanish by the author. Note: rather than "save" Martí from his masculine language, I chose to faithfully translate his gender exclusive words.

Chapter 6

Niin Naandamo

The Cultural Logics of Kinship and the Theological Detour of Prayer

Mark D. Freeland

Much more thought needs to be given to the question of whether the Indians had 'gods' in the same sense as Near Eastern peoples.

—Vine Deloria, Jr. (1973: 95n1)

The process of decolonization has proven to be a tricky endeavor. For several generations now, American Indian peoples have worked to untangle the threads of colonization woven into our landscapes, communities and into our very minds. Each historical fact uncovered, each movement of direct action, each ceremony rekindled since the 1960s has provided promise and new avenues of action to mobilize. At the same time, colonial methods of erasure, distraction, and confusion continue to reinscribe themselves, sometimes by indigenous peoples in our own communities. Is coyote teasing us with another dead end or are we just not digging down deep enough to root out the colonial frameworks of thought that we are forced to use on a daily basis? We must ponder, just what are those methods of decolonization that can take us from struggle and return us to the flourishing that is remembered in the narratives embedded in our communities and ceremonies?

When we look at the work of an individual, we can see these processes of shifting decolonization as a microcosm of the macro cultural events that have taken place over the last fifty years. The work of Tink Tinker helps to exemplify these shifts in decolonization. From his early work as an ordained Lutheran biblical scholar to his recent publications, Tinker demonstrates a significant shift in thinking in the role that Christianity, missionization and decolonization has had in our communities. His early thought involving hybrid ceremonies and Indians as Christian demonstrate an initial wrestling with the Gospel that work to make sense of colonialism in the 1980s and 1990s. These early texts function as an inclusionary endeavor, challenging some of the most problematic concepts of Christianity, like the role of Jesus as Conqueror, Salvation, and suffering. Like others at the time, Tinker demonstrates how American Indian cultural concepts mirror or can be included in Christian thought and practice. This early bending of Indigenous ceremony and thought would radically shift with the publication of *Missionary Conquest*. His engagement with the unadulterated violence associated with the missionary function in colonization left a lasting impact in Tinker and his subsequent publications. This process of looking at colonization in its Christian face provided the necessary force to question American Indian participation in Christianity in any form. An essential question is then posed, is it possible for an American Indian person to participate in Christian thought and action without causing harm to their American Indian self, identity, and community?

This question would drive Tinker's thought and action for the next three decades. His writing would shift from inclusionary treatises to discussions of worldview and frameworks of thought that go deeper than the surface ideologies represented in Christianity. In *American Indian Liberation*, Tinker elaborates on this idea of worldview by naming

> *four fundamental, deep structure cultural differences* between American Indian cultures (including religious traditions, social structures, politics and so forth) distinctly apart from amer-european cultures and religions. They are spatiality as opposed to temporality: attachment to particular lands or territory: the priority of community over the individual; and a consistent notion of the interrelatedness of humans and the rest of creation. (2008: 7, emphasis in the original)

This analysis, itself an extension of the work done by Vine Deloria, Jr. in *God is Red*, marks a significant shift in Tinker's work as it moves away from Christian foundations and centers Indigenous frameworks of thought as the solid footing for the development of life-giving systems for Indigenous peoples. I would suggest this discursive shift is the culmination of years of work, searching for sustainable analytical methods, which can promote life-giving systems of thought and action.

Tinker's work on worldview can be seen to develop in a piece he wrote in 2013 entitled, "Why I Don't Believe in a Creator," as part of a collection of essays titled *Buffalo Shout, Salmon Cry*, addressing contemporary environmental issues. In this essay, he elaborates on several points of worldview by critiquing the ongoing use of the concepts of "creation" and "creator" in the discourse of indigenous peoples and the presumption of universality that comes with these terms. First, the concept of "creator" is usually called God (with the capital G) and comes preloaded with a particular framework of power associated with that understanding of a deity. Here he borrows from the work of cognitive linguists the notion of identifying this structure of thought and power as an "up-down image schema," which identifies a hierarchical model of thought and power. Tinker explains,

> It is . . . crucial to notice that imposing these religious metaphors of a religious divine as an overlay on Indian cultures irredeemably distorts the Native culture and destroys the intricacies and the beauty, that is, the coherence, of the Native worldview. An up-down linguistic cognitive image functions to structure the social whole around vertical hierarchies of power and authority. (2013: 169)

He goes on to give examples of this imposed phenomenon, including the use of the "Great White Father" language in treaty negotiations and the medieval imagery of royalty as associated with god sitting on a throne in the sky. These examples help to demonstrate this up-down image schema at play and in the imposition of these concepts onto American Indian peoples. Tinker's argument helps to recognize that this divine sanction of a culturally particular ordering of relationships is at the heart of the colonialism. If we are going to continue to work through the process of decolonization, these foundational forms of colonization must be rooted out and replaced with authentic lifegiving Indigenous structures of thought.

Tinker then turns to Indigenous conceptualizations as a remedy. He terms this Indigenous worldview of relationships as a "collateral-egalitarian image schema" (Ibid.: 172). He goes on to explain that this model is based in a logic of reciprocal balance embedded in the number two. In the Indigenous world two halves come together to make a larger whole. This is fundamentally different than the eurowestern reliance upon monotheistic logic based in the number one. In eurowestern logic when the "one" is put into relationships with anything else it must overpower that other so that the singular logic stays intact. This is the animating logic behind the missionary endeavor. The "one" god as conceptualized in the culture of the eurowest must overcome all others. This is also representative of the divine sanction of hierarchy embedded in the up-down image schema, and is what played out in the genocide of American Indian peoples and cultures throughout the colonial period. Tinker gives numerous examples of the indigenous relational logic in play, including the earth/sky, male/female and above/below dualities. Tinker explains this colonial shift,

> What was a powerful reciprocal duality of collateral balance becomes a male-dominant monotheistic modality. Wakonda moshita ski wakonda udseta, Life Maker Above and Life Maker Below, Grandfather and Grandmother all get

reductively suppressed into "Dear Heavenly Father." And that dear heavenly father, we are assured by that missionary voice, is the english equivalent of the original Native wakonda. *What a tragic loss, the loss of cosmic balance.* (Ibid.: 173–174, emphasis in the original)

He makes clear the distinctions between an indigenous worldview and eurowestern worldview. These fundamental differences between the cultures must be understood if we are going to be able to return to our life-giving ways of interacting with the world. For Tinker, and for many other Indigenous people around the world, there is an emphasis on clearing the path for others to follow. This analysis of clearing up some of the confusion around missionary endeavors and their eurowestern frameworks of thought helps Indigenous peoples to find firm ground on which to make a stand for their very survival.

What we see then in the trajectory of Tinker's work is the development of a methodological test to see if Christian language is compatible with Indigenous thought. His answer to the above question whether or not Christian thought is damaging to Indigenous thought and communities is a resounding yes. That the fundamental structures at the level of worldview are so different between the two cultures demonstrates that Indigenous ceremony and thought is not parallel, complementary, or equivalent to that found in Christianity. Hence, Indigenous adoption of and participation in Christianity represents a challenge to the ongoing reproduction of Indigenous thought and ceremony. Tinker's demonstration of difference functions as a corrective to the colonial presumption of a single cultural framework as applicable to all cultures. It is this homogenization of frameworks of knowledge that must be combated for Indigenous thought to survive. While Tinker's work sets us down the path of understanding difference at the level of worldview, we must continue this trajectory into the particularities of different Indigenous cultures to fully demonstrate the ongoing problems of colonization that Indigenous peoples face. For the remainder of this essay I will further this analysis by critically defining worldview and mobilizing that definition in the particulars of my own Indigenous language, *Anishinaabemowin*, to demonstrate the unintelligibility of Christian thought within indigenous languages. *Anishinaabemowin* is the language of the Three Fires Confederacy of the Ojibwe, Odawa, and Potowattamie peoples.

WORLDVIEW

In its contemporary use worldview is rarely defined which has allowed for the concept to expand its meaning to the point of ineffectiveness. Without a critical definition, its deployment runs the risk of failing to communicate the depths of cultural difference. In an attempt to combat this issue, I define worldview as an interrelated set of cultural logics which describe fundamental relationships to land, time, the rest of life, and provides a prescriptive methodological lens for understanding those relationships. For Indigenous peoples, this set of logics can be described as an intimate relationship to localized space, a cyclical conceptualization of time, living in a web of relatedness and a methodological lens of balance. This is contrasted with a eurochristian worldview as dominion over land, time as linear progress, living in a hierarchy of life, and a prescriptive methodological lens of Manichean dualism, that is, the binary of good and evil. Furthermore, in defining worldview it is important to differentiate between what is the underlying logics of culture (worldview) and the consciously constructed manifestations of those logics (ideology). If ideology and worldview are conflated it creates confusion in the analysis. For example, the origin narratives of a people provide tangible demonstration of the underlying worldview, but they are not the worldview themselves. The worldview is the logical mooring for the culture, making sure that the people do not stray too far from their prescribed center. Keeping worldview defined as logics allows for is the deep analysis of culture. I will move to demonstrate how this definition functions within a particular culture. Makwa niindoodem, anishinaabemo, Mackinakong n'donjibaa. (Bear is my clan, I am speaking the Anishinaabe language, and I am from the Turtle's Back). The language of a particular culture provides the proper medium to demonstrate cultural difference and the problems associated with translating Christian concepts into and out of an indigenous language.

PRAYER

As a concept prayer represents a particular form of communication. It is usually considered to be a devout petition, praise or thanks to a God, deity or other higher power, often as a form of worship. In America, these actions are most often associated with Christian worship, and it is these concepts that were imposed as universal translations onto Indigenous communities in the colonial period. Because they are in common usage they are often not given much thought, by Indigenous and nonindigenous peoples alike. However, when we delve into the realm of worldview as a method of analysis, much more needs to be unpacked about the use of prayer as a translation for our actions in Indigenous ceremony and everyday life.

It is important to demonstrate the cultural particularity associate with a concept like prayer. Language is not a static medium, but dynamic and the result of multiple experiences and interactions with their respective environments over time. Mikhail Bakhtin provides a method of engaging in this complex relationship of language, meaning and translation. He elaborates on a "dialogical orientation of a word" to help get at this underlying complexity in thought and language (Bakhtin, 1981: 275). Bakhtin demonstrates that this dialogical orientation of a word spoken in a relationship with another person is

> directed toward its object, enters a dialogically agitated and tension-filled environment of alien words that have already been spoken about it. It is entangled, shot through with shared thoughts, points of view, alien value judgements and accents, weaves in and out of complex interrelationships, merges with some, recoils from others, intersects with yet a third group; and all this may crucially shape discourse, may leave a trace in all its semantic layers, may complicate its expression and influence its entire sylistic profile. (Ibid.: 276)

This interrelatedness of words and concepts is essential to understand the role and function of prayer as a concept in Christian thought. First, if someone prays, they usually are praying to a god, or deity of some design. One of the functions of prayer is to praise or to worship this god. Furthermore, when one prays, the body position is often head bowed, or even kneeling and communicating in an upward direction to god. These descriptions of the action of praying illuminate the underlying logics of worldview associated with the eurochristian social hierarchies. This omnipotent and omnipresent deity is placed firmly on top of a hierarchy of existence. Whether it is an Aristotelian chain of being or a Christian hierarchy of God (in trinitarian formulation), with the pope or council of bishops below and the people below them. This hierarchy of existence is given divine ordination in Genesis 1:28 with god giving "dominion" to humans over the world, with the rest of creation open to the use of humans as they see fit. To continue with the definition of prayer, this god then must be praised and worshiped. Here the power differentials are obvious, with the eurochristian hierarchy being maintained in the act of prayer. Praying, as an essential action of the Christian religion, is best understood in light of its particular usage. It comes from a specific doctrinal heritage and its interrelatedness with the concepts like god, praise and worship, help us to understand this concept. It is emblematic of a particular cultural phenomenon of Christianity and its social organization of hierarchy.

The deeper elaboration of prayer demonstrates that this concept, if it is to be translated into and out of another language must share some common "socio-ideological conceptual horizon" for those translations to effectively communicate what is being uttered (Bakhtin, 1981). The concept of prayer may have a common understanding within the Abrahamic faiths, even though there are a number of cultural and linguistic differences to contend with. There are at least some commonalities to draw upon within the sacred texts.

However, when the concept of prayer is communicated to people with a much different worldview, we cannot presume there is a cogent translation. As we will see, when prayer is communicated beyond the "socio-ideological conceptual horizon" of Europe during the colonial period, the concept was unintelligible among Indigenous peoples within their own cultural context. Prayer does not become a cogent concept until forced removals, genocide and assimilation imposed the concept in both English and Indigenous languages.

The translation of Christian concepts into indigenous languages offers an interesting take into the colonial contest of Indigenous North America. There can be no misunderstanding here that the missionization of Indigenous peoples was done in any neutral sense. Missionaries were the tip of the spear for the transplanting of European empire. That they actively participated in the pacification, destruction and ethnic cleansing of Indigenous peoples has been well established (Tinker, 1993). When discussing the process of translation this is an essential starting point for analysis since more often than not, indigenous peoples had little to no participation in that process. In its inception then, the process of translating Christian concepts was asymmetrical. Bending indigenous languages into Christian thought was part of the colonial method of "civilizing" us by attaching our languages to their concepts. These early translations of Christian thought demonstrate a concerted effort to change indigenous peoples through language and action.

One of the early translators of *Anishinaabemowin* into Christian thought was Bishop Frederic Baraga. He was a Slovenian born missionary whose work for the Catholic church brought him to *Anishinaabe akiing*, the homeland of *Anishinaaberg* of what is now Northern Michigan, Wisconsin and Minnesota. He first published his *A Dictionary of the Ojibway Language* in 1853, for the express purpose of converting *Anishinaaberg* to the Catholic Church. *Ojibwe* linguist John Nichols suggests that "of the hundreds of dictionaries and grammars of the North American languages that European missionaries made as tools in their campaign to supplant indigenous beliefs, few have proven as useful and durable as Baraga's" (1992: v). Baraga was a skilled linguist, speaking not only his native Slovenian and Latin, but also English, German, and Italian. He used those skills to quickly pick up the *Odawa* language when he was stationed in Arbre Croche (present day Harbor Springs, Michigan), then shifted to the *Ojibwe* dialect of western Lake Superior when we was transferred to Madeleine Island. His purpose in that area was to missionize American Indian peoples, so his dictionary provides a useful look into the world of missionary translations.

Baraga's translational work on prayer helps us to understand not only the methods of the missionary endeavor, but also the long standing colonial effects of those actions. In Baraga's dictionary, we see his entry for pray as "Pray, I Pray, nind anamia" (1853: 198). Here "nind" is personal pronoun

I, and *anamia* is the word for pray. For the untrained eye, language learner or even scholar looking for translations, this may be accepted without much thought. However, upon deeper analysis we can unearth the colonization of the *Anishinaabe* language and mind embedded in this word. *Anamia*, has the root of *nam*, which refers to something being above you. Another term, *name* (sturgeon) is also representative of the spatiality associated with this morpheme. The sturgeon is a bottom feeding fish. Within *Anishinaaberg* thought, this spatiality of *name* does not communicate hierarchical importance, the sturgeon is a *doodem* (clan) name and a fish of significance within *Anishinaaberg* culture. Therefore, it is not representative of a social hierarchy. However, that the morpheme *nam* is the root of prayer, does suggest a hierarchical order of communication. This conceptualization of communicating in a hierarchy does not have a cogent spatial equivalent in *Anishinaaberg* culture. Here the importance of the logics of a web of relatedness are essential to invoke as it provides a basis for testing these translations. The hierarchical communication associated with prayer is logically foreign. While there is a spatial recognition of an above and below, communication is rarely conceptualized as directed up or down. While the communication of help and thankfulness is evoked on a daily basis, it is not in a hierarchy. More often than not, this type of communication is negotiated with many different types of phenomenon that are spatially lateral. Often, we are in close proximity with those entities, easily within reach. It is this world of close relationship that would come under assault during the colonial period.

That Baraga's intent was to missionize, to fundamentally alter the lifeways and thought of *Anishinaaberg*, is clear. Furthermore, the time that Baraga was active in *Anishinaabe* communities, roughly 1836 to 1868, was a time of dramatic shifting and migration among the Indigenous peoples of the Great Lakes. This period witnessed the shift from Indigenous proprietorship of these lands to the official statehood of Michigan (1836), Wisconsin (1848) and Minnesota (1858). This cataclysmic altering of lifeways saw the free movement of a people shift to the establishment of the reservation system. Economically this meant the move from flourishing to poverty under capitalism and politically shifted from a *doodem* (clan) leadership/kinship system to tribal councils located on reservations. This complex destruction of lifeways put a significant strain on the people and the language as they worked to make sense of their quickly changing world. This context of destruction and genocide is important to keep in mind as the dynamic elasticity of language was used by colonial powers like Baraga for his own ends, and for the ends of nation and empire building. It is in this Bakhtinian "socio-ideological conceptual" context that the translation of prayer is being made. That there is a power imbalance associated with this process is clear. This is the context in which the word, in this example prayer, is being imposed in *Anishinaaberg* communities in particular ways. The ceremonial life of Christianity is fundamentally different from what the *Anishinabeg* were used to. Even though Christianity could now be practiced within their own language, we cannot presume that the concept of prayer, church, worship, god, Jesus and salvation have direct linguistic or conceptual equivalents. Therefore, it would make sense that Baraga would have to invent and transform words by necessity.

So was *anamia* being used prior to colonization? Since there is linguistic diversity regionally, it is difficult to definitively say whether or not *anamia* was a word already in use. *Anamia* is used in a contemporary context as the dictionaries demonstrate. When speaking in English, the language of most *Anishinaaberg* currently, prayer is used to speak of both Christian and Indigenous ceremony. However, when we shift the focus to other *Anishinaabemowin* words that are also used in ceremony we find alternatives. According to Mike Zimmerman, an *Odawa* and *Ojibwe* language instructor, *anamia* is not always used in ceremonial situations. He suggests "The word with longer ties to *Anishinaabe* practices would be "naandamo" in *Ojibwe* and *Odawa* and "matmo" in Potawatomi. The morpheme "naanda" represents searching and the "mo" represents the speech that is related to the act of searching for what to say."[1] Here it is important to discuss what constitutes ceremony. In an Indigenous context, this type of communication represented in *naandamo* is something that happens in the everyday. It is not set apart into particular situations and places, it is done as you go about your day. According to Zimmerman, "The average way in which a person who speaks these languages "prays" is to offer thoughts based on common themes in the moment."[2] Here communicating in the moment refers to the relationships in the daily experiences one has with the web of relationships in their environment, not the hierarchical supplication associated with prayer. This distinction is important to understand as it demonstrates a need for Baraga to invent, or at least twist the meaning of a word to fit his purposes of communicating to a god from a prostrate position. *Ojibwe* linguist Dr. Margaret Noodin suggests that *anamia*, "is related to the concept of being in a lower position and is likely the term used after colonization because it maps onto the idea of genuflection or prostration."[3] The *Anishinaabe* communication patterns with relatives is fundamentally different than that associated with Christianity so it makes sense that Baraga would need to invent an Indigenous word to communicate the difference in spatial configurations of the world.

Naandamo is associated with the daily acts of communicating to your relatives, human, non-human and other-than-human. This entails many things, including picking food, fishing, planting, meeting people during your day, eating, picking medicines, administering medicines, and cooking, among many others. The point here is to demonstrate that communication with all of our relatives is part of the fabric of *Anishinaabe* life. This is where the discussion of worldview as a web of relatedness comes into play. *Anishinaabe* life is conceptualized as related to all other things. From our origin narratives we understand ourselves to be younger relatives to a world that was already in existence. Through these sets of narratives, we are told how to properly interact with our relatives by giving thanks and following particular protocols when hunting, fishing, planting, harvesting, cooking and eating. We interact with our relatives and are required to treat them well for our own sustenance and well-being. Failure to do so, we are told through millennia of Indigenous experience, results in our own difficulty of potential starvation, disease or social conflict. To properly negotiate our lives as *Anishinaabe*, the good-hearted people, is to call on help from and communicate with all of our relatives. When hunting one is expected to go with a good mind (having positive thoughts about what they are doing), and offer tobacco for the animal killed. Many people also communicate with that animal to say *g'miigwech'in* (you are being thanked by me) for offering itself as food so that the hunter and their family can eat well. This protocol of offering tobacco and giving thanks is very common among Indigenous peoples and is a manifestation of the logic of a web of relatedness.

This is the ceremonial life that the concept of *naandamo* would be associated with. While hunting, one is searching for what to say. When my oldest son shot his first deer, we followed the blood trail to where it lay. I handed him tobacco and told him to go speak to that animal that he had just killed. While the protocol of giving thanks is a useful framework to think about, it is in these particular situations where *naadamo*, one is searching for something to say. I never asked him what he said, that would be inappropriate. It was up to him to make sense of that coming of age moment where he was now in the position to help feed his family. While this example is of greater significance to us as a family than most situations we come upon, it does exemplify the role of everyday ceremonial protocol. As Zimmerman explains of this type of communication, "The object is to communicate not just with a higher being, but to communicate with ancestors and manidoog. There is a difference between Christian practices performed for an audience to earn membership into an earthly community or afterlife and Anishinaabe practices which are developed as everyday praxis."[4] What *naandamo* helps to elucidate is the fundamentally different experience of relationships associated with the concepts of *anamia* and *naandamo*. While some may argue for the interchangeability of these concepts and say that *anamia* represents the above example of communication with that deer, I would suggest that this is a mistake. Since *anamia* is etymologically associated with a hierarchical logic of relationships embedded in Christian praxis, its usage along with the English utterance of prayer continually colonizes our thought in ways that cannot comprehend the myriad of important relationships embedded in *Anishinaaberg* culture. When we take seriously the role of worldview and the logic of relationships that are deeply embedded in our respective cultures, the role of language becomes crucial in understanding these differences.

KINSHIP

To further illustrate the *Anishinaabe* logic of relatedness, we can analyze the linguistic-conceptual field used to communicate with and speak about our human, non-human and other-than-human relatives. There are four main points to address in this illustration. First, *Anishinaaberg* naming is very different. Second, *Anishinaaberg* family systems and naming are not based in the nuclear patriarchal family. Third, the *Anishinaaberg* language of relationships is inclusive and provides a conceptual field of knowledge that relates us to the rest of life. Finally, this inclusivity is extended to all of life, human, non-human, and other-than-human. This analysis will demonstrate that the colonial imposition of eurochristian family structure, names, social and political hierarchies associated with missionization have fundamentally shifted kinship relationships in *Anishinaabe* and other Indigenous communities.

One of the rituals in Christianity that marks the convert is baptism. In colonial missionization this was an important process and often the converts would receive a Christian name. Naming was not only a power move but a sign of "civilization" on the part of the convert. This transformation was voluntary at first, but then became forced with the theft of our children into the Boarding School system. Here, children were fundamentally changed into a eurochristian image, often beginning with a new Christian name. The naming process in *Anishinaabe* communities is quite different. First, the individual receives a name early in life. This name is usually given by an elder whose skill is to help our children live into their full responsibilities to the community. This name is not in a first, middle, last configuration, but represents a relationship to an action, event, or other person in the environment that is supposed to help the child live into their full potential. An individual may have more than one name during their life, representing a shift in their community role. However, these names are rarely spoken and are usually known only by a relatively small group of people.

People in *Anishinaaberg* and many other Indigenous communities are identified by their relationship to others. Therefore, a person may respond to many relationship names, depending on the context of the situation. Some of the relational concepts translate to English words like *ossae* (father) and *gushih* (mother). Usually the personal pronoun *niin* (my) would be added so when spoken it would be *niin ossae*, often shortened to *n'ossae*. Aunt and uncle are similar, but are more complex to identify cross and parallel aunties and uncles. So *n'inzigos* and *n'inzhishenh* are cross aunt (father's sister) and uncle (mother's brother), and *n'ninoshenh* is parallel aunt (mother's sister) and *n'nimishoome* is parallel uncle (father's brother). However, it is important to note that aunt and uncle are also more inclusive than blood relative. These relational terms are used to describe many other older male and female relatives with whom one may interact. The concepts of siblings further this demonstrate this inclusivity. A younger sibling regardless of gender is callend *n'nishiime* and an older male sibling is called *n'nisayenh* and older female sibling is called *n'nimisenh*. These are same terms used to describe cousins respectively. *N'niijikiwenh* is also used for brother, as well as male friend, and *n'niijikwe* is used for female friend. There is also the general concept of *n'nawengawin* (my relative) which can be used as a general recognition of relationship. While there are clear distinctions between nuclear family, extended family and non-family in eurochristian language and thought, this hierarchy of blood relationship is not intelligible within *Anishinaabemowin* and thought. Family language is extended to everyone, and it is these relational names by which we know and call each other on a daily basis. We communicate and live a relational life.

It is important to note that the *Anishinaaberg* relational concepts are embedded in a *doodem* (clan) socio-political system. The *doodem* is an extended family of people organized around a relationship to an animal (usually) and considered to be the primary social identity in *Anishinaaberg* life. One does not marry within a *doodem*, as that would be incest, whether or not they are blood related. Marriage is only between *doodemag* (clans, plural). The difference in family structure is important to analyze as it provides a demonstration of difference between the eurochristian patriarchal nuclear family and the inclusive *doodem* extended family of the *Anishinaaberg*. Again, this family structure was being fundamentally reconfigured to mimic the eurochristian model during the same time that the hierarchical concepts of *anamia* were being imposed by the church. The move from extended family dwellings to nuclear family households would prove to be devastating to the social fabric of the *doodem* as the political structure of *doodem* councils would be forcibly reconfigured into male led tribal councils. When we look at the imposition of the religious language and thought happening simultaneously with forced removals, conversions, and social and political structures, we can see that the hierarchy associated with a concept like *anamia* is combined with the hierarchical institutions of the church, government relationships and the remaking of *Anishinaaberg* social and political life into hierarchical institutions as well. While these changes all took time, they worked in unison as a social engineering experiment to remake the *Anishinaaberg* culture and land more palatable to the eurochristian colonizers.

However, so far we have only discussed human relationships and the inclusivity of *Anishinaaberg* linguistic conceptual fields extends far beyond humans. There are two general categories in which to discuss these extended familial relationships, the non-human and other-than-human. First, the non-human category here refers to the surrounding flora and fauna in *Anishinaabe akiing*. The life that surrounds us is discussed in familial terms. Most *doodemag* are associated with animals and members of that *doodem* are considered to be closely related to that animal. This includes taboos of killing and eating the *doodem* animal by the *doodem* members. However, the family language does not stop at *doodem* animals, but is extended to all of our relatives. The above named *Anishinaaberg* family terms would be used to communicate with fish being caught, animals being hunted, food and medicines being harvested and most any other interaction with the environment. So when hunting the general term *n'nawengawin* (my relative) could be used, or *n'nimisenh* (older sister) or *n'nisayenh* (older brother) to communicate with those animals. The relationships to the rest of our environment are in the same linguistic conceptual field of knowledge as our human relationships. This familial closeness to the environment as represented in our language provides an ethical basis in our treatment of them. This is a manifestation of the logic of relatedness in the *Anishinaaberg* worldview.

The second conceptualization of other-than-human life refers to the *manidoog*, the ancestors and the cosmic entities that play a large role in our annual cycles. First, the sun and moon are also familiarized as *n'nisayenh* (my brother) and *n'okomis* (my grandmother) respectively. The ancestors, *n'aanikoobijiganag* (plural) are also considered to be important for keeping proper relationships and as well as some of the important characters of the origin narratives, the *aadizookaanag*. The structure of the language is important to name here in that there are two types of nouns, *maaba* and *maanda*. *Maaba* roughly refers to living entities and *maanda* to entities that are not alive. So a story, *dibajimowin*, is *maanda* and not considered living, but the origin narratives and their characters, *aadizookaanag* are *maaba* and considered to have power, or life. When those narratives are told, the relationship to the characters in the story are considered to be present during the narrative, and can be accessed through those narratives. In a similar fashion, the *manidoog*, or other-than-human living energies are also accessible and considered to be integral parts of the *Anishinaaberg* conceptual world. *Manidoo* (singular) is often translated as "spirit," but that eurochristian concept does not carry the spatial necessity associated with *Anishinaaberg* ontology. Therefore I prefer the translation of a quasi-material life energy. These *manidoog* are conceptually present in our environment and available to help in a number of different ways. The non-human and other-than human energies are linguistically considered alive and part of the large extended kinship system that we live in. These non-human and other-than-human persons further demonstrate the inclusivity associated with the *Anishinaaberg* worldview and its manifestation in the daily experiences of the people.

This discussion of human, non-human and other-than-human helps to demonstrate that "the concept of 'person' is not, in fact, synonymous with human being but transcends it" as anthropologist A. Irving Hallowell has noted (2010: 537). What constitutes a relative is not broken into an anthropocentric framework as it is in eurochristian thought. The relatives with whom we interact are all around us every day. They are persons that provide help, guidance and sustenance for us as we negotiate our lives. It is this conceptualization of the inclusive experience of the world that is embedded in *Anishinaabemowin* as people communicate with all of their relatives using familial language. It is this large inclusive kinship system that provides the foundation for *Anishinaaberg* relationships of our daily experiences in our environment. These familial concepts in *Anishinaabemowin* as applied to our communication with our relatives are the institutional, systematic manifestation of the web of relatedness in our worldview. When *naandamo* is uttered, we are communicating with this large extended family.

A THEOLOGICAL DETOUR

The work of Mikhail Bakhtin helps us to understand the complex dialogical relationships associated with the communication of words. We must not fall into the colonial trap of presuming a universal framework of knowledge in the act of translating between cultures. Each cultural context comes with its own rich dialogical world which intimately informs the meanings of words and their actions. As we dig into the logics of worldview associated with the colonial contest and missionization, the role of the translations offered by people like Baraga show a significant shift in the direction of communication. In this eurochristian framework of prayer the person communicates directly to god. Prayer, as a hierarchical form of communication between a person, community of people led by a priest to a god, comes with this whole conceptual field of knowledge attached to it. No need to communicate with the corn during planting time, one would pray to god for help. No need to communicate with the deer that was killed, one would thank god for the kill. No need to communicate with the medicinal plants for healing, one would go to a doctor instead. Whether in the *Anishiaabemowin anamia* or the English prayer, the hierarchy of the colonial culture is reproduced and functions as a theological detour which continually negates the complex kinship system of the *Anishinaaberg*. As Tinker states, *"What a tragic loss,"* the loss of our kinship ties to this world (2013: 174). In the aftermath of colonization, *doodemag* are broken into nuclear families, plants and animals are reduced to object status on lower rungs of a hierarchical existence and *manidoog* are demonized. There is no eurochristian sociopolitical equivalent to the complex relationships embedded in *Anishinaaberg* culture and the larger sociopolitical shifts in colonization help further reinscribe this hierarchy.

The eurochristian field of knowledge is fundamentally different than the *Anishinaaberg* community that Baraga was instructing. *Anamia* as a translation for prayer is a reproduction of this theological detour set up by missionaries to destroy the *Anishinaaberg* kinship system. This detour cuts off communication with the plants and animals in relationship for food and medicine. It cuts off communication from the numerous narratives that tell the *Anishinaaberg* how to properly interact with their world. It cuts off communication with the *manidoog* who help them navigate their lives. The continued use of prayer as a concept continually reproduces the hierarchy that negates the *Anishinaaberg* kinship system. It is an ongoing threat to our worldview and hinders our ability to reestablish life giving relationships with all of our relatives. As long as *Anishinaaberg* pray to a deity, we will follow this theological detour up and away from the relatives that are all around them, the relatives that our ancestors communicated with on a daily basis.

However, as we decolonize our own languages, we recreate options for ourselves. A shift in emphasis from colonial language to the integrity of our own as in the move to *naandamo* opens up the possibility of reinvigorating that complex kinship system. Our relatives, the human, non-human and other-than-human are still available. We can return to the flourishing of our ancestors if we ignore the colonial detours and clear the linguistic-conceptual paths available in our own language. Through language and analysis, we can reopen the paths of our ancestors if we choose to walk them.

NOTES

1. Michael Zimmerman, Ojibwe Instructor at ICS, Pokagon Potowatomi, Interviewed on April 14, 2019.
2. Ibid.
3. Margaret Noodin, associate professor, University of Wisconsin-Milwaukee, Anishinaabe and Metis, Grand Portage Band of Lake Superior Chippewa Descendant, Interviewed on April 14, 2019.
4. Zimmerman, Interviewed on April 14, 2019.

Chapter 7

Impostor God

De-Christianization

Barbara Alice Mann

Any spiritual system is secondary to the culture that invents it, reflecting that culture's values back to its members, now as reified. Thus, to understand the spirituality of any culture, it is first necessary to grasp the core impetus behind its system. A patriarchal, raiding culture will, for instance, emphasize hierarchical male kin/g/ship, so it is hardly surprising to find that culture projecting its values spiritually as "the kingdom" of one "father god." Problems arise when that father-god culture then raids a collective, parallel culture of female-male covalence, forcing its father-god religion onto the invaded culture to facilitate the permanent form of raiding called "colonization."

Once the dominance of the raider begins to exhaust itself, the spiritual sanity of the invaded requires a return to the pre-raid set point, but unscrambling original spiritual ideas from those of the religion imposed by the invader requires perspicacity. During the period of subjugation, traditions will have been mangled to suit the dominant culture, with the spiritual values of the two systems conflated and jumbled, favoring the dominant message. Scraping superimpositions off original thought is an operation as delicate as restoring a Renaissance painting. It requires a careful analysis of the target culture in such areas as its original methods of sustenance, its landscape, and its gender-relations, with surviving traditions understood in terms of that recovered knowledge. The greatest reliance belongs on the pre-raid versions of tradition. This chapter reviews the father-god religion installed by the invader in Europe and in North America, demonstrating a method of recovering original thought, through examples of spiritual concepts, as disentangled.

Euro-Christians hardly invented the father-god. It is pretty well established that the patriarchal Christian ideas of the father-god were imported into Europe from the desert lands of the eastern Mediterranean basin, largely as spun-off through Middle Eastern Greek to European Roman cultures. Originally in the Middle East, multiple gods abounded, and whichever god tickled a ruler's fancy was his people's god, too. Because the ancient Hebrews picked up on these commonplace ideas, it is not unlikely that the biggest raider around, then Persia, heavily influenced Hebrew thought concerning warlord gods (Bremmer, 2008: 339–345). This explains why even the Jewish god had to prove himself by slugging it out in a *"deity war"* with the Babylonian honcho, Marduk, as recounted in *Daniel*, 1–5(6) (italics in the original, Bruyn, 2013: 626). Thus, despite the misimpression of the Jewish god that most Christians have, as his always having been the only god in the cosmos, he actually emerged as just one among many. "I will take you to be my people, and I will be your God," *Exodus*, 6:7, is not a plenary but a particular claim. The breakaway Christian sect claimed the Jewish god, purportedly in his one-and-only status, although Christianity immediately appended a son-god and a holy ghost, their god emerging as the apex of an isosceles triangle. Luckily, the permanent raid of colonization does not require monotheism to be present among the invaded, but just a favorite father-warrior-god.

Euro-Christians similarly inherited the idea of the permanent raid. Early on, crude raiders discovered that their greed could easily outrun their targets' ability to supply goods. However, should the raiders claim sovereignty over their targets' land, as enforced by violence, then they could organize their raiding on a predictable schedule. This not only allowed the productive targets enough time to amass a surplus but also to know when the next raid was scheduled to hit, thereby to ready their "tribute" and forestall its violent theft. This scheduled raiding was first called feudalism. Once it moved out of Europe, it came to be called colonialism, but in both instances, it was protection racketeering. Only after the producers and the raiders merged into a shared system of (always unequal) "exchange" did majestic theories of economics arise to disguise the fact that the raid still sat at its core. Because of the force required to maintain the permanent raid, it is a system of diminishing returns, but raiders are day traders.

In Europe, the permanent raid had been going on since at least the Spartans first seized Laconia to lord it over the Helots (Rahe, 2016: 11, 24, 127–128). Many terms borrowed from Ancient Greek—the secondary language of early Christendom—bespoke its raiding mindset, for instance, ηγεμονία (*hegemonia*, hegemony), especially as it connected with leaders and rulership (Lavan, 2013: 117–118; note 133, 118). Greek and Roman systems of tributary states comprised polytheistic raiding under Zeus/Jupiter, with assists from his subordinate yet godly kin. The domination mindset central to Roman raiding was also embedded linguistically in Latin, the primary language of early Christendom. From Latin, the language of domination (*dominus*, "he who has subdued") transferred wholesale into European warlord Christianity, generally, as ably demonstrated by Steve Newcomb (2008: 23–29). Because Christianity ran barefoot through the ruins of Rome's first empire, as Rome's second empire, it picked up on the permanent raid by amassing its own vassal states. The claimed "spirituality" of the Euro-Christian conquest should not blind anyone to the violent nature of its spread.

Raiding typically continues until the raider runs face-first into a force as big and mean as itself. In Europe, Christianity was stymied by two such rivals: Islam and Odinism. Entering Europe about the same time as Christianity, Islam was the twin of Christianity, sired by the same Mediterranean father. Working from a cultural play book identical to Christianity's, Islam made considerable inroads into Spain, starting in 710 (Watt and Cachia, 2007: 8). It failed to reach France in 732 only when *Abd al-Rahman ibn Abd Allah al-Ghafiqi* was killed during his invasion by the Norman Charles Martel, at *Balāṭ al-Shuhadā'* (Battle of the Highway of the Martyr), the Christian-called Battle of Tours (Watson, 2003: 152–153). Farther west, Islam solidified in the Balkans under the Ottoman Empire in 1345, with Islam alive there to this day, whereas the Christian invasion of Western Europe won out generally enough to begin styling itself "Christendom," or the king/god-run domain of Christianity (Sugar, 1977: 3). Both Islam and Christianity featured forced conversion to their own systems, but evenly matched, neither could overcome the other, having to make do, instead, with Islamic (Ottoman) and Christian (European) territories squaring off against one another, regularly.

Christendom's second rival was the same as that which had dismantled the first Roman Empire: the Germanic invaders. Interestingly, Western European culture has a long history of denigrating the Vikings, especially, as irretrievable heathens, bad to the bone. Notwithstanding, all Western European cultures derive from the Germanic invasions of Europe: the Visigoths, Burgundians, and Franks in France and Spain; the Vendels and Goths in Germany and Austria; the Anglo-Saxons in England; and the Dönsk in Scandinavia, with the Dönsk eventually moving east to found Kiev and become the Rus. Odinism neither welcomed Christian conversion nor played well with others. Norse racism kept the Vikings from intermingling with the *Skrælings* ("wretches," that is, the Beothuk of Newfoundland), just as it kept Vikings in Greenland from intermarrying with the Inuit, even though intermingling would have ensured Viking survival in both locales (Hansen and Curtis, 2010: 290). The Greenland Vikings literally preferred starving and freezing to death over mixing with their successful, near neighbors. As archeologist Thomas McGovern noted, "You don't have this kind of barrier between cultures for so long without someone working very hard to maintain it" (Svitil, 1997: 30). By way of contrast, as long as someone expressed fealty to the Christian war god, Christendom incorporated the convert. It literally swallowed its competition whole.

With the conversion of all but the most northerly Germans to Christianity, Barbarians magically transformed into Bearers of Christian Light. For instance, Rollo the Feared Odinist Viking besieged Paris from 885 to 886, taking by force what became most of Normandy. When in 911, Charles the Simple "granted" Rollo land, he was just formalizing land that Rollo had already seized, his acknowledgment made on the understanding that Rollo would become Christian, in return. Thus did Rollo, Duke of Normandy, emerge as the respectable begetter of Franco-Christian kings, giving rise to the "Williams" of Normandy in 928 by fathering William Longsword. In true Viking-*cum*-Christian fashion, Longsword was assassinated, so that other warlords might move in on his turf, but the Williams hung on (Haggar, 2017: Paris siege, 45; Rollo and Charles the Simple, 50; Non-Religious Conversion, 190; William Longsword, 47, 54; Assassination, 60, 199; Timeline, 697). In 1066, Rollo's great-great-great-grandson, William the Conqueror, entered England for no other reason than to plunder it, but creating the permanent raid of a Norman colony in England was just fine, because it was "linked to a self-asserted Christian purpose" (Douglas, 1999: 1111).

The act of Christian conversion did not involve spiritual enlightenment let alone, piety, but was the equivalent of major sports teams trading star athletes among themselves, realigning players for mutual "owner" benefit (Melnikova, 2011: 90–92). Loyalties might easily shift again, thereafter. In no case were Rollo or Longsword particularly devoted to Christianity. It was a bargaining chip in their war-lording. The fanaticism of Euro-American evangelicals today, then, completely misses the point of Christian conversion, at least during the period of the Christian invasion of Europe. It was not about faith in some saccharine Jesus yearning to save them on a personal level, but about the raw, naked, material wealth and power gained through an alliance with the right crime family, and Roman pope ran the best enterprise in Europe (Dubois, 2008: 5; Mellor, 2008: 35–36; Dubois and Ingwersen, 2008: 155).

The permanent raid was, therefore, hoary by the time Christians stumbled onto American shores in the fifteenth century, its mechanisms of coercion all well in place for immediate plying against Turtle Islanders (North American Indians), although America's generalized absence of any supreme spirit stupefied early Europeans (Mann, 2000: 71). Entrenched in their ONE-THINKING—one god, one life, one soul, and so on—missionaries scrambled to cram the matriarchal, Twinned Cosmos of Indigenous America into their patriarchal, lonely-only God structure (Mann, 2003: 176–179; Mann, 2010: 29–48). It was not that they did not see the multiplicity of spirits, existing in a halved whole—in fact, they recorded the Iroquoian *erienta* and *gonnigonrha*—but that they found the binary fractals spinning throughout Indigenous culture to be demonic (Lafitau, 1974: I: 230). Ramifications of the Indigenous Twinship principle challenged Christian notions of male supremacy, for on

Turtle Island, the majority of the cultures were matriarchally structured, with Blood (lineage) women as powerful as Breath (spatial) men, with both respecting their own spheres of action and not meddling in the business of the other half. Missionaries fingered the self-directed power of the women to guide clan and national domestic policy as an emblem of devil-worship, to be rooted out, immediately (Anderson, 1991).

Any time that Euro-Christians wished to commit a crime against humanity, their father-god was there to justify it, so that the Christian invasion of America looked an awful lot like the Christian Crusades against Islam, using the same lures of gold, slaves, land, and power. Cruelly extracted, group conversions remained the primary method of the Spaniards of La Florida, but the French Jesuits in Québec, a century later and 1,500 miles north of St. Augustine, hit upon the time-consuming method of detaching the Breath, or Up ↑, half of the Cosmos for artificial elevation to their own godhead, while casually consigning the Blood, or Down ↓, half of the Cosmos, to Christian hell (Mann, 2016b: 111–112). Missionary conquest set up its little "praying towns," or demonstration villages, inhabited by converts, but these lacked success (Mann, 2000: 296; Tinker, 1993: 29–38). The simplistic, straight-line thinking of Europe was very confusing to Turtle Islanders, who were used to the Twinship of covalent, interactive haves, both considered "good" (Mann, 2016b: esp. 41–77).

Mutual confusion quickly gave way to raw military might, gleefully deployed, as true to their separatist Viking roots, the incoming Euro-Christians articulated their "manifest destiny" to rule, promulgating convoluted theories of their biological supremacy by way of evidence (O'Sullivan, 1845: 5; Mann, 2003: 10–34). Concomitant destruction of the environment, especially through the deliberate impoverishment of the fur trade, and the encouraged destruction of "the Indians' commissary," the buffalo, disrupted lifeways (Jefferson, 1903–1907: fur trade, Vol. X: 369–370; McHugh and Hobson, 1979: "Commissary," 285). The wanton deforestation that followed the invasion of the Americas actually brought on the Little Ice Age (Koch et al., 2019: 27). Worse, the erosive mold-board plow of Europe destroyed the topsoil of the Americas, carefully created by the women (Blood), while intrusive European crops and weeds supplanted the abundant Indigenous crops, raised in non-eroding mounds (Gaston and Mays, 2012: II: 57–58; Mann, 2000: 220–221; Warren, 1994: 37–41, 49). For ease of control, Euro-Vikings of the nineteenth century unilaterally declared any *Skræling* hold-outs remaining east after Jacksonian Removal to be no longer Indian, while isolating western Indians on military-patrolled, Christian-run "reservations" (*The Eastern Band of Cherokees v. The United States and the Cherokee Nations*, 1885: 479; *Eastern Bank of Cherokee Indians v. United States and Cherokee Nations*, 1885; Springer, 1898: 485; Prucha, 1984: 512–513).

Today, unscrambling the Christian omelette imposed wherever Christians set up their permanent raid is a trying, tedious task, but it can be undertaken, starting with an insight assist from an Indian experience totally distinct from the American kind. The Nobel prize-winning Hindu economist, Amartya Sen came at dismantling the colonized mind in India by first examining the three ways in which the British colonizer had denatured Indian culture and thought. He dubbed these categories the magisterial, the curatorial, and the exoticist (Sen, 2005: 141). Christian Europe had already perfected these methods against the Norse and the Ottomans, so that by the time Euro-Christians reached India and the Americas, the missionaries' bag of tricks was already bulging. Because the United States was, essentially, a British spin-off, it inherited the parental British methods of cultural dissolution used both on India and Turtle Island.

The British magisterial method sought to disempower Indian culture by, essentially, denying that it was a culture, at all. Official denigrations were first articulated by James Mill in his confabulated *History of British India* (1817). Its primary function was to proclaim the makeshift poverty of Indian thought, from which premise Mill concluded that anything the Indians knew about philosophy, they had learned from the English. It was short leap from there to Winston Churchill's infamous quip that India was "no more a country than is the equator" (Lyon, 2008: 43). Consequently, the British Christians had to "reform" education in India, to bring Indians up to Western speed (Sen, 2005: 146–147, 149). Curatorially, India was collected, with Sen's exemplar here the philologist, William Jones, who is West-credited with inventing linguistics, particularly in tracing Greek and Latin back to ancient Sanskrit (Ibid.: 145). In reality, Jones was simply working from the original method of grammatical analysis invented by the fourth-century Afghan scholar पाणिनि (*Pāṇini*), and had, in fact, learned ancient Sanskrit using the पाणिनि method. Although this is well known—Jones credited पाणिनि in his work—the derivation of Jones's knowledge remains almost uniformly ignored in Western texts (Jones, 1801: "Desiderata," I: viii). Exotically, Westerners viewed Indian spirituality as their little pull toy, its foolishness deemed relatively harmless and amusingly safe for Westerners to play with, and they did, from Friedrich von Schlegel and Samuel Taylor Coleridge to The Beatles (Sen, 2005: 152).

The magisterial approach effectively excised from its consciousness any of the target culture's knowledge that might produce intellectual "achievements" based on "formal training," allowing Euro-Christians to draw a "false contrast" between themselves and Others (Ibid.: 158). Just as Mill "disputed and dismissed" every Hindu accomplishment as "totally primitive and rude," so did Westerners defame every Indigenous American or Viking achievement as fraudulent or nonexistent (Ibid.: 147). Thus, we have the spectacle of Western scholars admitting, on the one hand, that they have no idea how Machu Picchu was constructed and that Viking ships showed profound engineering skills, while on the other hand, portraying Indigenous Americans and Vikings as unredeemable, bloody-minded menaces to civilization. Because of their savagery, both had to be god-schooled right out of their traditional knowledge and right into Christian ignorance.

Both resisted magisterial control as best they were able. An arguable, if seldom argued, reason that Vikings died on Greenland and struggled to survive on Iceland was to evade forced, Christian assimilation, although they were followed even to Greenland and Iceland by the indefatigable missionaries (Barnes, 2001: 2–83). Christians stalking them may be one reason that the Vikings continued on to Newfoundland. Evading forced conversion was even harder for Indigenous Americans. Regardless of whether they lived east or west of the Mississippi, starting as toddlers, Indian children were scooped up for imprisonment in Christian-run, government-funded "boarding schools," with devotion to the solitary father-god presented to Indian children as their only hope of continued existence (Mann, 2016a: 139–148; Adams, 1995). The boarding-school era is not studied in modern American scholarship as forced, mass conversion, but it should be, for it was an orchestrated effort to strip entire generations of traditional ways knowing. The effort succeeded, to an appalling degree.

Magisterial control resulted, for instance, in too many modern Turtle Islanders swearing fealty to the federal quantum-counting enrollment system, without knowing that it was an expression of eugenics, violently imposed by the U.S. government from 1893 to 1907 as the "final solution" to the "red-race problem," its aim being to "shrink" the number of "dependent Indians" to zero (U.S. Department of the Interior, 1906: I: 5). Too few today know that Indians east of the Mississippi were not allowed to enroll, although (or because) there were thousands; that traditional chiefs forbade enrollment, blocking it when they could; or that, of those defying their chiefs to attempt enrollment, two-thirds were denied inclusion by the capricious Dawes Commission (Mann, 2003: 283–297; Carter, 1999: 148–149; U.S. Senate, 1907: 641–642). Many modern Turtle Islanders are unaware that, traditionally, the women alone controlled identity, because it was a "water" (amniotic fluid, Blood) matter, with identity flowing solely through the mother. Still less do they know that, once adopted (i.e., granted citizenship), despite the adoptee's ethnic origin, s/he was fully Indian (Mann, 2006: 98–99). Engrained ignorance of these facts leads to many cruel, internecine fights over who gets to be an Indian. In this perfectly played, Euro-game of *divide et impera*, quantum counting aids the government's "final solution" by shrinking the "recognized" pool of Indians, in a perfect realization of Sen's magisterial method.

Curatorially, there can hardly be any question that cultural objects, euphemized as "artifacts," were stolen from both the Vikings and the Indigenous Americans for display in museums, including Harvard's Peabody and DC's Smithsonian (Mann, 2003: 7–8, 40–47). There is a standing "Native American Collection" at Chicago's Field Museum, while it was only in 2019 that the noted Museums Victoria of Melbourne, Australia, woke up to the distress of Viking descendants over the cavalier display of their peoples' remains and objects.[1] Although these displays form as clear a signal of Christian *dominatio* as imaginable, the mindset thus forced is hard to dispel. To this day, published discussions are overwhelmingly *about* Native Americans and Norse peoples, not *by* them. The resultant skew perpetuates father-god interpretations over the "pagan" imagination.

Traditional Native Americans regard artifact museums as dead places to be avoided, not only because of their ghost-making interruptions of the spirit journeys of the dead, but also because ceremonial items have been displayed without the slightest sense of their mystical potency or their need for care and feeding. I recall being shocked by the February 2016, Diker exhibit of Native American "artifacts" at the Toledo Museum of Art.[2] I was horrified not only that it included a ghost-dance shirt, but also that Native Americans were going through the exhibit, as if they did not know the danger in which all those potent items put them. Neither death nor disrupted potency departs from a place once it has been polluted, so that the recent, forced repatriations of Indian remains and objects to their peoples does not smooth the wrinkles in museums that housed them.

The exoticist method of demoting a culture is the most insidious of all, precisely because it looks the most benign. The "shiny object" approach to Viking and Native American culture pulls items out of their original context for use as cheap thrills. No Euro-Christian viewer need know anything at all about Norse tradition to watch *Thor: The Dark World* (2011) or *Thor: Ragnarok* (2017). Absent respectful Norse input, Thor transmutes into a vulnerable Hollywood Hunk with a magic hammer (all Hollywood superheroes have a visible power tool). Similarly, Ragnarok is made to echo the lurid Christian apocalypse, when it more likely referenced Norse knowledge of the procession of the equinoxes, as argued in *Hamlet's Mill* (Santillana and Dechend, 1969: 59–60, 156–159). Compared to the number who have seen the *Thor* movies, those who know of the elegant, informed, and original arguments in *Hamlet's Mill* are miniscule. Thus, without the slightest reference to or respect for their original meaning, Western cultural appropriations cement into millions of minds the Euro-Christian interpolation of an apocalyptic Ragnarok and a user-friendly Thor as a sort of proto-Jesus, come to save them.

Similarly, because Hollywood said so, all Native Americans are mystical savages who live in tipis and hunt buffalo from horseback (Hilger, 2016).

Because of exoticism, Euro-Americans invite themselves into Indigenous ceremonies, demanding that medicine lodge secrets be spilled in their laps, with some Indigenous people flattered enough by the attention to indulge them. The worst expression of Christian presumption came, however, early on, after Europeans learned that Turtle Islanders had no idea of a solitary mover and shaker. They responded by inserting into the official record a solitary "Great Spirit," pseudo-Indian speak for the Christian god. Missionaries worked overtime to conjure up this impostor god as indigenously conceived and then, through their converts using Christian formulations, attributed it to Real, Live Indian philosophies (Mann, 2016b: 22–28).

To accomplish this, first, missionaries picked out a Breath spirit scooting around in the atmosphere—say, male Thunder—and, second, elevated it to a godhead, regardless of Indigenous "informants" assuring them that Thundererers was not so recognized. This was how the Seneca *Hawenio* ("He, Majestic Voice") temporarily became a phony "Great Spirit" (Parker, 1989: 8; Mann, 2000: 304–305). *Hawenio*'s promotion to a Christian-style godhead was oblivious not only of the fact that Indian "sky" is outer space, not the blue atmosphere, but also that everything UP ↑ necessarily has a mirror-image DOWN ↓ so as to form a Twinship ‖. Moreover, this male unit has to be counterbalanced by female soil = latitudes cooperating dynamically to form one expression of the completed Cosmos ╬. This was not the kind of philosophy to countenance raiding-culture, male domination, let alone structured socio-economic inequalities, so that manifestly destined missionaries set about supplanting it with Christianity's UP-DOWN ↕ hierarchy, in which all the benefits ran UP ↑ and all the immiseration ran DOWN ↓.

The initial step in recovering tradition is to recognize, pinpoint, and surgically remove the remnants of Christian magisterial, curatorial, and exoticist projections about the culture being resuscitated. To highlight these for ease of extrication, I launch a dedicated hunt for "speed bumps," the jarring add-ons with their ill-fitting components, and next identify the patterns common to those disjunctures. At that point, the original thought structure peeks through its prison door. For instance, the Vikings were segued into Christianity through their "All-Father" meme, Odin. The Odin-God conflation was successful because both Christianity and Odinism served a warlord culture, although interestingly, Vikings originally countenanced women among their warlords—another hint.

Typically, the least dedicated to Odinism were the first converted to Christianity, for they stood to gain the most by sleeping with the enemy. Rollo was wishy-washy enough on the score of Christianity that his son Longsword enjoyed a somewhat Viking boyhood before Rollo converted, but the price of passing Normandy along to his son was that Longsword be a Christian (Haggar, 2017: 190–191). Throughout both their lives, securing

Aquitaine to themselves seems to have been the overriding draw, so that by the time of Richard I, son of the Christianized Longsword, it was lost that Odin was not THE Viking creator-god, in a replication of the Christian creator-god. Grandpa Rollo had presumably known, but if Longsword knew, his reputation as a pious Christian meant that his son Richard, was unlikely to have heard any pure, Odinist traditions, assuming he heard any, at all (Ibid.: 190–192).

Odin was thus the first casualty of Christian god-erasure. The best place to look for the bumpy ride over the formidable form of Odin is in the manipulation of *Yggdrasil*, the Central or World Tree, as it was pruned into a Christianized, proto-Tree of the Knowledge of Good and Evil. Here is the rub with that: it was not bipedal creatures scurrying about Eden that interfaced with *Yggdrasil*; it was Odin himself. This speed bump represents a major departure from the Christian story, for presumably, the Christian father-god had nothing to learn, whereas Odin stole his knowledge (the Runes) while hanging from *Uggdrasil*. Moreover, he was engaged in what Christians would regard as the wizardry of gazing into *Urd*, a reflective well, which allowed him to see all the knowledge and events of the past (Dougherty, 2017: 23–24, 28). The father-god conflation falls apart at this point, as a scrying Odin after wisdom has more in common with Christianity's Satan in revolt than with the Christian father-god.

Another speed bump came in Odin's marital relations, for unlike the Christian bachelor God, Odin was not only married, but twice-married, simultaneously to Frigg and Jord, perhaps explaining why Rollo took not just one Christian wife but, in interesting shades of Odin, two Christian wives, Gisela and Popa (Haggar, 2017: 47). Jord's son Thor spent most of his time whacking giants, while his uncle, Loki, was Odin's half-giant half-brother, and his mother, Jord, was the primary Earth spirit, the *Fjörgyn* (Dougherty, 2017: Frigg and Jord, 28; Giant-Whacking, 30; Loki, 31–32). Thus Thor, can be twisted into the Jesus mode, only if people do not know his context, for the last I heard, Jesus did not walk around with a stone lodged in his head from giant fighting run amok (Davidson, 1993: 82). At this point, all that Odin and the Christian god have in common is a deep propensity to violence, the original connection that facilitated such conversions as Rollo's to begin with.

Next, our sleuths must stop at each of the speed bumps around the lore, to consider what they meant in relation to fellow speed bumps, until the Odinist context can be descried moving behind the Christian curtain. Odin's friends and family do considerable axel-damage in the strong female fertility principle embodied by Freyja, whose magical chariot was pulled by cats (Dougherty, 2017: 30, 35). In the form of a bird, Freyja could travel to the land of the dead, an ability she shared with Odin (Crossley-Holland, 1980:

xxx, 7–8, 65–69, 95–99). There was no way that the Odinist Freyja could be transformed into the Christian Eve, for with her cat-drawn sky chariot and her ability to shape-shift into a bird to match Odin's feats, she was less the doormat Eve than the Midrashic Lilith, first wife of Adam who left in him disgust over his male supremacy, and was demonized for her pains (Baskin, 2002: 56–60). Jord offered a more likely conflation with Mary, until one considered the power of her *Fjörgyn* context. Women of the Odinist pantheon were simply not Christian-compatible. Like Lilith in Judaism, Jord and Freyja signal female power in Norse culture, and to be sure, we turn up historical Viking women wielding considerable authority in their own right. For instance, Leif Erikson's half-sister, Freydis, made her own voyage to Newfoundland as captain of her own longship to establish a trade route with her brother's colony (Horsford, 1892: 125–127).

Thus, if I were looking to reclaim Norse lore, I would certainly reevaluate the women's stories, seeking speed bumps in the texts, including sudden mentions without context or, as Christianized, in finger-wagging mentions, like styling Freydis's self-direction as her "crimes" (Ibid.: 125). How was it, for example, that Freydis had "men," whom she could order to "cut timber for her ship," while Lief's men were, instead, engaged in work on his house (Ibid.: 126)? There is evidently a lot of excised lore here, so figuring out the relationships among Freydis, Freyja, and the Jord-*Fjörgyn*, especially as they interfaced with men and the larger culture, is pretty important. It looks as though Odinist culture was not as lopsidedly male as it was portrayed in the Christian chronicles but was something of a parallel culture. In that light, perhaps Odin did not marry twice. Perhaps Frigg and Jord simply both had him. Polyandry was inconceivable to patriarchal Euro-Christians drawing up the texts, but polyandry is not uncommon among societies with strong female spirits (Mann, 2000: 284–285; Singh, 1988).

For *Hahnunah* (Turtle Island), the same methodology can be deployed. Again, because women are banned from Christology, women form an obvious point of entry. Why, for example, do traditions continent-wide so heavily feature first women: *Atensic* (Iroquois), *Kokomthena* (Shawnee), *Selu* (Cherokee), *Ptesan-Wi* (Lakota), *Stenatliha* (Apache), *Na'ashjé'íí Asdzáá* (Diné), and so on? This indicates something important, especially when the women are seen in balance with the male half. For instance, for the Iroquois, *Deheyhyondyesok*, The Ancient (Breath, that is, outer space │), counterbalances *Katsitsioniionte*, Her Fruits Are Hanging (Blood, that is, earth soil ─). This is clear a juxtaposition of Breath and Blood (+), with the necessary halves of the completed Cosmos propounding a cooperative interface as the highest Indigenous value. It is, therefore, hardly surprising to find matriarchies on Turtle Island, or patriarchies depicted in outer space. When the grid of interactive, halved wholes is applied to Turtle Island, freeing it from the heavy interpolation of Christian ONE-thinking, the necessity of everything happening by equally halved wholes begins to make sense.

We still know, for instance, that UP ↑ and DOWN ↓ play a major role in Indigenous American thought, because they were eagerly co-opted by the Christian missionaries to push their own Manichean ideas of heaven↑ and hell↓. If one also knows, however, that for Native America, if a thing exists, then it must be good, one has just encountered a significant speed bump, for Christians see Up ↑, only, as good. This draws into question the entire interpolation of Good UP ↑ and Evil DOWN ↓ as imposed on, say, day (sun UP↑, good) and night (sun DOWN↓, evil). If both up and down, night and day, are good, then it must make sense to look for their points of contiguity.

The retained tradition of the Mississippi River as sacred now comes into UP/DOWN focus, for the indigenous version of the Mississippi River arcs south from the Allegheny through the Ohio to the Lower Mississippi (Hale, 1978: 14). Anyone unafraid of the night will look up at the stars to notice the matching arc of the Milky Way mirroring the bending of the continent's main river. The two are twinned, both shining routes of travel, one on the ground, visible in the day, and one in the sky, visible in the night. If water travel (Blood) is used by the living, then star travel (Breath) is used by the dead. As with the suppressed Norse references to the procession of the equinoxes, what we see in the Mississippi Blood – juxtaposed with the Milky Way Breath | is a necessarily sacred expression of the Twinned Cosmos ✛. When taken together with another Sky/Earth replication – say, of the Hohokam canals (Blood)—replicating the Cygnus constellation (Breath) creating its own bisection, ✛, then together with the Mississippi/Milky Way, the Twinned Cosmos is perfected ✤.[3]

This same land-outer space parallelism explains the iconography of the Woodlands mound complexes, with their balanced circle-square motifs: ○=□. The circle ○ of UP ↑ sky balances the square □ of DOWN ↓ earth, the two parts connected by a narrow causeway = (Mann, 2003: 197–205). One logical conclusion is that there must be two spirits in everybody—one of ○ UP ↑ Breath and one of □ DOWN ↓ Blood, as coordinated by the "name," the = pathway of any particular life, running between the halves to coordinate them ○=□. In keeping with the multiplicity principle, each half can spin out fractals of itself, large and small, for instance, with the Lakota positing four indwelling spirits plus a name (Mann, 2016b: 97–103).

At this point, de-Christianization has begun. For Turtle Islanders, the spelunking might be a bit easier than for the Norse, who were plied with Christianity for a good 500 years longer than were Native Americans. Most indigenous Americans have at least heard that there is something off about the Christian father-god, because he lacks his "other half." Where is his clan cousin, from the other side of the longhouse? The Christian god must be an outcast, pacing a continent not his own, his kin elsewhere. Born on the eastern end of the Mediterranean Sea, whether invading the cold north of Scandinavia or the distant shores of Turtle Island, claiming to be Odin, here, or *Deheyhyondyesok*, there, he is and remains a desert god specializing in the raid. A raider god's needs must be portable, but as carried into the Americas or Scandinavia, he is an impostor god. If he is the Sky spirit he claims to be, then he cannot possibly hold dominion over the Blood/Water/Earth. If he is, instead, the earth spirit that I strongly suspect he is, then his desert medicine on running-water *Hahnunah* (Turtle Island) or frozen-water *Fjörgyn* (Scandinavia) can do only damage. Let him return to his dusty homeland, the deserts of the eastern Mediterranean basin, and do earth waters no more harm.

NOTES

1. Steve Johnson, "The Milder Side of Vikings, Now at Field Museum," *Chicago Tribune*, February 25, 2015; "Why Has Museums Victoria Decided Not to Display Human Remains in Vikings: Beyond the Legend?" *Museums Victoria*, Australia Website, 2019, https://museumsvictoria.com.au/article/museums-victorias-position-on-displaying-human-remains/.

2. Roberta Gedert, "American Indian Museum Exhibit Connects Primitive with Modern," *Toledo Blade*, January 31, 2016.

3. Omar Turney, "Hohokam Canals: Prehistoric Engineering," *Arizona Experience.org*, Accessed August 3, 2019, http://arizonaexperience.org/remember/hohokam-canals-prehistoric-engineering.

Chapter 8

On the Use of the Bible for Mental Colonization

Steven T. Newcomb

INTRODUCTION

In *American Indian Liberation* Osage theologian "Tink" Tinker, points out that the "'classic liberation theologies" that are "read in north America almost always begin with a radical interpretation of Jesus and the gospel" (2008: 128–129). He continues:

> To be absolutely fair, they [such theologies] actually begin with the people—that is, with the "experience" of the poor and oppressed—and then move decidedly toward a people's liberating interpretation of the gospel. (Ibid.: 129)

We ought to ask ourselves, "What has caused Indigenous peoples to be poor and oppressed?" They have generally found themselves in that predicament as the direct result of Euro-Christians having invaded their physical space, meaning, their territories, which the invaders justified on the claim that the native people were in need of "the Gospels" and "baptism" (Lewis, 1988: 200–245). Prior to the Christian European worldview first identifying the geographical location of a given non-Christian place, however, the people were neither poor nor oppressed. They were still living their original free and independence existence on their own lands, with their own language, culture, spiritual traditions, and ecological systems for satisfying their own needs (Mann, 2005; Martin, 1999; Harney, 1995).

For thousands of years native nations and peoples had fed and sheltered themselves and maintained a free and independent way of life within their own territories. It was as a direct consequence of the Christian world invading the native peoples that they were *reduced down* to a "poor and oppressed" existence, under a Christian form of control. A regime of Christian domination resulted in the Original Nation of that place no longer being able to live a free and independent existence, and thereby meet their own economic needs because they were being imposed upon by the invading system of domination (Williams and Macedo, 2005: 2). As one author put the matter with regard to the Caribbean, "For the original inhabitants, . . . the arrival of the three caravals from Spain in 1492 meant inexorable doom" (Knight, 1978: 22). The scope of that statement is accurately widened to include the entire Western Hemisphere, Australia, New Zealand, Tasmania, and Oceania.

George Tinker recognizes that indigenous peoples today are not in need of the gospel. They are in need of liberation from the invasive and imperial mentality of the Christian world, and, as he succinctly states: "Any Indian notion of liberation must attempt to break away from the way language is used so easily and comfortably by our colonizer[s]" (Tinker, 2008: 132). It is that Christian language and imperial mentality which arguably keeps indigenous peoples in a poor and oppressed condition. George Tinker explains this connection in the following manner:

> For American Indians, on the contrary, the radical interpretation of Jesus would be an unproductive and even counterproductive starting point for a liberation theology because the first proclamation of Jesus among any Indian community came as the beginning of a colonial conquest that included total displacing of centuries-old religious traditions and the replacing of those traditional ways with the imposition of a one-size-fits all euro-western Jesus. And even the occasional contemporary move to correct Jesus' ethnicity historically to some shade of mediterranean brown helps little to obviate our historical experience of the way missionary preaching about Jesus was used destroy our cultures and legitimate the theft of our property. (Ibid.: 129)

Tinker's assessment is refreshing because he's a theologian who is opposed to the standard euphemistic approach to writing about the Christian missionary tradition of colonization. He makes a direct connection between Christian proselytizing and what he terms "colonial conquest," which is simply another phrase for a tradition of "colonial domination," a tradition typically hidden behind easy-listening cover words such as "civilization" and "humanity." He insightfully points out "how the cultural values of the missionaries regularly became confused with the gospel they proposed to preach to Indian peoples" (Tinker, 1993: 113). In other words, "To the missionaries, conversion to christianity meant conversion to Euroamerican economic and political structures, structures that entailed the long-term subjugation [domination] of tribal peoples to a conquering [domination] people" (Ibid.).

Euphemisms (nice sounding words for negative things), obfuscate the point that genocide is the dark side of the imperial Christian missionary tradition undertaken ostensibly to propagate a Christian version of "civilization," a loaded word which *Webster's Third New International Dictionary* defines as "the forcing of a particular cultural pattern on a population to which it is foreign." Raphael Lemkin, the man who coined the word "genocide," explained the term to mean the effort to destroy, in whole or in part, a national group, or nation, by destroying those aspects of that society that hold it together, and without which it cannot exist (Power, 2002: 42–43).

There seems to be some question as to whether the colonizing peoples of Christendom were *intending* to *destroy* the existence of entire peoples, or whether they were simply intending to "bring" the native peoples to "the Catholic faith and Christian religion." The English phrase "bring them" translates in Latin as "reduce them" (e.g., "*reducere*") (Davenport, 1917: 73). The Holy See's language from the document *Dum diversas* of 1452 is but one document that enables us to clarify the matter of the Church's colonizing *intentions*. In that document, Pope Nicholas V exhorted King Alfonso V of Portugal to travel to non-Christian lands and to engage in acts of war against the original peoples living there: "Invade, capture, vanquish, and subdue" them, "reduce them to perpetual slavery," and "take away *all* their possessions and property" (Ibid.: 23).

The question that arises is whether the explicitly stated intention to wage war by engaging in those acts against the nations of the non-Christian world matches the criteria that Lemkin created and labeled genocide. According to Samantha Power:

> In *Axis Rule* he [Lemkin] wrote that "genocide" meant a "coordinated plan of *different* actions aiming at the destruction of the essential foundations of the life of national groups, with the aim of annihilating the groups themselves." The perpetrators of genocide would attempt to destroy the political and social institutions, the culture, language, national feelings, religion, and economic existence of national groups. They would hope to eradicate the personal security, liberty, health, dignity, and lives of individual members of the targeted group. (Power, 2002: 43)

As Power points out, "A group did not have to be physically exterminated to suffer genocide. They could be stripped of all cultural traces of their identity" (Ibid.). "It takes centuries and sometimes thousands of years to create a natural culture," wrote Lemkin, "but Genocide can destroy a culture instantly, like fire can destroy a building in an hour" (Ibid.). Power further quoted Lemkin as follows:

> Genocide has two phases: one, destruction of the national pattern of the oppressed group; the other, the imposition of the national pattern of the

oppressor. This imposition, in turn, may be made upon the oppressed [dominated] population which is allowed to remain, or upon the territory alone, after removal of the population and colonization of the area by the oppressor's own nationals. (Ibid.)

Christian invaders and colonizers engaging in oppressive processes of forcible "imposition" on non-Christians matches the previously mentioned definition of "civilization," that is, and Lemkin's idea of "the forcing of a cultural pattern" (the pattern of the oppressor group) on an oppressed group (or nation). The papal bulls or Vatican documents of the fifteenth century are commonly cited as the very basis of "the doctrine of Christian discovery and domination" (Newcomb, 2008). They ought to be regarded as Exhibit A, in the historical record so to speak, because, *by means of the papacy's own words*, those documents clearly demonstrates the *intention* of the Church leadership to destroy, *by a process of reduction (reducere)* (Davenport, 1917: 73), *the free existence* of native peoples living a free and independent non-Christian way of life (Tinker, 1993: 119).

The goal of the Christian world was to replace that non-Christians' way of life with a Christian idea and behavioral system of domination. In chapter 7 of *American Indian Liberation*, "Culture and Domination" (2008: 144), Tinker makes this connection explicit. The fifteenth-century decrees of various popes provide the documentation to show that the Holy See *intended* and *planned* to forcibly impose a system of domination on what Pope Alexander VI called, "barbarous nations" that he characterized as *"sub actuali dominio temporali aliquorum dominorum Christianorum constitute non sint"* ("not constituted under the domination of Christian dominators") (Davenport, 1917: 59). Wherever the Christian dominators went, they engaged in the forcible process of constituting an actual temporal Christian domination on the original nations, and this served to genocidally "destroy the political and social institutions, the culture, language, national feelings, religion, and economic existence of" the non-Christian "national groups," or nations.

The Vatican papal bull documents appear to match Lemkin's understanding of genocide: The free non-Christian way of life of the native nations and peoples was viewed by the Catholic leadership, and by the Christian world generally, as "destined" to be replaced by forcing a Christian "national pattern" on the oppressed (dominated) non-Christian nation or people. The Christian world was to accomplish this state of affairs by acts of war committed against all non-Christian peoples wherever they could be located, which is usually expressed as "discovered." The Christian world fully intended to wage a genocidal war against "heathens" ("a word of christian origin") and "infidels" (those who do not believe that Jesus Christian was the true Messiah), wherever non-Christians could be located by the Christian world. The papal bulls were a declaration of war against non-Christian worlds on every level of their existence. In this sense, then, war was the means by which "the gospel" was to be carried to the non-Christian places of the planet so that Christian domination could be constituted there.

MISSIONARIES OF DOMINATION

When such violent processes were engaged in over a long enough period of time, the resulting forcible imposition ended up stripping a native nation or people of all or nearly all cultural traces of their free and independent existence. Their own language and customary behavioral patterns were their most effective means of holding together their unique physical and mental world, and their best means of maintaining their own reality. Once the people were cut-off from their own cultural and linguistic repository of knowledge, by massive numbers of the people being killed off, and by their cultural knowledge not being transmitted to each new generations of young people, thousands of years of oral history and tradition could be largely eradicated within several generation through a genocidal process of mental and physical colonization. This is especially so given the estimates of incredibly high death rates throughout the Western Hemisphere; historian David Stannard noting that "population loss among native societies routinely reached and exceeded 95 percent" (Stannard, 1992: 268). For a cultural world held together on the basis of oral history and oral knowledge transmission, that is an incredibly high rate of cultural death through epistemological loss.

One main technique used by the Christian world to achieve its goal of eradicating non-Christian cultural and mental worlds was to prevent traditional inter-generational knowledge from being transmitted to native children, which was partly achieved by indoctrinating those children into the language and cultural tradition of what many of us as Indigenous scholars consider to be Christian *oppressors* (dominators). Although her example is illustrative of a Protestant rather than a Catholic context, Elizabeth Graham's book *Medicine Man to Missionary: Missionaries as Agents of Change among the Indians of Southern Ontario, 1784–1867*, provides a detailed record of native children being indoctrinated to a Christian cultural and mental milieu. Graham provides evidence of the pattern of schooling used by the Mennonites. In 1858, for example, we read of a missionary at New Credit "finding himself in the position of having to teach school for a month," and who "expressed his dissatisfaction with the progress the children had made in reading and writing English with understanding." This teacher suggested:

> We want a Geography of our country, also a Spelling book with definitions of words, a short Grammar in catechetical form, and then burn or destroy all Indian Books and put an end to talking Indian in school. (Graham, 1975: 73–74)

Preventing Indian children from speaking their own native language prevented them from acquiring their own forms of cultural knowledge, which meant they were not learning their own language and culture. Graham points out that "at Alnwick a manual labour school was started in 1839, with the emphasis on farming for boys and household economy for the girls, and the report for 1841 on the progress of the school" (Ibid.: 77) reads as follows:

> The School is a Manual Labour school; entirely under the control of the Missionary. The pupils are all boarded at the Institute. . . .They are taught reading and other branches of a Common English Education, including Geography, in separate buildings, the young men. . . about 25 little boys, by an Indian teacher; . . . who was instructed in this place:—the girls with 8 or10 little ones that are day scholars, by a lady.—the young men spend six hours a day in school; except in sowing time. During the remaining hours, they are instructed in agricultural business. The girls spend also six hours a day in school: the afternoon half of which time is devoted to needlework.—during the rest of the day they are engaged in housework. The following is the daily routine of this department.
> They rise during winter at 5 o'clock: and in summer at half past 4our. The girls proceed to milk the cows: then prepare the breakfast; attend family prayer; and hear a lecture, or exposition of a portion of the Scriptures.—The singing, and all the exercises, are in English. The girls then set the cheese, and do housework—School closed at half past four p.m.—at five, supper, at six, milking the cows. Prayers at eight p.m., at half past, they retire to rest. (Ibid.)

This arduous schedule provides an example of how the primary socialization process for thousands of native children was spent learning the language and knowledge system of the dominating society, including the mentality of the gospels ("the Scriptures"), and not learning their own native linguistic and cultural identity as "indigenous peoples," in this case, as Delaware (Lenape) Indians.

NON-LIBERATING IDEAS OF THE GOSPEL

There is another way that Christian proselytizing and the gospel have posed a threat to the indigenous worldview, and it is related to the account of native children being socialized to biblical thinking. By means of its categories for non-Christians, the Christian worldview has cast a judgmental stigma on the traditional lifestyles of native nations, as well as on the language systems of indigenous peoples. The original non-Christian peoples of a given geographical area are dehumanized by means of such Christian categories as, "pagans," "heathens," "infidels," "uncivilized" (i.e., not yet dominated), "barbarous," and so forth.

In Matthew 6:7, the following quote is attributed to Jesus: "But when ye pray, use not vain repetitions as the heathen do: for they think that they shall be heard for their much speaking." With these words, the Christian world casts a negative judgment on the prayers of the "heathen" "Indians." In Matthew 5:17 we find "Think not that I am come to destroy the law, or the prophets: I am not come to destroy, but to fulfil [the law]." This portrays the biblical figure Jesus as being committed to a fulfillment of the Jewish law, including the covenant to take over the "heathen" promised land. Biblical teachings do not provide an effective way of dealing with the onslaught brought on by the Christian empire and the Christian colonizers.

Take, for example, Matthew 5:39, where we find advice that if taken would play directly into the hands of the Christian invaders: "But I say unto you, That ye resist not evil: but whosoever shall smite thee on thy right cheek, turn to him the other also." Perfect words for advising an oppressed people to remain weak and submissive when dealing with their oppressors. At Matthew 5:43: "But I say unto you, Love your enemies, bless them that curse you, do good to them that hate you and pray for them which despitefully use you, and persecute you." Again, this is senseless advice to give to oppressed "heathens" being crushed under the boot and chastised under the lash of the Christian oppressors. This "gospel-thought-process" provides no basis for Indigenous nations and peoples to resisting their Christian colonizers in an effort to achieve liberation from a system of domination.

If taken to heart, that way of thinking ensures that the colonized will not resist their colonizers. Other such biblical words include: "That ye may be the children of our Father which is in heaven: for he maketh the sun to rise on the evil and on the good, and sendeth rain on the just and on the unjust." This passage seems to be saying that the Christian "God" does not discriminate against those who commit "evil" acts. The "sun" and "rain" of "His" blessings automatically fall upon those who commit evil acts, just as they fall on those who engage in acts of "good." This goes with Romans 13:1: "Let every soul be in subjection to the superior authorities, for there is no authority except by God; the existing authorities stand placed in their relative positions by God." From a traditional Indigenous viewpoint, this language seems to be saying that "God" placed the invading "superior authorities" of the Church and the State where they are. This "Gospel" thinking is inimical to an Indigenous worldview and path of liberation.

DOMINATION DISGUISED AS "CIVILIZATION"

The biblical socialization process that native children were been made to undergo in the residential ("Canada") and boarding schools ("U.S.") was integral to what George Tinker terms "missionary conquest." By that phrase he means a complex and comprehensive set of processes whereby a system of domination was carried by Christian voyagers to a geographical area where a Christian system of domination had not been previously extended. The Christian invaders intended to establish a system of Christian domination in that location by means of a violent social and physical imposition on the people of the non-Christian society. We might say that the effort to extend a system of Christian domination to lands where it did not *yet* exist was "the mission" of "the missionary tradition." "At stake here," says Tinker, "are those structures of Western, Euroamerican societies that generated the attitudes of the missionaries, as well as the attitudes of the political and military leaders who shared so many of the missionaries' beliefs and ultimate goals for dealing with the aboriginal inhabitants of North America" (Tinker, 1993: 115). Tinker continues:

> From the renaissance world of ideas, Europeans were empowered to begin the ongoing process of imposing their political and economic structures on the rest of the world for their own political and economic gain. The beginning of this colonial process coincided with the voyage of Columbus and with the emergence of a new, and now pervasive, political idea, that of the modern nation-state. (Ibid.: 116)

Such processes of domination were carried out in the name of advancing "civilization," which is a euphemism for "the mission" of spreading a system of *Christian domination*. With his profile of such evangelists as John Elliott, Junípero Serra, Pierre-Jean de Smet, and Henry Benjamin Whipple, George Tinker has illustrated key figures who have played a significant role as part of the vanguard of that "mission." Such well-meaning Christian missionaries have played a direct role in the subjugation and decimation of the original peoples of North, Central, and South America by means of various linguistic and physical processes of domination. Insight into the kind of language commonly used to discuss this framework and this process is found in Robert B. McCoy's Foreword to Francis E. Leupp's *In Red Man's Land*.[1] McCoy writes:

> A great many Whitemen have devoted their lives to Christian ideals. One of which consists in bringing Christianity to the aborigine wherever he might be found. In the eyes of most of these well-intentioned people (long gone, and contemporary,) Christianity and civilization were (are) synonymous, i.e., if the aborigine could be Christianized, he would automatically be "civilized.". . .The Whiteman was motivated thus by his own milieu—Christianity meant civilization; civilization meant Christianity. (1914: Foreword)

To reveal a deeper meaning found in McCoy's explanation, however, we must use the power of inference on the term "civilization." The process of *forcing* a cultural pattern of domination on a free and independent nation or people, under the guise of "spreading the gospels" of Western Christendom, constitutes an oppressive process that has been cleverly disguised by means of positive sounding words.

What is termed "a civilizing process" is, in actuality, *a dominating process* that has been used to make free and independent original nations and peoples no longer free (i.e., "Indigenous"), by forcing them to live in subjection to the agents working on behalf of a "Christian" idea-system of domination. This matches Claus Mueller's definition of domination in is amazing work *The Politics of Communication.* Mueller mentions the way in which "the structure of domination remains virtually unchallenged" (1973: 86). He defines domination as "the control by a limited and relatively small number of people over the allocation of resources and the access to significant participation in the decision-making processes" (Ibid.).

"Civilization" and "Christianity" are two names given to that process and the end result of that process. "Civilizing," "civilization," and "conquest," are euphemistic synonyms for a system and process of domination. It is accurate to restate the phrase "missionary conquest" as "missionary domination." When the terms "civilization" and "Christianity" are used without an understanding of this background interpretative framework, however, the association between domination and "civilization" remains out of focus.

According to McCoy, Christianity and civilization are synonymous. And since a forcible process of imposition was used as the means of "making" "uncivilized" (un-dominated) nations and peoples "civilized" (dominated), spreading "the gospels" ("Christianity") involved spreading a system of Christian domination to those geographical places where it had not yet been previously extended. We find evidence of this pattern in the papal bull of May 4, 1493. Pope Alexander VI calls for "barbarous nations" to be "reduced" ("*deprimantur*") by "the propagation of the Christian empire," ("*imperii Christiani*") (Davenport, 1917: 73).

The pope wanted the system of Christian domination ("dominio") extended by Christian dominators ("dominorum Christianorum") to places already "discovered" and to be "discovered." The Christian empire evidently had no knowledge of those un-dominated non-Christian locations prior to the representatives of the Christian world traveling there. Thus, the Christian desire to "discover" and seize the location of still free and independent (un-dominated) peoples and places was the result of the Christian empire's desire to "seek out, discover, and find" any and all non-Christian ("heathen" and "infidel") places where that Christian system of domination, politely termed "civilization," did not *yet* exist.

The above ideas lead to a seemingly unavoidable conclusion: In this context, of "the gospel" (i.e., "Christianity"), "civilization," and "domination" are synonyms. Because the Christian world's system of domination has worked for centuries to destroy the languages and knowledge systems of

Original Nations and Peoples, the Christian world's message of domination in the form of the gospel is destructive to the traditional Indigenous worldview.

The gravity of this truth is found in British travel writer Norman Lewis's exposé published by the Sunday London Times in 1969, "Genocide-From fire and sword to arsenic and bullets—civilization has sent six million Indians to extinction."[2] This accurately translates as, "—*domination* has sent six million Indians to extinction." Let us now turn to a further discussion of the threat that the gospel poses to the Indigenous worldview because of *mental* and physical colonization of those who survive the genocidal onslaught.

Indigenous languages create an Indigenous worldview. Those languages also serve as repositories of indigenous knowledge systems, and the means of human thought among indigenous peoples which has been evolved over many thousands of years. When massive numbers of Indigenous people died or were killed—such as the six million that Norman Lewis said perished in the Amazon during the twentieth century—indigenous languages, and the worldviews created by those languages, are, to that extent, lost as well. The amount of language death that has resulted from the physical deaths of tens of millions of Indians during the five centuries from the 1490s to the 1990s, is one way in which proselytizing based on the Bible has and continues to pose a threat to the indigenous worldview. To this, however, we need to add the centuries of intentional efforts by missionaries to destroy native languages, cultures, and spiritual traditions.

Travel author Norman Lewis chronicled some of those efforts in his book *The Missionaries: God against the Indians in 1988*. The video, "Norman Lewis: The Journey Man," is now available on YouTube. The narrator explains that Lewis "was an investigative journalist, who made journeys all over South and Central America, focusing world attention on the destruction of the Indians." During the interview, Lewis recounts:

> In 1968 and through the 70s, I made a number of trips to Brazil, Paraguay, and Venezuela, to report on the fate of the South American Indians . . . In 1968, the world was shocked by a report that the Indians of Brazil were being exterminated. Now the reason they were being exterminated is quite a simple one, and that was that people wanted the land they were living on, to turn into profitable ranches. And this was being done in a quite publicized and cold blooded fashion, that is to say in the leading Brazilian newspapers there were advertisements offering land for sale. And if you bought land which was un-cleared, which means Indians were or probably were still on it, it might be as low as a dollar an acre. If it were cleared land, which means the Indians had been exterminated, it was maybe ten dollars an acre or even twenty dollars an acre. Now this . . . work of extermination was done by the most fearful and brutal methods. For example, the Indians. . .that were squatting, or on their own territory, were issued with

clothing which [was] impregnated with the germs of various lethal diseases. Um, . . . they had sweets dropped . . . containing arsenic dropped on their villages from the air. They [were] machine-gunned and bombed from the air. They were attacked with napalm. And perhaps most fearful [of] all, expeditions were sent overland to kill 'em off. These were normally manned by psychopaths and these, these exterminations took place in circumstances of the most fearful cruelty. I went there for the Sunday Times, uh, towards the end of this process of extermination, uh, and traveled around as best I could, although I was not made welcome by the Brazilian authorities. And eventually the Sunday Times published an enormous article drawing attention to this.[3]

Christian Missionaries, working in league with massive corporations and the Central Intelligence Agency (C.I.A.) of the United States, were integral to these deadly efforts supposedly to "save" the Indians spiritually, while killing them physically (Colby and Dennett, 1995; Tinker, 2008: 119). It's the old formula, "the village had be destroyed so it could be 'saved'." During an interview, Lewis recounts traveling to the location of a missionary in Brazil. When Lewis and his photographer David McCallum entered a hut, they saw a native woman laying on her side. The missionary's son informed Lewis matter-of-factly that the woman had been shot while they were trying to capture her. "She's going to die," he said. Lewis later asked the missionary what happens to Indian people who die without being baptized. He was informed that according to their doctrine or teaching, such people burn for eternity in hellfire and damnation. When he asked the missionary if he had converted any of the Indians, he told Lewis he had not converted any, for the simple reason that he could not speak their language.

Flash forward to 2018. A Christian missionary, John Chau, from Vancouver, Washington, traveled to India with the goal of wanting to share the message of Jesus, based on the gospel, to an Indigenous people called the Sentinelese who are living on North Sentinel Island in the Bay of Bengal in India. They are said to have been living in that region for some 55,000 years. That island homeland that is closed to all visitors as a way to protect the Sentinelese people. The Sentinelese are fiercely independent and have been known to kill strangers who come to their island homeland. Although John Chau knew this, he paid some fishermen to take him to the island and drop him off so he could take the Bible to the unbaptized indigenous people.

Upon reaching the island, he was quite abruptly "called home" to "the Lord," so to speak, when the Sentinelese people killed him. When I read the report of Chau's quixotic journey and quick demise, I was struck by the fact that, as was also true of the missionary in Brazil, Chao did not speak any language that was intelligible to the Sentinelese. What I found even more striking was the fact that the population of the Sentinelese people had significantly declined by thousands of people as a result of colonization. Survival International works to advocate for the rights of native peoples. Stephen Corry, the group's director, issued a statement saying:

> The British colonial occupation of the Andaman Islands decimated the tribes living there, wiping out thousands of tribespeople, and only a fraction of the original population now survives. So the Sentinelese fear of outsiders is very understandable.[4]

Tens of millions of native people have died from various causes during more than five centuries of the Christian world traveling around with the stated goal of converting Indigenous people to the Bible and "the Gospel of Jesus Christ." As mentioned previously, in *American Holocaust*, historian David Stannard says that on average some 95 percent of the indigenous population of "the Americas" died as a result of the colonization of "the Americas" (Stannard, 1992: 256). Consider the overall population decline of tens of millions of Indigenous people throughout the hemisphere West of Europe during the past five centuries. Add to that the number of the native survivors who have been converted to Christianity, with their descendants having very little understanding of their own traditional language and worldview, and it is clear that the accumulation of all those events has been terribly destructive to the traditional worldviews of original nations and peoples.

CIVILIZATION, GENOCIDE, AND THE THREAT OF THE GOSPEL TO THE INDIGENOUS WORLDVIEW

The post-traumatic shock experienced by the survivors of genocide and death, can result in the survivors becoming committed to Christianity while rejecting their own traditional spiritual and ceremonial traditions. This phenomenon is well-illustrated by a 1927 letter written "in the Sioux language" to U.S. President Calvin Coolidge by Lakota Christian congregants gathered at the Pine Ridge Agency, on the Pine Ridge Indian Reservation (Burleson, 1932: xiii). The letter was written just three years after Congress passed the 1924 Indian Citizenship Act, and was originally written in Lakota and then translated into English by Reverend Dr. Edward Ashley (Ibid.).

Dated August 17, the letter was signed by Amos Ross, Philip J. Deloria, and Dallas Shaw. It was written a mere thirty-seven years after the Wounded Knee Massacre of 1890. The wording clearly demonstrates an effort on the part of the native people to use Christianity as a way to seek President Coolidge's protection from the political and military power of the U.S.

government, a government which had demonstrated at Wounded Knee its willingness to commit genocide against the Oglala Lakota Nation. The English translation of the Lakota letter opens as follows:

> To His Excellency the President of the United States of America:
> You have come to the land of the Oglala where dwell the descendants of those who offered the last resistance to the white man. Here are the children and grandchildren of those who fought on the Little Big Horn. It is the home of the last and the most stubborn of the fighting Sioux. A few miles to the east of you is Wounded Knee. Here your soldiers killed many of us. From the Black Hills you have come, where your summer home stands in the midst of our sacred region, the invasion of which by the gold-seeking white man brought on the final struggle. (Ibid.: xiv)

Notice the phrase "the descendants of those who offered *the last* resistance to the white man" (emphasis added), thereby implying that the "fighting Sioux" would be offering no further resistance to the United States. The letter goes on to state:

> We repeat these facts to show the contrast between yesterday and today. Fifty years ago those who killed Custer hated the white man; now in the same place are gathered hundreds of Christian Indians engaged in religious meetings. Members of the Episcopal church, representing the Sioux nation throughout the state of South Dakota, one hundred bishops, clergy, and lay workers, five hundred more delegates representing a body of five thousand communicants, greet you in the message of loyalty and respect.
> This is an example of the great change which has taken place in Indian conditions. No longer are the tomahawk and scalping-knife stained with white blood, nor will they ever be again; in fact, they no longer exist. We seek not the lives of our white brothers; it is rather some of them who seek what little we possess.
> To you, who are our Great White Father, we present our loyal and respectful greetings. You hold our fortunes in your hands; you and your successors control our destiny. With the passing of *the old free life*, the old world of the Indian disappeared forever. If we live at all, we and our children must live in the new world of the white man, and we must have your help to do this. . . .the hope of our people lies in education, industry, and religion, and we pray that you will help us find these necessities for a useful life. (Ibid.: xiv–xv)

The letter concludes by appearing to cast a negative judgment against the traditional Lakota people, "Many of us are still children of the primitive [free] world which has disappeared" (Ibid.: xv). The letter goes on to say:

And most of us have had little chance to learn fully the best things in the white man's way of life. Give to us, Great Father, understanding, sympathy, patience, and protection. In the America which was ours before it was yours, we desire to take our place in the ranks of Christian citizenship. (Ibid.)

There is much to critique in the above wording. We find ample evidence of a "Christian" or "Gospel" way of thinking on the part of some native people that has been deleterious to native nations and peoples. Referring to the president of the United States as "you, who are our Great White Father," reflects an apparent willingness to embrace an attitude of paternalism. To say to the U.S. president, "You hold our fortunes in your hands; you and your successors control our destiny," is to acknowledge a context of American domination without calling it by that name. To claim that with the "passing of *the old free life* [emphasis added], the old [free] world of the Indian disappeared forever," was to tacitly acknowledge that the Oglala Lakota people were living with the ongoing imposition of a U.S. system of domination on the "Great Sioux Nation," or *Oceti Sakowin*.

The letter's mention of "the America which . . . is now yours," and its mention of joining "the ranks of Christian citizenship" seemed to express a view that many of the Oglala Lakota people who had converted to Christianity not only desired to become Christians, but also *Christian citizens of the United States*. Although the letter was originally written in the Oglala Lakota language, its wording contains no trace of a traditional Oglala Lakota worldview. It concludes:

Praying God's blessing upon you, and his guidance in the discharge of the great duties of your high office, we are, Your Children of the West.
  Signed in behalf of the Convocation by Amos Ross, Philip J. Deloria, Dallas Shaw. (Ibid.: xv)

Vine Deloria, Jr., a grandson of Philip J. Deloria, was born in Martin, South Dakota a mere six years after the above letter was drafted. Roughly thirty-two years after President Coolidge received that letter from those Sioux clergymen, Vine enrolled at the Lutheran School of Theology. He received a master's degree in theology 1963. In 1969, during the era of the Red Power movement, Deloria published his first book, irreverently and humorously titled *Custer Died for Your Sins*. That was followed by *God is Red* (1973), and then *Behind the Trail of Broken Treaties* (1974). His final book, *The World We Used to Live In*, was published in 2006, not long after he passed to the Spirit World on November 13, 2005. Vine's intellectual leadership for Indian Country had a deep influence on George Tinker, who received his PhD in theology in 1983, two decades after Vine received his theology degree.

Those and many other books were efforts by American Indian intellectuals to come to terms with the phenomenon of original nations and peoples being deprived of their free and independent existence and being forced to live under a system of domination.

Vine Deloria and George Tinker represent what we might call a decolonizing generation of native theologians. This is clear based on what "Tink" has to say about the missionaries he profiles in *Missionary Conquest*. "Their own Euroamerican cultural blindness and self-righteous sense of cultural superiority," he writes, "meant that all missionaries inevitably assumed this posture" of complicity in what he calls "the European conquest [domination] of Indian people" and makes the missionaries "complicit in the destruction of Indian societies, economies, and self-determining freedom" (Tinker, 1992: 112). Every time I read the word "conquest" I prefer to translate it as "domination." Tink Tinker sees the gospel as damaging to a traditional native worldview because it is a blueprint for racism and domination. As George Tinker states:

> Five hundred years of conquest and domination, the ever-lingering trauma of mass murders, the loss of land, and, thus, of a self-sustaining economic base, and the continuing experience of racism and marginalizing disempowerment, combined with living in rather intimate closeness with our abuser and feeling constantly the colonizers' pressure to accommodate their culture and values has left Indian peoples in a state of chronic poverty and suffering a community-wide dysfunctionality that is similar in many ways to the typical psychological profile of the adult survivor of child abuse so common in north America today. (Idem, 2008: 154)

What I discern in the above quote is what I prefer to call *the claim of a right of domination* ["conquest"], based on a "notion of superiority" promoted in the name of the Bible, Jesus, and the gospel. The terms colonialism and colonization are synonyms for domination. Tinker clearly sees this, for he says: "More than just a convenient economic relationship, colonization has necessarily meant and continues to mean the domination of a people by another people [or of a nation by another nation]" (Idem, 1993: 119). He continues:

> Furthermore, colonization has necessitated and continues to necessitate the political, military, social, psychological, and economic domination that virtually requires the elimination of the culture and value system of the colonized and the imposition of the values and culture of the colonizer [dominator]. For the sake of economic control, the main impetus behind any colonization, the colonizer must devise ever new means of oppressing [dominating] the colonized [the dominated]. (Ibid.)

Tink Tinker then points out that "the Christian missionaries entered the fields of pagan harvest as an integral part of the colonizing effort of one European power or another" (Ibid.). The mission of the gospel is a mission of colonization and therefore a mission of Christian domination, which gave birth to the system of ideas called "U.S. federal Indian law," and the notion of "plenary power" *over* native nations (Newcomb, 1993: 305). U.S. federal Indian law is an outgrowth of "gospel-thinking," specifically the idea that—as the U.S. Supreme Court expressed the idea in its *Johnson* v. *McIntosh* ruling of 1823: The first colonizing "Christian people" to reach lands inhabited by "natives, who were heathens," asserted the "ultimate dominion" (a right of domination) to be in themselves,[5] explicitly *because* they were Christian! Being Christian gave the Europeans the complete and unquestionable right to claim a right of domination over non-Christians, to overrun their lands, and kill them if they resisted. That's what it meant to be Christian.

The Supreme Court said that they claimed and exercised as a consequence of that *claim* of ultimate dominion (or claim of a right of domination), the power to grant the "heathen" soil of Indigenous nations while it was still in their original possession. It is this *claim* of a right of domination by "Christian people" over "natives, who were heathens" that has resulted in the assumption that the United States has political and legal jurisdiction over native nations (Ibid.). A central problem that remains to be solved is how to dislodge and replace this way of thinking that has been institutionalized in law and policy in the United States, Canada, and many other countries. During his long career as a brilliant and cutting-edge thinker, Tink Tinker has contributed greatly to this much needed dialogue and discussion about the future of Original Nations and Peoples and the path that will one day liberate them from an idea-system of domination.

NOTES

1. Leupp was a former commissioner of Indian Affairs, and the book was published under the auspices of the Council of Women for Home Missions!

2. See Video: *Norman Lewis: The Journey Man*, https://www.youtube.com/watch?v=1gZ1_fOkLXw (at 55 minutes).

3. Ibid.

4. Nicole Chavez, "Indian Authorities Struggle to Retrieve US Missionary Feared Killed on Remote Island," *CNN*, November 26, 2018.

5. *Johnson* v. *McIntosh*, 21 U.S. (8 Wheat.) 543, 1823.

Chapter 9

jesus, the gospel, and Genocide
Tink Tinker

On the discovery of this immense continent, the great nations of Europe were eager to appropriate to themselves so much of it as they could respectively acquire. Its vast extent offered an ample field to the ambition and enterprise of all; and **the character and religion of its inhabitants afforded an apology for considering them as a people over whom the superior genius of Europe might claim an ascendency.** *The potentates of the old world [eurochristians] found no difficulty in convincing themselves that they made* **ample compensation** *to [American Indians for taking their Lands],* **by bestowing on them civilization and christianity.**

—Chief Justice John Marshall, 1823[1]

Much of the teaching at methodist missions was done by White women, which means in this context that much of the policing of Michi Saagiig Nishnaabeg bodies, intimate relationships, and parenting was done by and through White women. White women were the ideal, and missions were out to quietly destroy Nishnaabeg nationhood by erasing strong, powerful Nishnaabeg women who were skilled at fishing, hunting, trapping, sugaring, ricing, and medicine . . . . They were out to destroy our education system and spirituality . . . . White women were out to destroy us and our political systems. This is **genocide**.

—Leanne Betasamosake Simpson (2017: 96f).

For the Michi Saagiig Nishnaabeg in Ontario, it was the methodists.[2] For others it was episcopalians or catholics or calvinists of one stripe or another, just to name a few. Lutherans in northern Minnesota chose less to engage in missionizing Natives, choosing instead to form local chapters of the KKK, particularly anti-Indian branches of the Klan (Engelhardt, 2014: 92–103).[3] That is the Indian experience of colonialism, at times persecuted, excluded and more often forced into the eurochristian mold of assimilation. I chose the title of this volume of essays[4] in order to encourage American Indian folk to ask themselves the stark question: What deep cultural compromises did our ancestors (and perforce, we ourselves) have to make in order to comply with the eurochristian colonizers' expectation that we join a christian church, the eurochristian colonizer's religion? And how do those compromises affect our American Indian world beyond the category called religion, in terms of political structures, social structures, and in countless other ways? I want to show that it changed our languages and changed our relationships with one another and with the universe and that these changes were and are genocidal. We had better pay attention. Cherokee author Jeff Corntassel asks the simple but powerful question: "How will your ancestors and future generations recognize you as Indigenous?" (2012: 86–101).[5] Yes, pay attention indeed. I should add my presumption that our conversation about these matters will also be of interest to our eurochristian friends and allies as they engage their own process of decolonizing the eurochristian self.[6]

We Native folk have lost so much. Yes, everyone knows that Indians lost millions of acres of Land, actually more than 3.7 million square miles, nearly half a continent. But it is never patently clear HOW that happened. It gets buried in the romance of the american story, the narrative, for instance, celebrated still today with starry-eyed memes like "How the West Was Won."[7] Apart from the huge theft of our Lands and the murder of millions of Indian people, the colonizer found a variety of other genocidal means to weaken Indian Nations and facilitate their theft of Indian territory. One of those powerful inventions is euphemistically called "federal Indian law" (always capitalized) designed at every step to reduce Indian peoples to some ethnic minority population swallowed up by the colonialist whole.[8] But another central strategy was the imposition of radical change in Native cultures. Along with the boarding schools, christian missionaries were a front line in implementing this key u.s. government objective. As Marshall argues in our opening quote, giving Indians christianity (and perforce civilization) in return for taking Indian Land by force of conquest was a fair trade—"ample compensation."[9]

LIVING THE COLONIAL COMPROMISE

Like all Indigenous Peoples of the world today, I was born into the eurochristian colonial Landscape.[10] So, for over a half-century I have been actively involved in a complex process of decolonializing myself, my use of language, my thinking, and my habits of behavior. I am Indian on my dad's side and lutheran on my mother's side. In lutheran circles that is a pretty funny joke, since lutherans know that being lutheran in the united states is deeply ethnic (i.e., being of german or scandinavian extraction). That reality of divided ethnicity came increasingly, however, to define my personal struggle as a young adult. In 1979 on a trip back to the Osage Reservation, I visited with a relative who was then the elected chief of the Osage, Chief Sylvester Tinker. Discouraged with academia, I sought advice from *widseke* Ves,[11] asking what I might do if I quit school (without finishing the PhD) and came back to the Osage to help the people. Tinker, who had teased me no end for two days over being a Berkeley-Boy, suddenly got serious. Tink, he said, if you really want to help, do two things. First, finish your degree; second, wherever you go in the world, *be* Osage. That was it; those were my instructions.[12]

The hard part for me was sorting out the mother and father in me, the Osage and the lutheran. That quandary drove my early academic learning and studies. So, nearly four decades ago I did complete my studies for a PhD in christian bible, and for half a century I taught in christian graduate schools of theology—always trying to be Osage.[13] I used that academic life, that scholarly bent, in order to pursue the colonialism question and the parallel questions of decolonizing, which included the decolonizing business of trying to be Osage. Throughout my studies and then through my teaching and publishing career, my academic identity was persistently interrogated by my Osage identity. Consequently, I became more and more detached from my mother's faith and increasingly attentive to the culture and worldview of my father's ancestors. Even before I finished my doctorate in 1983, I began working directly in the urban American Indian community in the Bay Area,[14] and that same year I was participating in traditional Native ceremonies. Then, when I came to Iliff School of Theology in 1985 to take a teaching post, my primary focus was on American Indian communities, and my teaching at Iliff became focused on helping eurochristian folk understand their historic role in the colonization of Indian folk.[15] Yet at this point, I was still trying to rescue my mother's christian faith and struggling to hold the gospel in some creative tension with the traditional cultures of Native peoples. At the same time, I continued regular participation in Native ceremonial life, including going north to the Pine Ridge and Rosebud Lakota Reservations where Sylvester Tinker had assured me I would find Osage relatives.[16] My going back and forth between cultures seemed easy enough at the time. The tensive contradiction only became apparent to me over time as I continued the process of decolonization.[17]

I was born to a second generation norwegian immigrant lutheran mother and an American Indian father, a citizen of the Osage Nation—even as he came to adopt over time the religious affiliation of his wife. Dad was born to an Oklahoma Cherokee mother who had become a member of a baptist church in Fairfax—on the Osage Reservation, but he was forever alienated from that baptist church and the denomination by a church elder who assaulted him (sexually) when he was an adolescent. He also had an antipathy for the dominant catholic church on the Osage, something that mirrored his own Osage father's animosity, but the actual reasons for his antagonism were never clear to me. So, I was raised lutheran and did theological training in that tradition, both in the united states and in a german university. I went on to teach greek in a presbyterian theological graduate school for nine years, before Iliff discovered me at an annual meeting of the Native American Theological Association[18] and invited me for a job interview—out of the blue. It was a quirky happenstance, since I had largely given up looking for a teaching position.

FOUR WINDS AMERICAN INDIAN COUNCIL

By my fifth year on the Iliff faculty, I had experienced persistent interactions with my faculty colleagues and with Iliff staff that reminded me that my position at the school was indeed a colonial compromise. They really did expect me to mirror the structures of their own discourse. I was to teach about Indians, but to teach about Indians using the modalities that had been crafted by a century of eurochristian academics in anthropology and history, using their categories of analysis, their own theories, and their own jargon-laden language. They seemed oblivious to the possibility that Indian folk might want to talk about the Indian world using our own modes of discourse, our own theories and methods. So, I did have to make the compromise of studying and learning much of their sophisticated discourses—out of self-defense and in order to fight for a decolonizing project that they never quite understood.[19]

I had also come to assume leadership (volunteer) of an episcopal/lutheran Indian ministry in Denver—largely by default because of the lack of financial resources provided for the "mission" after an episcopal Indian priest left.[20] The urban Indian community that gravitated to Living Waters Indian Mission, later known as Four Winds American Indian Council (4Winds),[21] was from the beginning of my involvement an Indian community deeply involved in what Nishnaabeg author Leanne Simpson calls radical resurgence (2017: 48–50). While we maintained connection with two different christian denominations, we were self-consciously focused on the project of decolonizing ourselves. As we continued to use some semblance of an episcopal liturgical form,[22] we explored our Indian culture and values more openly and persistently, especially paying attention to Indigenous ceremonial life. For twenty-five years, my work with 4Winds helped me to maintain Indian community centeredness even as I taught in an elite eurochristian academic center. My volunteer responsibilities were like having a second job (albeit without pay), some fifteen hours a week generally. But I was living in community, the urban Indian community. And every weekend we brought the community together for an urban Indian ceremony, a place where we could be unashamedly Native, visit, make plans, plan protests, and help one another with the issues of life in a city. At the time, we were invested in the attempt to honor both our Indian ceremonial traditions and a form of christian identity that we hoped might be shaped more by our Indian-ness. That, at least, was my own agenda as titular leader, along with what turned out to be a very small segment of the regular community participants at 4Winds. In retrospect, it became clear that even though I had won respect from the community, I had failed in my attempt to convince them of my personal vision through those early years at 4Winds.

So, I spent the early years of my academic career in the attempt to hold traditional Indian culture in some balance with the colonized eurochristian church practice I had inherited. At the time, that seemed to me to be an important contribution to Indian wellbeing. I was convinced enough that I had done a PhD in christian bible in order to be able to hold that balance of christian colonialism with traditional culture and worldview. I became a greek scholar which allowed me to explore the biblical text in ways that I thought demonstrated some stray worldview similarities with American Indian traditional thinking. I certainly imagined I was on the right track in reinterpreting the colonialist eurochristian religion in ways that seemed to me to work within the Indian worldview. I was not alone, of course, in making the attempt to mitigate the distance between eurochristian religion and the traditional Indian world. And of course, there are yet today many American Indian ministers who are still trying to function in that in-between modality. The more I learned, however, it became increasingly obvious to me that my colonized genius simply did not work and that the two could not really be held together with any authenticity.

By the time I finished writing my book *Missionary Conquest* in 1993, however, it finally became ever clearer to me that my attempt to hold the gospel and Indian traditional culture in constructive tension was doomed to failure. Rather, I realized that ***any*** degree of conformity or assimilation to the christian gospel necessitated the deconstruction and ultimate extinguishing of a Native worldview, so that chief justice Marshall's legal language in *Johnson v. M'Intosh* about the ascendancy of a "superior [eurochristian] genius" necessitated a dramatic shift in worldview for Native folk—from Native to eurochristian. Reflecting on my volunteer work as leader at 4Winds, I came to the startled conclusion that I was really no better than the missionaries that I had critiqued in my book. In my struggle to make jesus and the gospel more palatable to Native folk, I had just as readily imposed a foreign (religious) value system and language as an overlay on top of traditional Indian culture. I came to understand that these are in actuality two very different worldviews, eurochristian and Indian, that stand in dramatic conflict with one another.[23] In my naiveté and with my mind still deeply enmeshed in (liberal, radical?) colonialized thinking, I had functioned to erase Indian traditional culture and replace it with this wholly different worldview, no matter how much I struggled to make jesus a Native and to interpret the greek gospel in terms more familiar to Indian cultures and worldview.[24] All we can expect from the more liberal colonizer missionary is to add a bit of familiarity and comfort for the colonized subject to entice us into the web of the eurochristian worldview, to wrest us away from our egalitarian world of community-ist harmony and balance and reduce us to the captivity of hierarchy and power structures with promises of individual salvation in heaven.[25] After all, the missionaries' allegiance is to their own eurochristian discourse, culture, and the narratives that have thrived in their own history and eurochristian practice. Adding familiarity and comfort is precisely what the (eurochristian/White) jesuits do in South Dakota, for instance, when they place a Lakota style pipe on the altar next to their sacrament of holy communion.[26] They even have learned to use Lakota words and phrases, except they have reinterpreted them with their own christian meaning.[27] So that at one point they renamed their confessional room in the church at Red Cloud mission the *hanblecea* room, totally erasing the traditional meaning of that ceremony and investing it with a new colonialist christian meaning.[28] Perhaps I was not as egregious as these jesuit priests, but my own efforts to make jesus palatable within Indian traditional cultures was nevertheless an act of colonial aggression, one that I felt an immediate need to end. I had become complicit in the very colonial compromise that I was supposedly challenging.

Until I became deeply involved in traditional Native spirituality, communion was the only ceremony I both knew how to do and was authorized to do by some outside authority, so I had put heart and soul into making it work for Indian folk. I knew the greek text, so I could translate with an intent to make the words universal, for all people. Yet, it never sold with the urban Indians 4Winds attracted. They brought such a traditional attitude to our ceremony that they could not quite wrap their minds around this lingering bit of colonialism. So we scrapped almost all of the liturgy with just the communion part, done with cornbread or corn tortillas and grape juice or occasionally in the late summer chokecherry juice. Things came to a head in 1994 when the Council and the larger 4Winds community actually requested that our ceremony finally exclude this last remaining christian identifier. As we sat down to discuss the issue, I discovered what I implicitly already knew, at least in part. A quarter of the regular participants at 4Winds gladly took communion because they came from reservation churches where, after all, that's what folk did. About half the folk who came to 4Winds ceremonies regularly declined communion and only came for Indian community fellowship and radical political conversation. They knew the talk would be radical Indian resurgence and that they would be fully enabled to be "traditional" Indian. I could explain my "universal" interpretation and they would certainly nod appreciatively; nevertheless, they would finally decline to participate at that key moment, turning down the offering of cornbread/tortilla and grape juice. The ceremony of communion was just too symbolic of colonialist power. What caught me off guard was the other quarter of the folk at 4Winds, who announced to my surprise that they did participate in communion, but only out of respect for me, Tink Tinker. That was the deciding moment. They were regular enough but participated not out of any respect for this jesus person; rather, they only did so because they thought I thought they should. I knew then that I had made a classic mistake and had to engage in a revolutionary transformation of our 4Winds identity in order to reclaim a traditional Indian identity. That was the moment that our decolonizing entered a new phase: 4Winds could no longer be identified with eurochristian religion.

For four decades now I have lived intensely in urban Indian communities with a quarter century as the identified spiritual elder at 4Winds. That experience revealed the irresolvable rifts between these two worldviews, eurochristian and Indian. Eliminating communion from our weekly ceremony was only one moment that laid bare the vastly differing approaches to spiritual practice and belief between our eurochristian benefactors and our own Indigenous ways. That chasm, however, has never been a clean split or an us-versus-them opposition. Indeed, Indian Country itself shows persistent signs of a jagged fracturing, a rupture that has exposed fault lines within Indian communities themselves. The initial point of rupture, the blunt force of colonial invasion, radiated historically throughout the differing Indian communities of the Americas, always in multiple patterns of diffusion. For many, who were left in the dust of the colonial destruction of their communities, conversion seemed early on as an easy solution, a way to protect their communities from further damage. Yet, the seismic cultural shifts that violent colonization left in its wake exploited that conversion of Native peoples to the spectrum of competing eurochristian denominations and doctrines. Eventually that modality of Indian conversion overran the continent and bent every Indian community toward a radical shift in worldview. Communities were split between converts to different denominations. Albert White Hat notes the tensive relationship between catholic and episcopal converts on his reservation and the shift in lakota language meanings brought by conversion:

In the 1950s Rosebud was pretty much equally divided between the episcopalians and the catholics. These churches and their missionaries used our language as a method of acculturation and assimilation into the fold. At the time we had fluent Lakota speakers in both churches, but the catholics taught and spoke Lakota according to catholic philosophy and the episcopalians did the same for theirs. As these two churches had different beliefs, the converts in them didn't get along very well, but before long they had one thing in common: they were both deathly afraid of traditional Lakota philosophy and ritual. Fluent Lakota speakers in both churches spoke the same words, the same vocabulary, and the same sentence structure as always, but the meanings that were put on the words had been redefined according to these two churches and were now different from our traditional meanings. (2012: 17)[29]

This, then, is where we begin to see a shifting from spatiality to temporality (eschatology: from a relationship with place to the reification of time as sacred) and from community to individual (balance versus salvation). And even among Indigenous communities that continue to embrace robust collateral-egalitarian worldview, we have been conscripted into a compromise that imposes the eurochristian hierarchical up-down image schema on each of our communities in different ways. That is, it imposes a whole new eurochristian worldview as an overlay on top of the Native way of being. That is precisely what Native resurgence must struggle against. Colonialism and its eurochristian worldview stand as the center of that rupture that has and continues to fragment, shatter, and divide the Indigenous communities and their cultures in this hemisphere. Yet, the original foundation of that Indigenous worldview and our cultures are still held firm by enough folk that we need not entirely despair. Through the first two decades of this twenty-first eurochristian century, for instance, urban Indians in Denver where I live are still able to gather in order to *"wada"* (talk[30]) with our relatives in the *wanagi* world in ceremony. That has been a moment and a place each week where Indian folk from various nations were able speak to their ancestral *wanagi* relatives, to reclaim languages that have been historically silenced by colonization.

The question of "Whose language will we use?" was never a question during 4Winds ceremonies or any other urban Indian ceremony.[31] At any time at 4Winds, one might hear two or three or a dozen different languages spoken in those moments of *wada* with the *wanagi*. Whether I understood what someone was saying to the *wanagi* was never at stake. They were not talking to me in any case but to the *wanagi* who came into our ceremonies. The colonial language aspect of the colonial compromise we rejected from the start, and that was followed by a developing resistance to eurochristian (denominational) doctrine, liturgy, and institutions.[32] In our struggle to decolonize ourselves, language was always key. It is deeply embedded in how we think as well as in how we think and talk about the consequences of colonial compromise for Indigenous Peoples. The words that we use reveal the embedded assumptions that mark the difference between an Indigenous worldview and a eurochristian worldview.

This was evident during two moments in our history of 4Winds. Early on our financial situation was becoming ever more tenuous because of our lack of conformity and growing distance from any idealized eurochristian congregational life. In 1989, I received a very short, three line/one sentence letter from the episcopal bishop proclaiming that we were no longer a part of the episcopal church.[33] I guess we had become too Indian and not nearly sufficiently anglophile.[34] The lutherans very nearly made the same move a decade and a half after that in the later 2000s, except that the sharp articulate rhetoric of the all-Indigenous council at 4Winds (speaking while I intentionally remained silent) was able to sway the lutheran synod council's thinking at that time.[35]

When the episcopal bishop sent the notification that 4Winds was no longer supported by the episcopal diocese, the unmentioned rationale was that 4Winds failed to comply with the eurochristian doctrinal tenets of the episcopal church—and most particularly because Indian folk at 4Winds were finding spiritual comfort from Native resources quite apart from jesus as the personal savior for each Indian at 4Winds. From the episcopal doctrinal position, conversion to jesus is not about salvation, *per se*, but rather it is about the use of particular language and the deep structure assumptions that are embedded in that language. In the final analysis it was about our failure to adhere to the episcopal up-down hierarchical structure.

A quarter of a century later the lutherans responded to 4Winds in an ultimately radical but stunningly honorable way in 2015—by returning the Land on which 4Winds was built to the Denver Indian community. They were nevertheless driven by their own eurochristian individualist worldview assumptions. When the Indians and the lutherans showed up at 4Winds for the ceremony marking the occasion, the Indians called it "making relatives" while the lutherans called it a liturgy for the "transfer of property."[36] And so, even in that historic, unprecedented, counter-intuitive, and transformative moment of upending the colonial compromise so that the colonizers were the compromisers, it still turned out that the eurochristian worldview remained intact. Despite their intentionally radical act, their eurochristian worldview was still incompatibly divergent from that of Indian folk at 4Winds. Yes, lutheran action spoke loudly and with honor, yet the problem of a dominating eurochristian worldview did not suddenly evaporate for Indian Peoples.[37] Of course, the sudden and outright abandoning of their eurochristian up-down image schema was not a possibility for lutherans at that moment, not if lutheran institutions were to continue. On the other hand, lutherans had the privilege of stepping into an Indigenous space for that moment and perhaps to appreciate briefly the Indigenous worldview of spatiality and communityism. When it was all done and said, however, lutheran folk went home to the comfort of their own languaging, practices and hierarchical worldview with its up-down image schema—but with a well-earned feeling of having done something worthwhile. That was necessarily the limit of their lutheran compromise (albeit at considerable monetary cost to themselves). Having completed their important act of reconciling themselves in an act of restorative giving,[38] they then returned to their own doctrinal and liturgical world of individual salvation and an up-down image schema of hierarchy.

Indian folk at 4Winds will forever remember their new/renewed relationship with lutheran folk of the Rocky Mountain Synod and can only hope that our lutheran relatives will also remember. We are close relatives now—without the colonialist jesus to hold us together. Unfortunately, however, even this radical moment of eurochristian restorative gifting reveals a truth about the colonial compromise that will forever place Indigenous Peoples on the back end of the best equations constructed by the colonizer class.[39] While the lutherans never intentionally forced us into their mold in 2015, the pressure was there automatically, because that is just how eurochristian folk think and act. To complete the legalities involved, we necessarily then used the colonial language to undertake negotiations together despite the Indian notion of making relatives. For us to continue to be in the space/place where 4Winds had been for twenty-five years, meant that we necessarily had then to deal with eurochristian structures of law, this thing called real estate, tax codes and their exemptions, and finally we took over responsibility for maintaining an old urban facility.[40] The colonial compromise never ends; we just learn to deal with it differently.

The lutheran repatriation of Land was a most liberal presentation of the colonizer. Yet, the worldviews are so disparate and the eurochristian community is so dominant (not the immediate fault of colorado lutherans, obviously), that there is almost always little room left for Native folk to breathe, or Native voices to speak, unless we are courageous enough to speak "out of turn." To speak in ways that might even offend our eurochristian relatives in the world around us. Yet domination (eurochristianDOMination) has captured the minds and languaging of so many of our own people. The threat of conversion is always a looming presence that silences authentic Native *wada*, whether *wada* is speaking with the *wanagi* or speaking back to the colonizer world.

This brings me back to my provocative assertion that the christian gospel, brought to us by eurochristian invading forces and their missionaries, has proven to be genocidal to American Indian peoples across this continent—as it has to Indigenous Peoples around the world.

GENOCIDE...

I have often argued in the classroom that the first eurochristian missionary to enter any Indigenous community immediately introduced division into that community with devastating effect. That these missionaries saw themselves from the beginning as working to replace Indian culture and values with their own value system becomes secondary in this claim, even though I have made that argument in a book, *Missionary Conquest*. While the destruction of Native cultures and value systems was ultimately the desired effect, the initial damage occurred more immediately. With the first convert to his church, the missionary's presence irrevocably split the community in two, between those who did convert and those who continued the traditional Native culture. It is important to note this effect quite apart from the content of that missionary's preaching. Eventually the community-ist structure of a Native social organization was split up into more parts as different eurochristian denominations came and laid claim to their share of the Indian community, splintering the community away from its own community-ist ceremonies.[41] The denomination of the missionary was hardly relevant, since every eurochristian group functioned to wrest Indian peoples' attention away from their community and to focus Indian attention on themselves and their new individualist allegiance to one colonialist denomination church or another. The community-ism of every Indian community was intentionally replaced with the self-focus the salvation of the individual. While this was the foundation for Luther's theology in the european christian reformation, it had already become a deeply embedded affect in the european renaissance. The radical eurochristian individual had risen from the ash heap of the plague of 1348–1352 that took the lives of some one quarter of the European population. The eurochristian individual replaced the community as the primary concern and focus—both from the preaching of the missionaries and the interests of the colonialist government.[42]

As a result, some important ceremonies of the People, those that typically involved the whole of community, could no longer happen because all those needed to perform the ceremony were no longer available to the people. In the case of my own people, the wazhazhe Nation, toward the end of the nineteenth eurochristian century, the process of conversion began to thin the ranks of the all-important society of old ones, the *noho^{n}zhi^{n}ga*. The most important ceremonies were whole community ceremonies and required *noho^{n}zhi^{n}ga* from each of the clans to complete. In the "defend the People" ceremony, euroformed by colonial interpretation as the Osage war ceremony,[43] the ceremony could not even begin until a *noho^{n}zhi^{n}ga* from one of the black pipe clans, the black bear or the panther clan, brought the appropriate pipe bundle. Then a *noho^{n}zhi^{n}ga* from the deer clan would bring the tobacco for filling the pipe. And that is only the very start of what would usually become a twelve-day ceremony. As life became more difficult for Osage folk after the eurochristian invasion, through the poverty of the Kansas strip reservation and the early years on the current Oklahoma reservation, more and more *noho^{n}zhi^{n}ga* put away their bundles and began to turn first to the peyote ceremony that became the Native American Church, a line of resistance to christian conversion (Rollings, 2004), but then finally to the eurochristian churches proper. As they put their bundles away, it became more impossible to perform any of these large whole-community ceremonies. And as the missionaries began to convert one individual at a time, the new converts were dissuaded from any participation in these community ceremonies in any case. A careful analysis of the ceremonies, however, begins to demonstrate how significant a compromise Osage folk were compelled to make in order to keep the colonizer happy (Ibid.).

Most Indian communities resisted the colonial missionary pressure to convert for as long as they could. The Osage were largely successful until the turn of the twentieth century (Ibid.), when they no longer had a full complement of *no^{n}ho^{n}zhi^{n}ga* necessary to conduct whole community ceremonies. Eventually, the erosion of Land holdings, the abduction of children, the deadly spread of epidemic diseases, the destruction of Native economies (e.g., killing off the buffalo and other animals), and a resulting depth of poverty took its toll on one Nation after another. To ensure the process they called civilizing, the eurochristians created the notorious boarding school system, which systematically removed Indian children from their homes and essentially incarcerate them in indoctrination centers, boarding schools, for up to a dozen years. These schools, euphemistically so-called,[44] implemented policies to outlaw Native language use in favor of an english-only policy. They structured training to erase the Indian cultural value of community in favor of radical eurochristian individualism. And most importantly they made christian conversion an important goal in the process of "civilizing" Native people (Prucha, 1973).[45]

... And the Genocidal gospel

Promising life in its preaching and sacred texts, jesus and the gospel have instead proven to be a deadly colonialist weapon intending our genocide,[46] that is, intending to erase our Indian-ness. The "[r]eligious aspects of genocide involve the overt attempt to destroy the spiritual solidarity of a People"

(Tinker, 1993: 7). In concert with the imposition of christianity, colonization assaulted Native Nations with strategy and tactics that began with the extermination of Indian Peoples, followed by the removal of Indian Nations from their homelands to reservations, and has endured to the present day with assimilation of Indigenous Peoples to eurochristian norms and behaviors. As I noted in *Missionary Conquest*,

> The missionaries seem to have believed a culture could be transformed by replacing some of the building blocks one at a time. Instead of transformation, the missionaries were most often faced with collapse, because they failed to realize that the block they had removed for exchange provided the foundation for much of a tribe's life. (Ibid.: 77)

Colonization's effects of eliminating Native populations, dislocating Indigenous Peoples from their Lands, and dismantling the cohesion of their cultures left Native Peoples in a post-extermination vacuum, vulnerable and available to the totalizing power of eurochristian political and religious institutions and structures.

Robert Williams, Jr. argues, "Divergence from the conqueror's religion, if allowed to continue, would make 'the conquest less decisive'" (1990, 198). The politically enduring decisiveness of the conquest has been achieved through jesus and the gospel. The colonialists came with a unified intellectual universe, shared by politicians and missionaries alike, that was wholly different from the Native perception of the world. That unified and reified understanding, imposed on Native folk with all the power of conquest, could and would not permit deviance of any real kind. As Williams argues, the political whole of the colonizer insisted on a compulsory ideology of normativity called civilization. Normative divergence would not be tolerated. Essential to making this conquest firmly decisive was the enforcement of eurochristian power that was, from the beginning of the invasion, the power to murder Native Peoples and take Native lands by force (extermination and removal). But generations and centuries after the invasion, eurochristian power continues to exert itself through conformity to languaging and institutions (assimilation and erasure by absorption).

By the late nineteenth eurochristian century, six decades after Marshall's famous decision in *Johnson v. M'Intosh*, we see a single-minded u.s. government focus on teaching Indians the radical individualism of the eurochristian worldview. Teach them to say mine instead of ours, and me instead of us, railed the government policy pundits. By 1883, these u.s. government policy wonks began meeting annually at Lake Mohonk, New York, to shape u.s. Indian policy.[47] Commissioners of Indian Affairs, future presidents, high ranking churchmen like bishop Whipple, senators, and the like had a single overall focus, namely, to structurally, socially and politically convert savages into White eurochristian individualist americans, to assimilate Indians as citizens into the united states, to finally erase Indian-ness and all of its savage values and ways of life. From the beginning the Lake Mohonk conferences established a consistent platform for action for solving the "Indian Problem." (1) Teach Indians individualism along with the private ownership of property; (2) Use education, along with replacing all Indian languages with the colonizer's english; (3) Assimilate all Indians into american citizenship. And (4) the glue that was to hold all of this social disruption together for these u.s. government policy experts was the conversion of Indian folk to their christian religion. That was the key step toward teaching their cultural value of individualism.[48] Take Indians' focus off of their communities and off of their persistent community-ist concern for harmony and balance and get them to focus on the notion of individual salvation, concern for the self, me instead of us. Ultimately, that is the only way eurochristian capitalism can work, and it was the only way Indian peoples could be separated from their Lands in order to turn their Lands and natural resources into eurochristian capitalist commodity.

So conversion to eurochristian christianity became a dominant political goal of colonialist governments before and after the formation of the united states. And indeed, the christian conversion of American Indians (and other Indigenous Natives around the world) has been an exercise in what Seneca author Barbara Mann calls "euro-forming."[49] Mann discusses the various ways that colonizers have euroformed the Indian past through misinterpretations of Indian cultures, stories, and the like. I want to extend the concept to the physical euroforming of Indian peoples through eurochristian governmental policy and missionary activity. Colonialism has shaped us into what we have become today, or, rather, eurochristian colonialism has mis-shaped us through a series of compromises Indians have been forced into. Conversion to colonizers' religion has been an important part of that mis-shaping. We recall that the material mis-shaping of Indian cultures starts with the beginning of the eurochristian invasion. Remember that puritan missionary John Eliot, a civil servant of the "new england company," would not let his converts form a "church" until they had proven themselves by learning to make and wear wool pants and dresses, fence Land, and build architecture that might result in an english style church building and in english style homes (Tinker, 1993: 21–41).[50]

What this had to do with the presumed salvific death of jesus is totally unclear, of course, but it does thoroughly initiate the euroforming the Native. But that was just the beginning. The realm of faith was the "final frontier" in the threat of the gospel to Native peoples of the continent, and it persisted from Eliot's seventeenth-century new england to the turn of the twentieth century with the Lake Mohonk government crowd and on to the present. We were asked to trade our Native experience of the world, our knowledge of the world, for the eurochristian notion of belief, and for the Native, belief meant first and foremost belief not in jesus or the gospel, *per se*, but belief in the preaching of a colonialist invader who so coveted Indian Lands.[51] Faith was first of all belief in colonial government promises (think Treaties) for whom conquest was the ulterior motive and belief in the missionaries that came with the invasion and conquest.

It is important to reiterate that the eurochristian gospel became the seedbed for genocide against Indigenous Peoples of the continent. Even as I make this claim I can hear the voices of so many Indian friends and relatives rushing to make the counterclaim, to defend their own participation in colonial religion and various churches where they continue to find comfort. But hear me out. I am speaking about much more than just religion here. I am much more concerned with cultural and political compromises Indians have been forced to make that ultimately distort and mutilate the whole of our American Indian worldview. It is not just about religion. These compromises are deeply embedded even in the colonialist christian religion of individual salvation.

Converting Indian folk to eurochristian individualism was a colonialist u.s. government goal that was increasingly voiced through the nineteenth eurochristian century, and conversion to christianity was likewise seen as the appropriate vehicle for accomplishing this goal. At the Lake Mohonk conferences the goal was articulated by nearly every speaker and in every paper. Yet, hidden in this Lake Mohonk concern for teaching individualism and conversion to christian religion was the devastation of the looming Dawes Act or General Allotment Act (1887),[52] which aimed to extend this lesson in individualism by weakening "tribal" governments and teaching Indians the private ownership of property (real estate), individualism at a whole new level. And tucked away in this Dawes Act was the promise of relieving Indians of the vast majority of their still existing Land base to open it up for eurochristian occupation and cultivation by christian farmers (intended to give Indians a good example for learning eurochristian agriculture[53]). This Dawes Act succeeded in "legally" stealing about 100 million acres of remaining Indian Lands and making that Land available to invading christians. This law is not in any way separable from the movement to convert Indian folk to the eurochristian gospel religion.

Dawes was the key to the colonial religious compromise, to turn the Earth from grandmother, from *mo^{n}zho^n*, into property, to shift the reality from a close personal interrelationship to one of ownership, a hierarchy of human over non-human, of owner over owned, not much different from the christian ownership (chattel slavery) of imported African folks. And here owned meant and means not just the Land but everything on the Land, including particularly her natural resources. Indian Land is now owned as private property by the anthropocentric hierarchical human individual to serve the eurochristian economy of extraction. Now instead of persons other-than-human who share the Earth with us, we have the less-than-human who are to be controlled and used as extractable resources solely to enhance the human, a radical hierarchicalizing of the world.[54] That is what we gave up in this compromise. We were asked to betray our non-human relatives and to focus merely on the salvation of our individual souls.[55]

As the general American Indian worldview shifted under the weight of the conquest, Indian peoples were morphed more and more into the radical eurochristian individual. Increasingly as individuals, we find ourselves embedded in a world of hierarchy that has replaced too much of our community-ist, collateral-egalitarian world. To this extent, Indian folk have been coerced, whether we recognize it or not, into eurochristian mimicry. Our lives, our performance, is likewise shaped by this new social, economic, legal and political reality. It is not without irony that the urban Indian community at 4Winds discovered this powerfully when we took over the corner of 4th and Bannock from the lutheran synod. For us, there was no escaping the new "property" realities (even as we held the Land at 4th and Bannock as a close relative). All of a sudden there were issues of property title, tax codes, permits, and even the city's listing of 4Winds as a historical building.

Remember, my argument here is intentionally controversial, hoping to generate intense conversation about worldview and culture among both Native folk and our colonizer relatives. My intention is not a mere bashing of other peoples' religious beliefs, whether the beliefs of eurochristian churchgoers or Indian folk who have converted to their religion and find some satisfaction there. That would be too simplistic. What is important at this point is some deeper reflection on the history and development of what I call eurochristian culture through the past two millennia and the colonizer imposition of that culture on American Indian communities for half a millennium. That imposition of eurochristian culture then came with deep cultural compromises that are always attached to conversion, that is, to colonizer religion and the eurochristian worldview.

My aim here is that Indian folk who have become evangelical christian converts might begin to interrogate themselves and ask how their commitment to individual salvation might be contributing to the erosion of our traditional community-ist unity as Indian Nations.

CONVERT THE NATIVES AND TAKE THE LAND: COLONIALIST STRATEGIES FOR CONQUEST

Converting American Indian "savages" to christianity, and to the eurochristian culture and worldview, was a fundamental colonialist strategy from very early in the eurochristian invasion of north America. By 1823 it was clearly articulated by supreme court justice Marshall in the official court decision we have already cited, and as such it is embedded in u.s. law. By the 1880s it was a persistent government policy recommendation that came out of the Lake Mohonk u.s. government policy think-tank conferences. They called themselves "Friends of the Indian," and whether they personally knew any Indian person or not, they surely did presume to know what was best for Indians. And let's be perfectly clear, conversion to the colonialist christian religion would indeed make Native folk much easier to control, and, most importantly, it gave the colonizer much easier access to Native Lands and resources.[56] That in turn allowed for the deeper cultural/worldview conversion of Land, Native Land, the Earth itself, into the invented eurochristian legal category of "property" (Hall, 2010). Today, instead of Native communities living in close relationship with the Land, with their territory, we have reservations owned (on our behalf, in reserve) by the colonialist u.s. government. And within that reservation Indian individuals own (in fee simple, the intent of the Dawes Act, 1887) private pieces of what we now call property—even though it can and often is still managed by the colonialist government on behalf of individual property owners.

Conversion to colonialist religion required our American Indian ancestors to make horrendously significant cultural compromises that could not yet have been clearly understood in their day. Given the nature of Indian cultures, those ancestors were still trying to find common ground with their eurochristian invaders and could not have understood the extent to which the invaders' culture would replace the deepest foundations of the Native worldview and its cultures. That deep understanding of the eurochristian culture and its oppositional contrast to their own values and traditions would only come with much longer exposure. On the other hand, the eurochristian politicians and policymakers who met at Lake Mohonk knew exactly what they were doing. Forcing the conversion of Indian folk to eurochristianity (i.e., to christianity) was explicitly intended to shift the culture and worldview of Natives to encourage assimilation to the eurochristian social whole, to erase Indians entirely—and just as readily to put Indian Land and natural resources at the disposal of eurochristian invaders.

Of course, the real surprise is that American Indians still have substantial chunks and pieces of the surface structure of the old worldview and cultures and pieces of our Lands. We are still here.[57] We still dance, and powwows are ubiquitous, of course. Even the public likes our powwow regalia, the beads and feathers, the drum, moccasins and clothing. There is always frybread, but even that is a reservation invention. And we still talk about some of the old traditional values. But powwow is a more modern phenomenon. Frybread and handcrafts are not culture in and of themselves, and they are especially not worldview. And even the remaining traditional ceremonies, where they continue to exist, can show clear signs of having been transformed by eurochristian thinking and individualism. I am arguing that eurochristian thinking on a day to day basis has largely replaced the old American Indian thinking that held our ancestors' communities together, even as some people in every reservation struggle to hold on to the old ways of thinking and seeing the world. The boarding schools took their toll; White eurochristian teachers in the reservation schools took their toll; the u.s. federal government forced their mode of governance on each reservation (particularly the Indian Reorganization Act, 1934). Those are very tough odds against which some are still trying to maintain the values and traditions of the old cultures. These, and countless other colonizer-imposed shifts in our thinking, acting and daily living, have been a greater source of American Indian genocide than the actual killings. Killing, extermination, is only the first stage of colonialism, followed by removal. The third stage of colonialism, and most important for our attention now, is assimilation. And the foundation for this colonialist strategy has been the actual conversion of Indian individuals to colonial christianity. That, too, I am arguing, is genocidal. The real telling argument, however, has to do with what is left of our worldview. We must work to reclaim, to resist, to engage in radical resurgence—for the sake of those who have not yet been born.

So, we return to Corntassel's pointed query: "How will your ancestors and future generations recognize you as Indigenous?" (2012: 86–101).[58] Of course, if our ancestors were long ago consigned to burning in hell as those who never did "believe" in jesus, if they were no more than demonic savages, devil worshipers of some satan, then we should not waste our time even thinking about them. If, on the other hand, they are alive in the wanagi world waiting for us to join them, then we should indeed be concerned to maintain our relationships with them now, in the present. Then we do need to be thinking about how they might recognize us as their close relatives, even if we arrive in the *wanagi* world with a cellphone in our hands and earbuds attached. And equally important in the American Indian worldview is a concern for future generations. What will our generation preserve for them? For the seventh generation yet to be born. Will there yet be an Indian worldview? Or will there only be culture clubs where people can dress and dance and eat what by then will be ethnic food?[59]

In this light, as Native peoples, we need to be asking ourselves the radical resurgence question of the day: How do we reclaim ancestral wisdom? And how do we safeguard that for future generations?

How will our ancestors recognize us when we go to that *wanagi* world? Or does it matter? Perhaps many Indians will prefer to join that mob of eurochristian democratic capitalists crowding around a bewildered *wanagi* named jesus who is utterly baffled by what has happened to himself over two millennia.

NOTES

1. *Johnson v. M'Intosh*, http://www.utulsa.edu/law/classes/rice/u.s.T_Cases/ JOHNSON_V_MCINTOSH_1823.HTM.

2. I strongly encourage the reader to pay attention to my annotations, since I continue a great deal of the discussion here in the notes. Throughout this chapter, my capitalization and non-capitalization convention is very intentional—even as it may seem idiosyncratic. It is an attempt to diffuse the sense of reification that comes with much of capitalization in the usual english language conventions.

I decided to use the lower case for jesus, arguing that the jesus that is so central to eurochristian religious thinking and faith is not a real person by the name of jesus, but rather has become a powerful, larger-than-life symbolic value that has emerged from 2,000 years of eurochristian historical and intellectual development, both in the more heady environment of church doctrine and theology and in the popular faith of the masses. Indeed, it seems to me that this is the only jesus readily available to modern eurochristian religious believers. Indeed, I am one of those scholarly researchers who is of the decided opinion that the "quest for the historical jesus" is an impossible task. The biblical text is not at all a reliable historical source for the historical jesus, but is evidence for an emerging religious movement using the jesus name. It is what caused Rudolf Bultmann to speak of the christ of faith as opposed to the historical jesus. Hence, when I use the word jesus with a lower-case initial letter, I am referencing a theological term rather than as a personal name—even though the two are regularly intertwined with one another in both theological and popular usage in the united states. I find it helpful to distinguish between the usages this way.

A good balanced assessment of the scholarly historical issues at stake *is* Bart D. Ehrman, *Did jesus Exist? The Historical Argument for jesus of Nazareth* (New York, NY: HarperCollins, 2012). Ehrman is a former evangelical and graduate of Moody Biblical Institute who considered the bible to be the inerrant word of god. He completed a PhD under a very conservative mainline scholar at Princeton, and now teaches at the University of North Carolina. He remembers as a doctoral student:

> I did my very best to hold on to my faith that the Bible was the inspired word of God with no mistakes and that lasted for about two years . . . I realized that at the time we had over 5000 manuscripts of the New Testament [original greek texts], and no two of them are

exactly alike. The scribes were changing them, sometimes in big ways, but lots of times in little ways. And it finally occurred to me that if I really thought that God had inspired this text . . . If he went to the trouble of inspiring the text, why didn't he go to the trouble of preserving the text? Why did he allow scribes to change it? https://www.wunc.org/post/sunday-school-teacher-turned-skeptic-meet-bart-ehrman.

3. In 1922 a lutheran pastor and professor at Concordia College spoke publicly at a Klan rally in Ulen, Minnesota, just about ten miles west of the White Earth Reservation. In northern Minnesota, the Klan was much more about anti-Indian race sentiment than it was about black Americans. Concordia College is in the heart of Anishinaabe and Dakota Territory with reservations close by in every direction.

4. I should acknowledge at the outset that I am deeply honored by the essays included in this volume and thankful to each of the authors for their contribution to the topic of the volume. And I certainly need to acknowledge the wonderful assistance of my wife, Dr. Loring Abeyta, whose copy-editing skills have for thirty years worked to make my written text much more readable.

5. Cited from Simpson, *As We Have Always Done* (2017: 192). This is a critical question in every Indigenous community. It should be noted that Indian folk have an entirely dispirit notion about what happens to the human at death.

6. I am using the term eurochristian to signal the sociopolitical cultural group that invaded Native Lands in the Americas and began what is now a 528-year history of colonial conquest. In a recent article, I make the argument for using this term in place of the usual color code word White as a more precise designation. White people are not really white; Indian folk are not red; nor are African American folk really Black. Those are just unworkable metaphors. I am not using the term eurochristian as a mere religious signifier. See my essay: "What Are We Going to Do with White People? *The New Polis* (December 17, 2019), https://thenewpolis.com/2019/12/17/what-are-we-going-to-do-with-white-people-tink-tinker-wazhazhe-osage-nation/.

My use of the lower case in cases where it seems to violate common english language convention is intentional. It is always my personal attempt to decenter the power and privilege inherent in the colonial contest and particularly in the written discourse of that colonialist power.

7. I articulated my resistance to any participation of American Indians in romance of the american story in my essay: "American Indians, Conquest, the christian Story, and Invasive Nation-building," (2011: 255–277). The romanticization of the conquest continues in many forms. In 2014 I was invited to speak at the Chautauqua Institution in New York right at the moment when they decided to celebrate the winning of the west, placarding the infamous 1872 John Gast painting titled American Progress, where the angel of progress floating westward has all the wild and savage animals on the run away from herself, including American Indians, the wildest of the animals. For their summer theme, they blatantly took the title of the 1963 romance movie, How the West Was Won. My talk on that occasion: "How the West Was Lost: An Indian Take on the American Romance of the West," can be viewed online at: https://www.youtube.com/watch?v=VkIRG9FvN3g.

8. Indian oppression included a forced inclusion (absorption into eurochristian social whole), just as Black folk after the end of slavery were forced into exclusion (segregation). Inclusion meant eventually the effective erasure of Native sovereignty by imposing u.s. citizenship on all Indians in a 1924 u.s. congressional act.

9. Marshall's unanimous decision in *Johnson v. M'Intosh* is the u.s. legal canonization of the infamous Doctrine of Discovery, which Lenape scholar Steve Newcomb insists on labeling the Doctrine of christian Discovery. Newcomb's point is that Marshall clearly finds legal basis for the conquest of north America rooted in the christian identity of the invaders. See Steven T. Newcomb, *Pagans in the Promised Land: Decoding the Doctrine of Christian Discovery* (Golden, CO: Fulcrum Publishing, 2008).

10. By the early 1900s, we are told, the british empire alone controlled nearly a quarter of the globe's Landmass and nearly a quarter of the world's population. By 1900 eurochristian colonialism covered some 80 percent of the global Landmass.

11. Chief Tinker was actually my dad's cousin, but out of respect I addressed him as *widseke*, uncle.

12. Actually, there was a third request, a more obscure, technical act. A 1925 federal government law required all Osages to have appointed legal guardians until they qualified for a certificate of competency. Ves asked me to go down to the agency and renounce my decree of competency, if I had one recorded. It turns out that I was never granted a certificate of competency and have always been a "non-competent" Indian, something my students had always suspected anyway. I had to explain to them, of course, the difference between non-competent and incompetent.

13. I have used the word "trying" here because being Osage, or being Indian generally, in this context of late colonialism is always a struggle. We are always fighting out of the colonial condition. If we blink, we can lose our way that quickly. I am remembering the title of a book by Russell Means (with Bayard Johnson): *If You've Forgotten the Names of the Clouds, You've Lost Your Way*, 2013. Perhaps the struggle for decolonizing ourselves is even greater for those of us who work in higher education.

14. I initiated something called the Bay Area Native American Ministry, a social-justice oriented agency that worked closely with the American Indian Movement. BANAM went on for another decade after I left, under the leadership of Paul Schultz (Anishinaabe) and Judy Wellington (Pima/Dakota). While it was formally attached to the lutheran and presbyterian churches, it was one of those *diversity* add-ons that never did enjoy the full financial support of the churches—no matter how articulate and effective Paul and Judy were (or I had been earlier).

15. To wit, the opening quote from Leanne Simpson. Iliff is a graduate school related to the united methodist church. I retired after thirty-three years of teaching on their faculty and was granted professor emeritus status by the institution in 2018. While I am not methodist, I have respect for Iliff as an institution and have gained respect for the united methodist church over the years. That makes the Simpson quote all the more poignant in my mind.

16. I ran into a dozen or so Lesserts and Artichokers, who are Lakota/Osage, their ancestor having left the Osage Reservation more than a century ago and are related to the Tinker Osages. And I also discovered then that there was a large wazhazhe tiospaye lying between the Oglala and the Sicangu Reservations, lakota wazhazhe folk, Osages who split off from the main Osage communities over a couple hundred years. Victor Douville, a professor in the Lakota Studies Department at Sinte Gleska University (on Rosebud Reservation), explained to me that some of the most important moments in Lakota history involved this wazhazhe tiospaye.

17. It needs constant repetition that after 528 years of eurochristian colonization, the process of decolonization is never a onetime deal but is a continuing process for every Indigenous person and community across the colonized world.

18. NATA was a coordinated attempt by american protestant denominations to do more culturally appropriate training of American Indian candidates for ministry in their denominations. They were strange meetings, after all. Virtually every Indian representative to NATA came escorted by eurochristian male overseer from their denominational office. Shortly after coming to Iliff, I was elected president of NATA. Unfortunately, NATA lost funding when it became clear to these eurochristian denominational escorts that they could neither be in charge of their Indian charges, nor could they ultimately control their theological thinking. As such, NATA was no longer useful to the denominations, and the organization died a couple years after my presidency. The denominations wanted faithful mimicry with just a touch of cultural color. Beads and feathers were encouraged, but independent theological thinking was a distinct no-no.

19. The downside of this compromise is that I began writing articles and books that were less and less readable by average folk in the Indian community. My Lakota/Osage relative Lessert Moore and my adopted Osage father Morris Lookout both read my book, *Missionary Conquest* and came to the same conclusion. Several hundred miles apart, each told me in almost identical words: uncle, son, this is a really good book. But I had to buy a dictionary! To this day, it seems, I write in an academic style to which I have become accustomed, but which is relatively thick with theoretical jargon. And after fifty years of academic writing, I am simply not quite smart enough to shift my written language. Yet that compromise is what it took for me to earn tenure and promotion in a self-professed liberal school of theology and to earn respect across the academy.

One example of my ongoing conversations with faculty colleagues was a question pressed on me one day right before we went into a meeting. "Tink, do you consider yourself a modernist or a postmodernist?" This colleague became irate when I responded that I rather thought of myself as a pre-modernist. He was mollified some months later when I modified my response and said, Bill, I think probably I am a post-pre-modernist. Whatever that might be . . . . But such is academic linguistic game-playing.

20. That priest, Father Joe Bad Moccasin, was also a part of NATA and had begun to embrace the traditional ceremonial life of Native Peoples. In what was at the time a remarkable surge in Indian ministers moving back towards traditional culture, he and I joined a significant number of other NATA Indian ministers in a traditional sun dance ceremony on the Rosebud Reservation before he left Denver.

21. The episcopals named it Living Waters Indian Mission about 1980. As we gained more autonomy through our acts of Indigenous resurgence and engaged in persistent and increasing decolonizing of ourselves and our organization, the community came to rename it Four Winds American Indian Council, as it is today under the leadership of Shannon Francis, a Hopi/Dine community leader.

22. We used what was then called Form 3 in the episcopal book of common prayer, a spoken liturgy that allowed for the insertions and transforming of big parts of the liturgy with Indian notions of ceremony.

23. Barbara Mann underscores this point on difference in worldview, arguing "none of the metanarratives of the two cultures coincide" (2000: 62f).

24. I think one can see here my continued attempt to rescue my mother's religion as well as trying to make the colonial religion palatable to Native folk. Even though I had made the shift towards the culture and worldview of my father's people, my personal process of decolonization was only beginning. There was a long way to go.

25. Since communitarian and communism have already been spoken for in eurochristian discourse to name different genres of eurochristian social structuring, I have opted for a new construction to name the American Indian notion of social structuring: community-ism. It is substantially different from those eurochristian forms of societal governance and structuring.

26. It should be clarified that we are talking here about pseudo familiarity rooted in a thoroughly falsified use of the pipe. The Lakota relationship with their pipes as family members is shifted to an object that is held by the colonizer on their behalf. It is no longer their personal relationship. Moreover, to make clear the eurochristian power structure, the pipe is place strategically on the altar at a notch below the vessels of holy communion. To that extent, then, the Lakota pipe has been thoroughly euroformed by the Jesuits.

That we are talking here of rank eurochristian power became evident on the one occasion I attended mass at the Red Cloud church. At the end of the liturgy, the Jesuit priest officiating (up-down image schema, hierarchy) announced that all *Catholics* were invited to come up and smoke the pipe with him. The rest of us, evidently, were free to go our way. This is, of course, a rank violation of Lakota and Indian culture and values generally. If we use a pipe in ceremony, all people are invited to participate at that moment. It is wholly consistent, however, with the missionary need for absolute control.

27. One great description of this colonizing process of the shift in Native language is Albert White Hat's memory of growing up on a Lakota reservation in the 1940s and 1950s. White Hat recalls that his reservation was divided between episcopal and catholic converts by the 1950s, almost all of whom were fluent Lakota speakers. "These churches and their missionaries used our language as a method of acculturation and assimilation into the fold." He goes on to report,

> ... but the Catholics taught and spoke Lakota according to catholic philosophy and the Episcopalians did the same for theirs. As these two churches had different beliefs, the converts in them didn't get along very well, but before long they had one thing in common: they were both deathly afraid of traditional Lakota philosophy and ritual. Fluent Lakota speakers in both churches spoke the same words, the same vocabulary, and the same sentence structure as always, but the meanings that were put on the words had been redefined according to these two churches and were now different from our traditional meanings. (2012: 17)

28. *Hanblecea* is the ceremony that Osages called *no^{n}zhi^{n}zho^n* and always requires a willing choice on the part of the person making the ceremony. It is a very rigorous endeavor and entails days and nights of dry fasting in some remote location away from the community, a time to reflect and to be open to communication from the Wanagi. Not everyone does this ceremony of *hanblecea*, and no-one is obligated to

repeat it. Now everyone can complete that days long ceremony quickly and easily in five or ten minutes by going into this room and telling a eurochristian non-Native in a robe, "Father, I have sinned . . . ." Snappy. It is much easier, but it involves a distinct erasure of the American Indian Self. And once a person has done that ritual, they are then obligated to repeat this sacrament of penance on a regular basis, at a minimum once a year. On a side note, one key problem for Native cultures is that none of our languages had any word for "sin," that is, until a missionary picked one of our words to serve their colonialist ends. And our old traditional Indian ways of rebalancing our communities with the cosmos are struggling against eurochristian erasure. Early Indian converts to chrisitanity invariably had to invent sins to confess—with the able assistance of the missionary. See my chapter on John Eliot in *Missionary Conquest* for examples of this (1993: 21–41). Indian sins always seemed to have to do with Indian people living daily life in violation of eurochristian culture and values. These days, of course, we have lots of sin in our Indian communities, a self-fulfilling prophecy.

29. This time also marks the shift among Indian community members on nearly all reservations who began to critique their ancient traditional ways as demonic, devil worship, and the like. Under early criticism from his own people, White Hat committed his life to radical resurgence, to decolonization, to reclaiming those ancient ceremonial ways.

30. *Wada* is the Osage word stolen by the eurochristian missionaries to signify their own concept of prayer, now suddenly meaning to "pray." It was everyday Osage language, meaning what we all do when we talk with one another—as well as when we talk with our *wanagi* relatives. But now it seems reserved for some sacred christian usage meaning (hierarchically, up-down image schema) to talk to some higher power. The *wanagi* are NOT a higher power. They live in a different world but on the same plane as we do and share our collateral-egalitarian status. I explain this difference between the eurochristian up-down hierarchical worldview and the Native collateral-egalitarian worldview in my essay: "Why I Don't Believe in a Creator," in *Buffalo Shout, Salmon Cry* (2013: 167–179). Indian terms like $wako^nda$, $waka_nta_nka$, or *gitchi manitou* are not names for a higher power god in those Native languages. Indeed, they are more important than that to Native cultures, even if the missionaries took them over to signify their own notion of god.

31. That was, of course, always the question among the eurochristian colonizer. Teaching the colonial language was the top of every colonialist government priority list for Native Peoples. See Francis Paul Prucha, *Americanizing the American Indian: Writings by the "Friends of the Indian" 1880–1900* (Cambridge, MA: Harvard University Press, 1973), inter alia, for excerpts from the government policy planners at the Lake Mohonk Conferences; and Gerard Colby and Charlotte Dennett, *Thy Will Be Done: The Conquest of the Amazon: Nelson Rockefeller and Evangelism in the Age of Oil* (New York, NY: Harper Collins Publishers, 1996), trace the abject religio-political goals of the Wycliff Bible Translators in the twentieth eurochristian century—always done in concert with the colonialist state governments in latin America to pacify Native Nations living within those artificial state boundaries.

32. At one point the episcopal diocese appointed a crisis intervention specialist to conduct a meeting at what was then Living Waters Indian Mission. Under the

leadership of this White eurochristian expert, we had the only "vote" that was ever taken in a meeting of this community organization. Aside from that moment, every decision was made by consensus. That act of voting was a low point in the existence of the group, a direct body-blow to Indian traditional culture.

33. In one sense, the episcopalian cut-off was not a big deal, since they never had followed through with their promises of funding.

34. The bishop at the time, Bill Frey, was a very conservative evangelical anglican who shortly thereafter resigned as bishop to become president of a small similarly conservative Anglican training center back east. I suspect the actuality is that as 4Winds became more "Indian," we fit less and less into Frey's ideal of evangelical orthodoxy. He made the move to exorcise 4Winds, however, with no conversation whatsoever, either with the Living Waters Council or with his lutheran bishop counterpart. When I called bishop Wayne Weissenbuhler to ask what he knew about the situation, he said the only thing he knew was that he had received a copy of the same letter I got and was left with the same questions. And that was Bill Frey's parting shot, since he left the diocese only shortly thereafter.

35. By 2015, under the leadership of a different bishop (Jim Gonia), the lutheran synod made the extraordinary move to return Land to Indian folk. Namely, the synod transferred their deed of property for the Land and the buildings where 4Winds had lodged for twenty-five years from the synod to 4Winds American Indian Council. See Terra Brockman, "A Church Returns Land to American Indians: 'This is Decolonized Land,' a Young Woman Said. 'This is a Liberated Zone'," *The christian Century*, March 3, 2020, https://www.christiancentury.org/article/features/church-returns-Land-american-indians. So 4Winds is today Indian through and through, but we hold a fixed place in our hearts for the lutheran folk of the rocky mountain synod, ELCA.

36. In March 2015, when the rocky mountain synod acted to forgo its "ownership" of the building which had housed 4Winds for twenty-five years, they conceived of it as a "transfer of property" to 4Winds. During that ceremony, our people responded by saying that we saw the interaction very differently. We, said one speaker, see this as making relatives, creating a new relationship! Very different from dealing in mere property or doing a real estate transaction. Regardless, for the rocky mountain synod to relinquish its legal (if wholly imaginary) hold on that urban corner and its market value was extraordinary. Note Terra Brockman, "A Church Returns Land to American Indians." In terms of the Land at 4th and Bannock, where eurochristian see a metaphysic of ownership as a natural category, Indians see relationship, relationship with the Land itself, our close relative.

37. For Native folk there is the persistent problem of an unchanged *worldview* and the overwhelming dominance of what I call eurochristenDOMination, building on the old notion of christendom [with thanks to both Steve Newcomb and Roger Green for the word itself]. It is worth noting that the lutherans did not apologize, but rather they engaged in restorative action, the gift of the old church building at 4th and Bannock near downtown Denver. And the lutherans' restorative gift came right at a time when they might have cashed in on a lucrative price for that Land qua property.

38. After months of negotiating this moment, both sides were clear that reconciliation was a eurochristian word that would not work for the Native folk involved. It is

a quintessential christian theological word. Yet, for Indian Peoples who have learned something of the colonial language, reconcile is a word that marks some repetition, some going back to a having-been-conciled in the past. Unfortunately for contemporary eurochristians the only point of having-been-conciled with Natives that either of us can remember is back when the Land was Indian Land, and our eurochristian relatives lived across the big waters where they had their own Lands.

39. There is a neoliberal tendency these days in academia to reference the colonizer in countries like the united states, australia, new zealand, and canada, as settler colonialism and finally as a settler class. That is a nice move toward obfuscation. It effectively blurs the damage caused by the colonial invasion and occupation. Please can we call it what it is without some liberal colonialist cover-up.

40. At the same time, 4Winds at 4th Ave. and Bannock Street is where a large slice of the Denver urban Indian community had lived its urban community life for twenty-five years. We made ceremony there; we married people there; we buried loved ones; Indian folk celebrated sobriety anniversaries at 4Winds; so did families celebrating kids birthdays and all sorts of other family occasions. We did extensive planning for political actions, including protests of everything from bogus holidays (Columbusday!) to extractive industries that lay waste to Indian Country still today (think Newmont Mining or DAPL/Suncor Energy). The American Indian Movement of Colorado had an office at 4Winds, and various other urban Indian agencies, including the Denver Indian Center, used our place for meetings and workshops. The corner of 4th and Bannock continues to be vitally important to the Denver Indian community—thanks in no small part to the lutheran rocky mountain synod, even if that claim is not uncomplicated. See again Terra Brockman, "A Church Returns Land to American Indians," *The christian Century*, March 3, 2020. And don't miss the comments of my Denver colleagues Sky Roosevelt Morris (Apache/Shawnee) and Jolynne Locust Woodcock (Lakota) published with this article: https://www.christiancentury.org/.../sky-roosevelt-morris . . . . And https://www.christiancentury.org/.../jolynne-locust.

41. Frank Fools Crow remembered being at a meeting of a group of headmen from different Tiospaye and how they sat together to divide themselves up between catholic and episcopalian—in order to satisfy the colonizer. Those families then joined that denomination. At that point, it had nothing to do with belief, none of these key Oglala leaders quit being Indian or participating in their own traditional ceremonies. But dividing themselves up to join these two powerful churches on their reservation Lands made life a little easier for their families (Mails and Dallas Chief Eagle, 1990: 44f).

42. Both the missionaries and the colonialist u.s. government particularly idealized the destruction of what they called "tribal" governments. Eventually, when they could not simply destroy Native governing structures, they shifted to replacing those government with (banana republic) governmental structures modeled after themselves, structures that were far more easily controlled by Washington. So they thought. Yet, Indian Nations are still today saddled with the notion of Indian governance structured by the Indian Reorganization Act of 1934.

43. Even Francis LaFlesche blatantly translates $dodo^n$ as "to go to war" (1932: 37).

44. Rather than engaging in actual education, the schools were "training" centers intended to reduce Indian folk to a hired labor force. Church schools and federal government schools functioned largely the same in this regard. For the federal schools, see especially Ward Churchill, *Kill the Indian, Save the Man: The Genocidal Impact of American Indian Residential Schools* (San Francisco, CA: City Lights Books, 2004).

45. Prucha's assortment of Lake Mohonk documents makes clear the intentions of these policy think-tank participants. From separating children from their families (boarding schools) to converting Indians (especially children) to their colonial eurochristian religion and its radical individualism. Again, the political lodestone was always conversion to christianity.

46. For those who still think simplistically that genocide must be merely the killing of a people, and killing all of a people, I would refer you to the u.n. "Convention on the Prevention and Punishment of the Crime of Genocide" (1948). For instance, taking children from a people (boarding schools!) is genocide. Article 2.e.

47. Tink Tinker, "Tracing a Contour of Colonialism: American Indians and the Trajectory of Educational Imperialism," in *Preface to Ward Churchill, "Kill the Indian, Save the Man": The Genocidal Impact of American Indian Residential Schools* (San Francisco, CA: City Lights Books, 2004c), xiii–xlI, my introduction to Churchill's *Kill the Indian, Save the Man*. Again, note Prucha's collection of excerpts of papers and talks given at Lake Mohonk, *Americanizing the American Indian*, 1973.

48. Besides my introduction to Churchill's book, "Tracing a Contour of Colonialism," see my chapter on Henry Benjamin Whipple in *Missionary Conquest*, 1993: 95–111.

49. Barbara A. Mann's very useful term. See her chapter, "Euro-Forming the Data," in *Debating Democracy: The Native American Legacy of Freedom*, ed. Bruce Johansen (Santa Fe, NM: Clear Light Publishers, 1998). Essentially, she is arguing that a huge quotient of what people today "know" about American Indians is actually totally misinterpreted through the imposition of eurochristian categories cognition. We are just like them; except Indians are primitive versions of the eurochristian self, lower down on the evolutionary scale—yet who can be taught civilized behaviors. Thankfully, I am from one of the uncivilized "tribes" and am still listed by the u.s. government as "non-competent," even with and perhaps especially because of the PhD, professorship, et al.

50. John Eliot, a puritan minister, was appointed by the "Massachusetts general council" as missionary to the Natik community near Roxbury in the mid-1640s.

51. That the eurochristian missionaries persistently worked in concert with the colonialist government is a point I demonstrated in my book *Missionary Conquest*.

52. Henry Dawes, a u.s. senator from Connecticut, the author of the Dawes Act, was the acknowledged national (eurochristian) expert on Indians. By then, of course, Connecticut was a long way from the heart of Indian Country in his day, but that has never stopped either eurochristian politicians or academics. Dawes, we should note, was a prime mover at the Lake Mohonk Conferences and a constant presence for many years.

53. That notion was built into the Dawes General Allotment Act, never mind that Indians were always excellent farmers before the invasion. 60 percent of the world's food supply today originated in Indian communities of the Americas.

54. This was voiced not too long ago in Denver by local conservative radio shock jock Mike Rosen in terms of radical eurochristian anthropocentrism: "Call me human-centric if you like, but in the final analysis, the only reason to preserve the balance of nature is to sustain human life. In the absence of humans, what would it matter if the Earth existed?" In an op-ed piece: "Warming 'watermelons'," *Rocky Mountain News*, July 7, 2006. Rosen has somehow failed to notice how insignificant he is, or our planet is within the cosmic whole. The whole only exists, evidently, for his enjoyment—and for his prosperity. Whereas, for Natives, the whole Cosmos has a life of its own and is experienced by Native communities as a relative and as a cosmic sky filled with relatives.

55. Note again the differing experience of the lutherans and Indian folk at 4Winds in determining the proper status of the Land at 4th and Bannock as we engaged in ceremony together to celebrate that urban corner as a piece of "Indian Country."

56. See the argument in Leanne Betasamosake Simpson, *As We Have Always Done: Indigenous Freedom through Radical Resistance* (Minneapolis, MN: University of Minnesota Press, 2017), particularly Chapter 7: "The Sovereignty of Indigenous Peoples' Bodies."

57. We are still here is a well-known saying among American Indian folk in this late colonial period.

58. Cited from Simpson, *As We Have Always Done*, 192.

59. *Johnson v. M'Intosh*.

Bibliography

Abel, Christopher. "Martí, Latin America and Spain." In *José Martí: Revolutionary Democrat*. Edited by Christopher Abel and Nissa Torrents. London, GB: The Athlone Press, 1986.

Abtahi, Hirad, and Philippa Webb, eds. *The Genocide Convention: The Travaux Préparatories*, Vol. 1. Boston, MA: Martinus Nijhoff Publishers, 2008.

Adams, David Wallace. *Education for Extinction: American Indians and the Boarding School Experience, 1875–1923*. Lawrence, KS: University Press of Kansas, 1995.

Alexander, Edward. "Stealing the Holocaust." *Midstream*, Vol. 26, No. 9 (November 1980): 47–51.

Anderson, Gary Clayton. *The Conquest of Texas: Ethnic Cleansing in the Promised Land, 1820–1875*. Norman, OK: University of Oklahoma Press, 2005.

———. *Ethnic Cleansing and the Indian: The Crime That Should Haunt America*. Norman, OK: University of Oklahoma Press, 2014.

Anderson, Karen L. *Chain Her by One Foot: The Subjugation of Women in Seventeenth Century New France*. New York, NY: Routledge, 1991.

Anghie, Antony. *Imperialism, Sovereignty and the Making of International Law*. Cambridge, UK: Cambridge University Press, 2005.

Asara, Viviana, Iago Otero, Federico Demaria, and Esteve Corbera. "Socially Sustainable Degrowth as a Social-Ecological Transformation: Repoliticizing Sustainability." *Sustainability Science*, Vol. 10, No. 3 (July 2015): 375–384.

Bakhtin, Mikhail. *The Dialogic Imagination: Four Essays*. Edited by Michael Holquist, translated by Caryl Emerson and Michael Holquist. Austin, TX: University of Texas Press, 1981.

Baraga, Frederic. *A Dictionary of the Ojibway Language*. St. Paul, MN: Minnesota Historical Society Press, 1992 [1853].

Barnes, Geraldine. *Viking America: The First Millennium*. Cambridge, UK: D. S. Brewer, 2001.

Barzan, Elazar. "Genocides of Indigenous Peoples: Rhetoric of Human Rights." In *The Specter of Genocide: Mass Murder in Historical Perspective*. Edited by

Robert Gellately and Ben Kiernan. Cambridge, UK: Cambridge University Press, 2003.

Baskin, Judith R. *Midrashic Women: Formations of the Feminine in Rabbinic Literature.* Hannover, MA: Brandeis University Press, 2002.

Bauer, Yehuda. *The Holocaust in Historical Perspective.* Seattle, WA: University of Washington Press, 1978.

Bediako, Kwame. *Theology and Identity: The Impact of Culture upon the Second Century and Modern Africa.* Eugene, OR: Wipf and Stock Publishers, 1999

Belnap, Jeffrey. "Headbands, Hemp Sandals, and Headdresses." In *José Martí's "Our America": From National to Hemisphere.* Edited by Jeffrey Belnap and Raúl Fernández. Durham, NC: Duke University Press, 1998.

Bernheimer, Richard. *Wild Man in the Middle Ages.* Cambridge, MA: Harvard University Press, 1952.

Boroditsky, Lera. "How Language Shapes Thought." *Scientific American*, Vol. 304, No. 2 (2011): 62–65.

Bremmer, Jan N. *Greek Religion and Culture, the Bible, and the Ancient Near East.* Leiden, NL: Brill Publishers, 2008.

Brooks, Rosa Ehrenreich. "Failed States, or the State as Failure?" *University of Chicago Law Review*, Vol. 72 (2005): 1159–1196.

Bruyn, Jacobus de. "Daniel 5, Elohim and Marduk: The Final Battle." *Old Testament Essays*, Vol. 26, No. 3 (January 2013): 623–641.

Burleson, Hugh Latimer. *Facing the Future in Indian Missions.* New York, NY: Council of Women for Home Missions and Missionary Education Movement, 1932.

Capriccioso, Rob. "The State of Indian Economic Development." *News from Indian Country* (April 26, 2012).

Carter, Kent. *The Dawes Commission and the Allotment of the Five Civilized Tribes, 1893–1914.* Orem, UT: Ancestry.com, Inc., 1999.

Catá Backer, Larry. "Hatuey to Che: Indigenous Cuba without Indians and the U.N. Declaration on the Rights of Indigenous Peoples." *American Indian Law Review*, Vol. 33, No. 1 (2008/2009): 201–238.

Chalk, Frank, and Kurt Jonassohn. *The History and Sociology of Genocide: Analyses and Case Studies.* New Haven, CT: Yale University Press, 1990.

Charny, Israel W. "Toward a Generic Definition of Genocide." In *Genocide: Conceptual and Historical Dimensions.* Edited by George J. Andreopoulos. Philadelphia, PA: University of Pennsylvania Press, 1997.

———. "A Passion for Life and Rage at the Wasting of Life." In *Pioneers of Genocide Studies.* Edited by Samuel Totten and Steven Leonard Jacobs. New Brunswick, NJ: Transaction Books, 2002.

Chomsky, Noam. "On the Aggression of South Vietnamese Peasants Against the United States (Review of Guenter Lewy, *America in Vietnam*)." In *Toward a New Cold War: Essays on the Current Crisis and How We Got There.* New York, NY: Pantheon, 1982.

Churchill, Ward. "Indigenous Peoples of the United States: A Struggle Against Internal Colonialism." *The Black Scholar*, Vol. 16, No. 1 (January/February 1985): 29–35.

———. *Struggle for the Land: Indigenous Resistance to Genocide, Ecocide, and Expropriation in Contemporary North America*. Monroe, ME: Common Courage Press, 1993.

———. *Indians Are Us? Culture and Genocide in Native North America*. Monroe, ME: Common Courage Press, 1994.

———. *A Little Matter of Genocide: Holocaust and Denial in the Americas, 1492 to the Present*. San Francisco, CA: City Lights Books, 1997.

———. *Perversions of Justice: Indigenous Peoples and Angloamerican Law*. San Francisco, CA: City Lights Books, 2003.

———. *"Kill the Indian, Save the Man": The Genocidal Impact of American Indian Residential Schools*. San Francisco, CA: City Lights Books, 2004.

———. "Self-Determination and the Fourth World: An Introductory Survey." In *Breaching the Colonial Contract: Anti-Colonialism in the US and Canada*. Arlo Kempf. New York, NY: Springer, 2010.

Churchill, Winston S. "The Atlantic Charter (August 21, 1941)." In *Winston S. Churchill: His Complete Speeches, 1897–1963, Vol. 6 (1939–1942)*. Edited by Robert Rhodes James. London, UK: R. R. Bowker, 1974.

Clavero, Bartolomé. *Genocide or Ethnocide, 1933–2007: How to Make, Unmake, and Remake Law with Words*. Milan: Giuffrè Editore, 2006.

Colby, Gerard, and Charlotte Dennett. *Thy Will Be Done: The Conquest of the Amazon: Nelson Rockefeller and Evangelism in the Age of Oil*. New York, NY: Harper Collins Publishers, 1995.

Coghlan, Andy. "Obama to Restore Science to Its Rightful Place." *New Scientist* (January 20, 2009). Available online at: https://www.newscientist.com/article/dn16452-obama-to-restore-science-to-its-rightful-place/.

Colón, Cristóbal. *Journal of the First Voyage of Columbus*. Edited and translated by American Journeys Collection. Madison, WI: Wisconsin Historical Society, 2003 [1492].

Conroy-Krutz, Emily. *Christian Imperialism: Converting the World in the Early American Republic*. Ithaca, NY: Cornell University Press, 2015.

Cooper, John. *Raphael Lemkin and the Struggle for the Genocide Convention*. New York, NY: Palgrave-Macmillan, 2008.

Corntassel, Jeff. "Re-envisioning Resurgence: Indigenous Pathways to Decolonization and Sustainable Self-Determination." *Decolonization: Indigeneity, Education and Society*, Vol. 1, No. 1 (2012): 86–101.

Cozzens, Peter. *The Earth is Weeping: The Epic Story of the Indian Wars of the American West*. New York, NY: Alfred A. Knopf, 2016.

Crossley-Holland, Kevin. *The Norse Myths*. New York, NY: Pantheon Books, 1980.

Davenport, Frances G., ed. *European Treaties Bearing on the History of the United States and Its Dependencies*, Vol. I. Washington, DC: Carnegie Institution, 1917.

Davidson, Hilda Ellis. *The Lost Beliefs of Northern Europe*. London, UK: Routledge, 1993.

Davidson, Laurence. *Cultural Genocide*. New Brunswick, NJ: Rutgers University Press, 2012.

Davis, Robert, and Mark Zannis. *The Genocide Machine in Canada: The Pacification of the North*. Montréal, CA: Black Rose Books, 1973.

de Certeau, Michel. *Heterologies: Discourse on the Other.* Translated by Brian Massumi. Minnesota, MN: University of Minnesota Press, 1986.

de Hueck Doherty, Catherine. *The Gospel without Compromise.* Combermere, CA: Madonna House Publications, 1995.

de la Fuente, Alejandro. *A Nation for All: Race, Inequality, and Politics in Twentieth-Century Cuba.* Chapel Hill, NC: University of North Carolina Press, 2001.

Deloria, Philip J. *Playing Indian.* New Haven, CT: Yale University Press, 1998.

Deloria, Vine Jr. *Custer Died for Your Sins: An Indian Manifesto.* New York, NY: Macmillan, 1969.

———. *God Is Red.* New York, NY: Grosset & Dunlap, 1973.

———. *Behind the Trail of Broken Treaties: An Indian Declaration of Independence.* New York, NY: Delacourt Press, 1974.

———. *God is Red*, 3rd ed. Golden, CO: Fulcrum, 2003.

———. *The World We Used to Live In: Remembering the Powers of the Medicine Man.* Golden, CO: Fulcrum Publishing, 2006.

D'Errico, Peter. "Whitewashing History, the Indian Wars and Denying Genocide." *Indian Country Today* (February 17, 2017). Available online at: https://newsmaven.io/indiancountrytoday/archive/whitewashing-history-the-indian-wars-and-denying-genocide-yet-another-bad-book-sEGDX4v8PkGyPDoJqHnMcQ/.

Dickason, Olive Patricia. "The Concept of *L'Homme Sauvage*." In *Manlike Monsters on Trial: Early Records and Modern Evidence.* Edited by Marjorie M. Halpin and Michael M. Ames. Vancouver, BC: University of British Columbia Press, 1980.

Dougherty, Martin J. *The Untold Story of the Vikings.* New York, NY: Cavendish Square, 2017.

Douglas, David C. *William the Conqueror: The Norman Impact upon England.* New Haven, CT: Yale University Press, 1999 [1964].

Drinnon, Richard. *Facing West: The Metaphysics of Indian-Hating and Empire-Building.* Minneapolis, MN: University of Minnesota Press, 1980.

Drost, Pieter N. *The Crime of State*, 2 vols. Leiden, NL: A.W. Sythoff, 1959.

Dubois, Thomas A. "Introduction." In *Sanctity in the North: Saints, Lives, and Cults in Medieval Scandinavia.* Edited by Thomas Andrew DuBois. Toronto, CA: University of Toronto, 2008.

Dubois, Thomas A., and Niels Ingwersen. "St. Knud Lavard: A Saint for Denmark." In *Sanctity in the North: Saints, Lives, and Cults in Medieval Scandinavia.* Edited by Thomas Andrew DuBois. Toronto, CA: University of Toronto, 2008.

Dudley, Edward, and Maximillian E. Novak, eds. *The Wild Man Within: An Image in Western Thought from the Renaissance to Romanticism.* Pittsburg, PA: University of Pittsburgh Press, 1972.

Eastern Band of Cherokees v. United States and Cherokee Nations. 20 Ct. Cl. 449, 479, 1885.

Eastern Bank of Cherokee Indians v. United States and Cherokee Nations, Commonly Called Cherokee Nation West. 117 U.S. 288, 1885.

Ehrman, Bart D. *Did Jesus Exist? The Historical Argument for Jesus of Nazareth.* New York, NY: HarperCollins, 2012.

———. *The Triumph of Christianity: How a Forbidden Religion Swept the World.* New York, NY: Simon and Schuster, 2018.

Eliade, Mircea. *The Myth of the Eternal Return; or, Cosmos and History*. Princeton, NJ: Princeton University Press, 1965.

Ellinghaus, Katherine. *Taking Assimilation to Heart: Marriages of White Women and Indigenous Men in the United States and Australia, 1887–1937*. Lincoln, NE: University of Nebraska Press, 2006.

Engelhardt, Carroll. "Modernity Confronts Tradition: Concordia College and the Turbulent Twenties." *Minnesota History Magazine* (Fall 2014): 92–103.

Estes, Nick. *Our History is the Future: Standing Rock versus the Dakota Access Pipeline, and the Long Tradition of Indigenous Resistance*. New York, NY: Verso, 2019.

Esteva, Gustavo, and Madhu Suri Prakash. *Grassroots Post-Modernism: Remaking the Soil of Cultures*, 3rd ed. London, UK: Zed, 2014.

Fein, Helen. "Genocide: A Sociological Perspective." *Current Sociology*, Vol. 38, No. 1 (March 1990): 1–126.

Fisher, Linford D. *The Indian Great Awakening*. Oxford, UK: Oxford University Press, 2012.

Fitzpatrick, Peter. *The Mythology of Modern Law*. London, UK: Routledge, 1992.

Forbes, Jack D. "Colonialism and American Indian Education." In *Perspectives in Contemporary Native American and Chicano Educational Thought*. Edited by Joshua Reichert and Miguel Trujillo. Davis, CA: D-Q University Press, 1974.

———. *A World Ruled by Cannibals*. Davis, CA: D-Q University Press, 1979.

———. *Columbus and Other Cannibals: The Wetiko Disease of Exploitation, Imperialism, and Terrorism*. Brooklyn, NY: Autonomedia, 1992.

Foucault, Michel. *The Order of Things: An Archeology of the Human Sciences*. New York, NY: Vintage Books, 1994

Fountain, Anne. *José Martí, the United States, and Race*. Gainesville, FL: University Press of Florida, 2014.

Freeland, Mark D. *Aazheyaadizi: Worldview, Language and the Logics of Decolonization*. Manuscript PDF. East Lansing, MI: Michigan State University Press, 2021.

Friedberg, Lilian. "Dare to Compare: Americanizing the Holocaust." *American Indian Quarterly*, Vol. 24, No. 3 (Summer 2000): 353–380.

Gallagher, Richard, and Tim Appenzeller. "Beyond Reductionism." *Science*, Vol. 284, No. 5411 (April 2, 1999): 79.

Garavaglia, Juan Carlos. "The Crisis and Transformation of Invaded Societies: The La Plata Basin (1535–1650)." In *The Cambridge History of the Native Peoples of the Americas, Vol. III: South America, Part 2*. Edited by Frank Salomon and Stuart B. Schwartz. Cambridge, UK: Cambridge University Press, 1999.

Gaston, Gregory, and Kacey Mays. "Carbon and Conservation Tillage." In *Food and Famine in the 21st Century*, Vol. II. Edited by William A. Dando, 2 vols. Santa Barbara, CA: ABC–CLIO, 2012.

Gillman, Susan. "*Ramona* on 'Our America'." In *José Martí's "Our America": From National to Hemisphere*. Edited by Jeffrey Belnap and Raúl Fernández. Durham, NC: Duke University Press, 1998.

Gould, Stephen Jay. *The Mismeasure of Man*, Rev'd ed. New York, NY: W.W. Norton, 1996.

Graham, Elizabeth. *Medicine Man to Missionary: Missionaries as Agents of Change among the Indians of Southern Ontario, 1784–1867*. Toronto, CA: Peter Martin Associates, 1975.

Greenblatt, Stephen. *Marvelous Possessions: The Wonder of the New World*. Oxford, UK: Oxford University Press, 1991.

Griffin, Susan. *A Chorus of Stones: The Private Life of War*. New York, NY: Doubleday, 1992.

Gwynne, S. C. *Empire of the Summer Moon: Quanah Parker and the Rise and Fall of the Comanches, the Most Powerful Indian Tribe in American History*. New York, NY: Scribner, 2010.

Haggar, Mark S. *Norman Rule in Normandy, 911–1144*. Woodbridge, Suffolk, UK: The Boydell Press, 2017.

Hale, Horatio, ed. *The Iroquois Book of Rites*. Scholarly Reprint Series. Toronto, CA: University of Toronto Press, 1978 [1883].

Hall, Anthony J. *Earth into Property: Colonization, Decolonization, and Capitalism*. Montreal, CA: McGill-Queens University Press, 2010.

Hallowell, A. Irving. *Contributions to Ojibwe Studies: Essays, 1934–1972*. Edited by Susan Elaine Gray and Jennifer S. H. Brown. Lincoln, NE: University of Nebraska Press, 2010.

Hancock, Ian. *We Are the Romani People*. Hertfordshire, UK: University of Hertfordshire Press, 2002.

Hansen, Valerie, and Kenneth Curtis. *Voyages in World History: Vol. 1, to 1600*. Boston, MA: Wadsworth, Cengage Learning, 2010.

Hardin, Blaine. "Croatian Militia Falling Back as Conflict with Serbs Intensifies." *Washington Post* (August 2, 1991).

Harney, Corbin. *The Way It Is*. Nevada City, NV: Blue Dolphin Publishing, 1995.

Harff, Barbara, and Ted Gurr. "Toward Empirical Theory of Genocides and Politicides: Identification and Measurement of Cases Since 1945." *International Studies Quarterly*, Vol. 32, No. 3 (September 1988): 359–371.

Hilger, Michael. *Native Americans in the Movies: Portrayals from Silent Films to the Present*. Lanham, MD: Rowman and Littlefield, 2016.

Horowitz, Irving Louis. *Genocide: State Power and Mass Murder*. New Brunswick, NJ: Transaction Books, 1976.

Horsford, Eben Norton. *Landfall of Leif Erikson, A.D. 1000, and the Site of His Houses in Vineland*. Boston, MA: Damrell and Upham, 1892.

Howitt, William. *Colonization and Christianity: A Popular History of the Treatment of the Natives by the Europeans in all their Colonies*, Vols. I and II. London, UK: Longman, Orme Brown, Green & Longman, 1838.

Hurtado, Larry W. *Destroyer of the Gods: Early Christian Distinctiveness in the Roman World*. Waco, TX: Baylor University Press, 2016.

Huseman, Jennifer. "Tar Sands and Indigenous People in Northern Alberta." In Damien Short, *Redefining Genocide: Settler Colonialism, Social Death and Genocide*. London, UK: Zed Books, 2016.

International Military Tribunal [IMT]. *Trial of the Major War Criminals Before the International Military Tribunal: Nuremberg, 14 November 1945 – 1 October 1946*,

42 vols., Vols. I, XVII, and XIX. Nuremberg, DE: International Military Tribunal, 1947.
Jackson, Robert H. "Minutes of the Conference Session of July 23, 1945." *Report of Robert H. Jackson, United States Representative to the International Conference on Military Trials*. Washington, DC: U.S. Government Printing Office, 1949.
Jacobs, Steven Leonard, ed. *Lemkin on Genocide: Written by Raphael Lemkin*. Lanham, MD: Lexington Books, 2012.
Jefferson, Thomas. *The Writings of Thomas Jefferson*, Vol. X. Edited by Albert Ellery Bergh, 20 vols. in 10. Washington, DC: Thomas Jefferson Memorial Association of the United States, 1903–1907.
Jennings, Francis. *The Invasion of America: Indians, Colonialism, and the Cant of Conquest*. Chapel Hill, NC: University of North Carolina Press, 1975.
Johnson v. M'Intosh. 21 U.S. 543, 5 L.Ed. 681, 8 Wheat. 543, 1823.
Jones, Adam. *Genocide: A Comprehensive Introduction*. New York, NY: Routledge, 2006.
Jones, William. *The Works of Sir William Jones*, Vol. I. Edited by John Shore and Baron of Teignmouth. London, UK: G. G. and J. Robinson and R. H. Evans, 1801.
Kahn, Paul W. "The Question of Sovereignty." *Stanford Journal of International Law*, Vol. 20 (2004): 259–282.
Kakel III, Carroll P. *The American West and the Nazi East: A Comparative and Interpretive Perspective*. New York, NY: Palgrave Macmillan, 2011.
Katanski, Amelia V. *Learning to Write 'Indian': The Boarding-School Experience and American Indian Literature*. Norman, OK: University of Oklahoma Press, 2005.
Katz, Steven T. *The Holocaust in Historical Context, Vol. 1: The Holocaust and Mass Death Before the Modern Age*. New York, NY: Oxford University Press, 1994.
Knight, Franklin W. *The Caribbean: The Genesis of a Fragmented Nationalism*, 2nd ed. New York, NY: Oxford University Press, 1990 [1978].
Koch, Alexander, Chris Brierley, Mark M. Maslin, and Simon L. Lewis. "Earth System Impacts of the European Arrival and Great Dying in the Americas after 1492." *Quaternary Science Reviews*, Vol. 207 (2019): 13–36.
Laclau, Ernesto. "The Death and Resurrection of the Theory of Ideology." *Journal of Political Ideologies*, Vol. 1, No. 3 (November 19, 2007): 201–220.
Lafitau, Joseph François. *Customs of the American Indians Compared with the Customs of Primitive Times*, Vol. I. Edited and translated by William N. Fenton and Elizabeth L. Moore. Toronto: The Champlain Society, 1974 [1724].
LaFlesche, Frances. *A Dictionary of the Osage Language*. Washington, DC: Smithsonian Institution Bureau of American Ethnology Bulletin 109, 1932.
Lavan, Myles. *Slaves to Rome: Paradigms of Empire in Roman Culture*. Cambridge, UK: Faculty of Classics, University Printing House, 2013.
LeBlanc, Lawrence J. *The United States and the Genocide Convention*. Durham, NC: Duke University Press, 1991.
León, Luis D. *La Llorona's Children: Religion, Life, and Death in the U.S. Borderlands*. Berkeley, CA: University of California Press, 2004.

Lemkin, Raphaël. *Axis Rule in Occupied Europe: Laws of Occupation, Analysis of Government, Proposals for Redress.* Washington, DC: Carnegie Endowment for International Peace, 1944.

_____. "Draft Convention on the Crime of Genocide: 'Secretariat's Draft'. U.N. ESCOR, 5th Session, U.N. Doc E/447 – A/AC.10/55 (June 17, 1947a)." In *The Genocide Convention: The Travaux: Préparatoires.* Edited by Hirad Abtahi and Philippa Webb, Vol. 1. Boston, MA: Martinus Nijhoff Publishers, 2008: 208–281.

_____. "Genocide as a Crime under International Law." *American Journal of International Law*, Vol. 41, No. 1 (January 1947b): 145–151.

Leupp, Francis E. *In Red Man's Land: A Study of the American Indian.* Glorietta, NM: Rio Grande Press, 1976 [1914].

Levinas, Emmanuel. *Totality and Infinity: An Essay on Exteriority.* Edited by Scott Davidson and Daine Perpich. Pittsburgh, PA: Duquesne University Press, 2012.

Lewis, Norman. *The Missionaries: God Against the Indians.* New York, NY: Penquin Books, 1988.

Lewy, Guenter. "Were American Indians the Victims of Genocide?" *Commentary* (September 2004): 55–63.

Lindsay, Brendan C. *Murder State: California's Native American Genocide, 1846–1873.* Lincoln, NE: University of Nebraska Press, 2012.

Lyon, Peter. *Conflict Between India and Pakistan: An Encyclopedia.* Santa Barbara, CA: ABC–CLIO, 2008.

Maddox, Lucy. *Citizen Indians: Native American Intellectuals, Race, and Reform.* Ithaca, NY: Cornell University Press, 2005.

Mails, Thomas E., and Dallas Chief Eagle. *Fools Crow.* Lincoln, NE: University of Nebraska Press, 1990.

Mann, Barbara Alice. "Euro-forming the Data." In *Debating Democracy: The Native American Legacy of Freedom.* Edited by Bruce Johansen. Santa Fe, NM: Clear Light Publishers, 1998.

_____. *Iroquoian Women: The Gantowisas.* New York, NY: Lang Publishing, 2000.

_____. *Native Americans, Archaeologists, and the Mounds.* New York, NY: Lang Publishing, 2003.

_____. *George Washington's War on Native America.* Westport, CT: Praeger, 2005.

_____. "Slow Runners." In *Daughters of Mother Earth: The Wisdom of Native American Women.* Edited by Barbara Alice Mann. Westport, CT: Praeger, 2006.

_____. "A Failure to Communicate: How Christian Missionary Assumptions Ignore Binary Patterns of Thinking within Native American Communities." In *Remembering Jamestown: Hard Questions about Christian Mission.* Edited by Barbara Brown Zikmund and Amos Yong. Eugene, OR: Pickwick Publications, 2010.

_____. "Native Americans, Christian Missionaries, and the Politics of the Forced School Movement." In *The Wiley-Blackwell Companion to Religion and Politics in America.* Edited by Barbara McGraw. Chichester, West Sussex: John Wiley & Sons, Ltd., 2016a.

―――. *Spirits of Blood, Spirits of Breath: The Twinned Cosmos of Indigenous America*. New York, NY: Oxford University Press, 2016b.
Mann, Charles C. *1491: New Revelations of the Americas Before Columbus*. New York, NY: Random House, 2011 [2005].
Margalit, Avishai. *On Compromises and Rotten Compromises*. Princeton, NJ: Princeton University Press, 2013.
Martin, Joel W. *The Land Looks After Us: A History of Native American Religion*. New York, NY: Oxford Press, 2001 [1999].
Martí, José. "The Truth about the United States." In *José Martí Reader: Writings on the Americas*. Edited by Deborah Shnookal and Mirta Muñiz. New York, NY: Ocean Press, 1999 [1894].
―――. *Obras Completas de José Martí*, 26 Volúmenes. La Habana, CU: Centro de Estudios Martinanos, 2001. Herein referred to as OC.
Marx, Karl. "Thesis on Feuerbach." In *Selected Writings*. Edited by Lawrence H. Simon. Indianapolis, IN: Hackett Publishing Company, 1994 [1888].
Marx, Karl, and Frederick Engels. *The German Ideology*. Edited by C. J. Arthur. New York, NY: International Publishing Company Inc., 2016.
Matsuda, Mari J. "Looking to the Bottom: Critical Legal Studies and Reparations." *Harvard Civil Rights-Civil Liberties Law Review*, Vol. 22 (1987): 323–398.
McDonnell, Michael A., and A. Dirk Moses. "Raphael Lemkin as Historian of Genocide in the Americas." *Journal of Genocide Research*, Vol. 7, No. 4 (December 2005): 501–529.
McHugh, Tom, and Victoria Hobson. *The Time of the Buffalo*. Lincoln, NE: University of Nebraska Press, 1979.
Means, Russell, and Bayard Johnson. *If You've Forgotten the Names of the Clouds, You've Lost Your Way: An Introduction to American Indian Thought and Philosophy*. Scotts Valley, CA: CreateSpace Independent Publishing, 2013.
Melnikova, Elena. "How Christian Were Viking Christians?" *Ruthnika*, Vol. 4, Supplement 4 (2011): 90–107.
Mellor, Scott A. "St. Ansgar: His Swedish Mission and Its Larger Context." In *Sanctity in the North: Saints, Lives, and Cults in Medieval Scandinavia*. Edited by Thomas Andrew DuBois. Toronto, CA: University of Toronto, 2008.
Memmi, Albert. *The Colonizer and the Colonized*. New York, NY: Orion, 1965.
Miller, Robert J., Jacinta Ruru, Larissa Behrendt, and Tracey Lindberg. *Discovering Indigenous Lands: The Doctrine of Discovery in the English Colonies*. Oxford, UK: Oxford University Press, 2010.
Mills, Kenneth. *Idolatry and Its Enemies: Colonial Andean Religion and Extirpation, 1640–1750*. Princeton, NJ: Princeton University Press, 1997.
Mohawk, John. "Technology as Enemy: A Short History." In *Thinking in Indian: A John Mohawk Reader*. Edited by José Barreiro. Golden, CO: Fulcrum, 2010.
Moore, Carlos. *Castro, the Blacks, and Africa*. Los Angeles, CA: Center for Afro-American Studies, University of California, 1988.
Mudimbe, V. Y. *The Invention of Africa: Gnosis, Philosophy and the Order of Knowledge*. Bloomington, IN: Indiana University Press, 1988.

Mueller, Claus. *The Politics of Communication*. London, UK: Oxford University Press, 1973.
Newcomb, Steven T. *Pagans in the Promised Land: Decoding the Doctrine of Christian Discovery*. Golden, CO: Fulcrum Publishing, 2008.
———. "The Evidence of Christian Nationalism in Federal Indian Law: The Doctrine of Discovery, Johnson v. McIntosh, and Plenary Power." *N.Y.U. Review of Law and Social Change*, Vol. 20, No. 2 (1993): 303–341.
Nichols, John. "Foreword to the Reprint Edition." In Frederic Baraga, *A Dictionary of the Ojibway Language*. St. Paul, MN: Minnesota Historical Society Press, 1992.
Nolan, Albert. *Jesus Before Christianity*. Maryknoll, NY: Orbis Books, 1992.
Norton, Marcy. *Sacred Gifts, Profane Pleasures: A History of Tobacco and Chocolate in the Atlantic World*. Ithaca, NY: Cornell University, 2008.
Nuernberg Military Tribunals [NMT]. *Trials of War Criminals Before the Nuernberg Military Tribunals Under Control Law No. 10*, 15 vols., Vols. III and IV. Washington, DC: U.S. Government Printing Office, 1950.
Okri, Ben. *A Way of Being Free*. London, UK: Phoenix House, 1997.
Ostler, Jeffrey. "Genocide and American Indian History." *Oxford Research Encyclopedia of American History* (March 2015). Available online at: http://oxfordre.com/americanhistory/view/10.1093/acrefore/97801993291 75.001.0001/acrefore-9780199329175-e-3#acrefore-9780199329175-e-3-note-13.
O'Sullivan, John L. "Annexation." *The United States Magazine and Democratic Review*, Vol. 17, No. 85 (July–August 1845): 5–10.
Oxford English Dictionary, Compact Edition, Vol. 1. Oxford, UK: Oxford University Press, 1971.
Pagden, Anthony. "Dispossessing the Barbarian: The Language of Spanish Thomism and the Debate Over the Property Rights of the American Indian." In *The Languages of Political Theory in Early Modern Europe*. Edited by Anthony Pagden. Cambridge, UK: Cambridge University Press, 1987.
Pagden, Anthony. *The Fall of Natural Man*. Cambridge, UK: Cambridge University Press, 1982.
Parker, Arthur Caswell. *Seneca Myths and Folktales*. Lincoln, NE: University of Nebraska Press, 1989.
Pine, Lisa, and Peter N. Stearns. *Debating Genocide*. New York, NY: Bloomsbury Academic, 2018.
Pinker, Steven. "Science Is Not Your Enemy." *New Republic* (August 6, 2013). Available online at: https://newrepublic.com/article/114127/science-not-enemy-humanities.
Power, Samantha. *"A Problem from Hell": America and the Age of Genocide*. New York, NY: Basic Books, 2002.
Prucha, Francis Paul. *Americanizing the American Indian: Writings by the "Friends of the Indian" 1880–1900*. Cambridge, MA: Harvard University Press, 1973.
———. *The Great Father: The United States Government and the American Indians*, Vols. I and II. Lincoln, NE: University of Nebraska Press, 1984.
Rahe, Paul Anthony. *The Spartan Regime: Its Character, Origins, and Grand Strategy*. New Haven, CT: Yale University Press, 2016.

Roberts, Adam, and Richard Guelff, eds. *Documents on the Laws of War*. Oxford, UK: Clarendon Press, 1982.
Rollings, Willard Hughes. *Unaffected by the Gospel: Osage Resistance to the Christian Invasion, 1673–1906: A Cultural Victory*. Albuquerque, NM: University of New Mexico Press, 2004.
Ross, John. *The War against Oblivion: The Zapatista Chronicles*. Monroe, ME: Common Courage Press, 2000.
Saignes, Thierry. "The Colonial Condition in the Quechua-Aymara Heartland (1570–1780)." In *The Cambridge History of the Native Peoples of the Americas, Vol. III: South America, Part 2*. Edited by Frank Salomon and Stuart B. Schwartz. Cambridge, UK: Cambridge University Press, 1999.
Saito, Natsu Taylor. *Meeting the Enemy: American Exceptionalism and International Law*. New York, NY: New York University Press, 2010.
———. *Settler Colonialism, Race, and the Law: Why Structural Racism Persists*. New York, NY: New York University Press, 2020.
Sale, Kirkpatrick. *The Conquest of Paradise: Christopher Columbus and the Columbian Legacy*. New York, NY: Alfred A. Knopf, 1990.
Santillana, Giorgio de, and Hertha von Dechend. *Hamlet's Mill: An Essay Investigating the Origins of Human Knowledge and Its Transmission through Myth*. Boston, MA: Gambit Incorporated, 1969.
Sartre, Jean-Paul. "On Genocide." In *Against the Crime of Silence: Proceedings of the Russell International War Tribunal*. Edited by John Duffett. New York, NY: O'Hare Books, 1968.
Schabas, William A. *Genocide in International Law: The Crime of Crimes*. Cambridge, UK: Cambridge University Press, 2000.
Scott, David. *Conscripts of Modernity*. Durham, NC: Duke University Press, 2004.
Sen, Amartya. "Indian Traditions and the Western Imagination." In *The Argumentative Indian: Writings on Indian History, Culture and Identity*. New York, NY: Picador, 2005.
Senior, Jennifer. "In Conversation: Antonin Scalia." *New York Magazine* (October 6, 2013). Available online at: http://nymag.com/news/features/antonin-scalia-2013-10/).
Shaw, Martin. *What is Genocide?*, 2nd ed. Cambridge, UK: Polity Press, 2015.
Shiva, Vandana. *Biopiracy: The Plunder of Nature and Knowledge*. Boston, MA: South End, 1997.
Short, Damien. *Redefining Genocide: Settler Colonialism, Social Death and Genocide*. London, UK: Zed Books, 2016.
Simpson, Leanne Betasamosake. *As We Have Always Done: Indigenous Freedom through Radical Resistance*. Minneapolis, MN: University of Minnesota Press, 2017.
Singh, Sarva Daman. *Polyandry in Ancient India*. Delhi, IN: Montilal Banarsidass, 1988.
Sleeper-Smith, Susan. *Indian Women and French Men: Rethinking the Cultural Encounter in the Great Lakes*. Amherst, MA: University of Massachusetts Press, 2001.

Smith, Andrea. *Conquest: Sexual Violence and American Indian Genocide.* Cambridge, MA: South End Press, 2005.

Smith, Linda Tuhiwai. *Decolonizing Methodologies: Research and Indigenous Peoples.* Dunedin, NZ: University of Otago Press, 1999.

Snyder, Graydon F. *Inculturation of the Jesus Tradition: The Impact of Jesus on Jewish and Roman Cultures.* Harrisburg, PA: Trinity Press International, 1999.

Springer, William M. "Cherokee Nation: Opinion of William M. Springer, Judge." *Annual Report of the Commissioner of Indian Affairs for the Fiscal Year Ended June 30, 1898*, Department of the Interior. Washington, DC: Government Printing Office, 1898.

Stannard, David E. *American Holocaust: Columbus and the Conquest of the New World.* New York, NY: Oxford University Press, 1992.

———. "Uniqueness as Denial: The Politics of Genocide Scholarship." In *Is the Holocaust Unique: Perspectives on Comparative Genocide.* Edited by Alan S. Rosenbaum. Boulder, CO: Westview Press, 1996.

Starblanket, Tamara. *Suffer the Little Children: Genocide, Indigenous Nations and the Canadian State.* Vancouver, BC: Clarity Press, 2018.

Stark, Rodney. *The Triumph of Christianity: How the Jesus Movement Became the Largest World Religion.* San Francisco, CA: HarperOne, 2011

Stiller, Alexa. "Semantics of Extermination: The Use of the New Term of Genocide in the Nuremberg Trials and the Genesis of a Master Narrative." In *Reassessing the Nuremberg Tribunals: Transitional Justice, Trial Narratives, and Historiography.* Edited by Kim C. Priemel and Alexa Stiller. New York, NY: Berghahn Books, 2012.

Stoett, Peter. "Shades of Complicity: Towards a Typology of Crimes Against Humanity." In *Genocide, War Crimes, and the West: History and Complicity.* Edited by Adam Jones. London, UK: Zed Books, 2004.

Sugar, Peter F. *Southeastern Europe under Ottoman Rule, 1354–1804.* Seattle, WA: University of Washington Press, 1977.

Svitil, Kathy A. "The Greenland Viking Mystery." *Discover*, Vol. 18, No. 7 (July 1997): 28–30.

Thiong'o, Ngũgĩ wa. *Decolonising the Mind: The Politics of Language in African Literature.* Portsmouth, NH: Heinemann, 1986.

Thomas, Robert K. "'Colonialism: Classic and Internal' and 'Powerless Politics'." *New University Thought*, Vol. IV, No. 4 (Winter 1966–67): 37–44, and 44–53.

Thornton, Russell. *American Indian Holocaust and Survival: A Population History Since 1492.* Norman, OK: University of Oklahoma Press, 1987.

Thorpe, Francis Newton, ed. *The Charter of New England: 1620. The Federal and State Constitutions Colonial Charters, and Other Organic Laws of the States, Territories, and Colonies Now or Heretofore Forming the United States of America.* Washington, DC: Government Printing Office, 1909.

Tinker, George E. ("Tink"). "Native Americans and the Land: 'The End of Living, and the Beginning of Survival'." *Word and World*, Vol. 6, No. 1 (1986): 66–74.

———. *Missionary Conquest: The Gospel and Native American Cultural Genocide.* Minneapolis, MN: Fortress Press, 1993.

———. "An American Indian Theological Response to Ecojustice." In *Defending Mother Earth: Native American Perspective s on Environmental Justice*. Edited by Jace Weaver. Maryknoll, NY: Orbis, 1996.

———. "Foreword." In Vine Deloria, Jr. *God is Red*, 3rd ed. Golden, CO: Fulcrum, 2003.

———. *Spirit and Resistance: Political Theology and American Indian Liberation*. Minneapolis, MN: Fortress Press, 2004a.

———. "The Stones Shall Cry Out: Consciousness, Rocks, and Indians." *Wicazo Sa Review*, Vol. 19, No. 2 (2004b): 105–125.

———. "Tracing a Contour of Colonialism: American Indians and the Trajectory of Educational Imperialism." In *Preface to Ward Churchill, "Kill the Indian, Save the Man": The Genocidal Impact of American Indian Residential Schools*. San Francisco, CA: City Lights Books, 2004c.

———. *American Indian Liberation: A Theology of Sovereignty*. Maryknoll, NY: Orbis Books, 2008.

———. "American Indians, Conquest, the Christian Story, and Invasive Nation-building." In *Wading through Many Voices: Toward a Theology of Public Conversation*. Edited by Harold Recinos. Lanham, MD: Rowman and Littlefield, 2011.

———. "Why I Do Not Believe in a Creator God." In *Buffalo Shout, Salmon Cry*. Waterloo, CA: Herald Press, 2013.

———. "The Irrelevance of Euro-Christian Dichotomies for Indigenous Peoples: Beyond Nonviolence to a Vision of Cosmic Balance." In *Peacemaking and the Challenge of Violence in World Religions*. West Sussex, UK: Wiley-Blackwell, 2015.

———. "What Are We Going to Do with White People?" *The New Polis* (December 17, 2019).

Todorov, Tzvetan. *The Conquest of America: The Question of the Other*. New York, NY: Harper & Row, 1984.

United Nations Development Programme Strategic Plan, 2018–2021. Executive Board of the United Nations Development Programme, the United Nations Population Fund and the United Nations Office for Project Services, DP 2017/38, 2017.

United States Commission on Civil Rights. *The Navajo Nation: An American Colony*. Washington, DC: U.S. Government Printing Office, 1975.

United States Department of the Interior, Bureau of Indian Affairs. *Annual Report of the Commissioner of Indian Affairs for the Fiscal Year Ended June 30, 1905*. Washington, DC: Government Printing Office, 1906.

United States Senate. "Report of the Select Committee to Investigate Matters Connected with the Affairs in Indian Territory with Hearings, November 11, 1906–January 9, 1907." *Congressional Serial Set. Issue 5062. Senate Reports (Public) in Four Volumes. Fifty-ninth Congress. Second Session. Report 5013*, Vol. 3. Washington, DC: Government Printing Office, 1907.

Veracini, Lorenzo. *Settler Colonialism: A Theoretical Overview*. London, UK: Palgrave Macmillan, 2010.

Viveiros de Castro, Eduardo. *The Inconstancy of the Indian Soul: The Encounter of Catholics and Cannibals in 16th-Century Brazil*. Chicago, IL: Prickly Paradigm, 2011.
Vizenor, Gerald. "Aesthetics of Survivance." *Survivance: Narratives of Native Presence*. Lincoln, NE: University of Nebraska Press, 2008.
Warren, Dennis Michael. "Indigenous Agricultural Knowledge, Technology and Social Change." In *Sustainable Agriculture in the American Midwest: Lessons from the Past, Prospects for the Future*. Edited by Gregory McIsaac and William R. Edwards. Chicago, IL: University of Illinois Press, 1994.
Watson, Irene. *Aboriginal Peoples, Colonialism and International Law: Raw Law*. New York, NY: Routledge, 2015.
Watson, William E. *Tricolor and Crescent: France and the Islamic World*. Westport, CT: Praeger, 2003.
Watt, W. Montgomery, and Pierre Cachia. *A History of Islamic Spain*. New Brunswick, NJ: Aldine Transaction, 2007 (1965).
Weaver, Jace. *The Red Atlantic: American Indigenes and the Making of the Modern World, 1000–1927*. Chapel Hill, NC: University of North Carolina Press, 2014.
White, Hayden. *Tropics of Discourse: Essays in Cultural Criticism*. Baltimore, MD: Johns Hopkins University Press, 1978.
White Hat, Albert. *Life's Journey: Zuya: Oral Teachings from Rosebud*. Salt Lake City, UT: University of Utah Press, 2012.
Whitehead, Alfred North. "Religion and Science." *The Atlantic* (August 1925). Available online at: https://www.theatlantic.com/magazine/archive/1925/08/religion-and-science/304220/.
Williams, Robert A., Jr. *The American Indian in Western Legal Thought: The Discourses of Conquest*. New York, NY: Oxford University Press, 1990.
Williams, Melissa S., and Stephen Macedo, eds. *Political Exclusion and Domination: NOMOS*. New York, NY: New York University Press, 2005.
Wolf, Eric R. *Europe and the People Without History*. Berkeley, CA: University of California Press, 1982.

Index

Adam (biblical figure), 60, 73, 113
Africa: Bantu, 6; continent, 8–9, 11, 15, 18–19, 21n2, 61, 80–82; northern, 12; people and cultures of, 6–9, 15, 18–19, 61, 80–82, 147; Shona, 6–7; slaves, 61, 80–82, 147–48, 152n8; southern, 6. *See also* Afro-Cubans; Mozambique; Rhodesia, Southern; Zimbabwe
African Americans, x, 49–50, 148, 152n2, 152n6, 152n8
Afro-Cubans, 79–84
Alexander VI, Pope, 120, 125
Alfonso V, King, 119
American Indian Liberation, 25, 34, 52, 88, 117, 120
American Indian Movement (AIM), 1–2, 50, 153n14, 158n40
Americas: continents, 8, 11, 15, 18–19, 31, 55, 59, 71–75, 79–80, 107–8, 115, 118, 121, 124, 128, 139–40, 152n6, 160n53; Latin (*latinoamérica*), 19, 55, 62–63, 71–76, 78–80, 83, 118, 124, 126, 156n31; north, 26, 52, 75, 80, 91, 93, 103, 117, 124, 130–31, 149, 153n9; Turtle Island, as, 55, 58, 67, 91, 106–9, 111, 113–15. *See also* Argentina; Brazil; Canada; Cuba; Guatemala; Mexico; Paraguay; Peru; United States; Uruguay; Venezuela
Andean people, 63
Anishinaabe, 58, 90–91, 93–101, 152n3, 153n14
Apache, 113, 158n40
Argentina, 71–72
Asia: continent, 19; southeast, 48. *See also* China; India
Asian Americans, x
Augustine, St., 12
Australia, 8, 19, 39n2, 110, 115n1, 118, 158n39
Aztecs, 65

Babylon, 104
Bakhtin, Mikhail, 91–92, 94, 100
Baraga, Frederic, 93–95, 100–101
Bhaba, Homi, 8
blanqueamiento, 75, 80–81
blood (soil, lineage), 107, 113–15
boarding schools, 26, 45–46, 53, 63, 77–78, 82, 97, 109, 122–34, 144, 150, 159nn44–47
Bolívar, Simón, 72
Brazil, 63, 126–27
Breath (outer space, spatial), 107, 109, 111, 113–14

175

Index

Britain, 7, 42, 44, 66–68, 105–6, 108, 126, 128, 153n10
buffalo, 7, 107, 110, 144

Calvinism, 16, 133
Canada, 46, 50, 53, 107, 123, 132, 158n39
Carmichael, Stokely, 49, 52
Castro, Fidel, 81, 84–85
Catholicism, 11, 16, 56–57, 70, 93, 119–21, 125, 133, 136, 139–40, 155nn26–27, 158n41. *See also* Franciscans; Jesuits
Chau, John, 127
Cherokee, 1, 51–52, 57, 77, 107, 113, 134, 136
China, 8
Cheyenne, 77
Christian: baptism, 64, 66, 69, 97, 117, 127; Bible, 5–6, 8–20, 21n6, 22n11, 63–64, 88, 117–18, 121–23, 125–28, 130–33, 135, 137–38, 142, 144–47, 151n2, 156n31; canon law, 16; colonizing, 3, 8–10, 14, 29–30, 33, 55, 58, 60–66, 71, 98, 103–5, 119–20, 123, 125, 134, 137–38, 141, 146–50, 153n10, 154n17, 156n31; conversion to, 19, 21, 29–30, 50, 56, 61–65, 69–70, 81, 93, 97–98, 105–7, 109, 111, 118, 127–28, 130, 139–50, 155–56, 159n45; creation story, 18, 27, 29, 60, 73, 88, 92, 113; christenDOMination, 56, 59–61, 142, 157; dominion, 28–30, 32, 56, 59, 91–92, 115, 132; heaven, 14, 16, 61, 81, 90, 103, 114, 123, 138; hell, 20, 81, 107, 114, 127, 150; hierarchy, 27–29, 32, 38, 58–60, 63, 66, 70, 89, 91–101, 111, 138, 140–42, 147–48, 155n26, 156n30; missionaries, 5, 7–8, 14–15, 19–21, 25–27, 30, 49–50, 52, 65–67, 69, 71, 87–90, 93–94, 97, 100–101, 106–9, 111, 114, 118, 121–27, 131–47, 154n21, 155nn26–28, 156n30, 156n32, 158n42,
159n48, 159nn50–51; prayer, 11, 27, 91–97, 100–101, 107, 122–23, 129–30, 154n22, 156n30; spirit/soul, 29, 73, 78, 104, 106, 123, 148; worldview, 8, 25–28, 59, 88, 91–93, 122, 138–43, 148–49, 156n30. *See also* Calvinism; Catholicism; God, Christian; gospel; Jesus Christ; Lutheranism; Protestantism
Christian Church: Baptist, 136; Catholic, 11, 16, 56–57, 70, 72, 93, 119–21, 125, 133, 136, 139–40, 155nn26–27, 158n41; colonial Spain, 56, 72; Episcopal, 60, 129, 133, 136, 139–41, 154nn21–22, 155n27, 156n32, 157nn33–34, 158n41; evangelical, 60, 64, 106, 124, 148, 151, 157n34; Lutheran, 16, 87, 130, 134–36, 141–42, 148, 152n3, 153n14, 157nn34–37, 158n40, 160n55; Methodist, 133, 153n15; Pope, 59, 92, 106, 119–20, 125; Presbyterian, 136, 153n14; Puritanism, 67–69, 146, 159n50; reservation, 139–40, 155n27, 158n41; schools, 53, 159; U.S., in, 2, 20, 25–26, 93, 95, 98, 120, 123, 129, 134, 136–41, 143–44, 146–47, 159, 151n2, 153nn14–15, 155nn26–27, 157nn35–37, 158nn40–41, 159n44
Churchill, Winston, 42, 108
Columbus, Christopher (Cristóbal Colón), 18, 50, 73, 124
Columbus Day, 2, 50, 52, 158n40
conquistadores, 56, 73, 81, 84–85
Constantine, Emperor, 13
Coolidge, Calvin, 128, 130
Cree, 53
Cuba, 72, 79–85

Dakota, 152n3, 153n14
Dawes General Allotment Act, 147, 149, 159n52, 160n53
de Castro, Viveiros, 62–63, 69
de las Casas, Bartolomé, 57, 69, 74

Delaware Indian. *See* Lenape
Deloria, Philip, 67, 128, 130
Deloria, Vine, 31, 38, 50, 87–88, 130–31
de San Martin, José, 72
de Smet, Pierre-Jean, 124
Diné, 113, 154n21
Doctrine of Discovery, 56, 59, 66, 69–70, 120, 153n9
dualism, 38, 65, 89, 91, 107, 111, 113–14

Eliot, John, 67, 146–47, 156n28, 159n50
encomienda, 60–61
environmental issues, 29, 88, 95, 99, 107
ethics and morality, 5, 10–11, 19–20, 32, 36, 43, 47–48, 65, 73, 76, 79, 99
Europe: colonization, 3, 6, 9, 23, 26–30, 32–33, 36–37, 56, 58, 62, 64, 66, 69–71, 73, 77, 80, 83, 97–98, 103–7, 118, 123, 125, 131, 134, 137, 142, 144–49, 152nn6–7, 153n10, 154n17, 156n28, 156n31, 159n45; continent, 8, 13, 16, 61, 93, 103–8, 128, 132–33; law, rule of, 8, 11, 16–21, 22n16, 43–44, 56–57, 59, 66, 132, 142, 149, 153; people of, ix, 2–3, 5–8, 14–16, 18–21, 25–27, 30–31, 33, 43, 47, 49–50, 55–59, 64–67, 70–71, 73, 78–81, 83–85, 87–90, 93–94, 97–98, 104–8, 100–101, 106–9, 111, 113–14, 117–18, 121–27, 131–50, 151n2, 154n18, 155nn26–28, 156nn30–32, 157n36, 158n42, 159nn50–52; worldview, x, 6, 12, 19, 21n1, 25–35, 37–39, 41, 49–50, 55–64, 66–92, 97–100, 103–4, 106–10, 117–18, 124–25, 131, 134, 136–51, 152n6, 152n8, 153n9, 154n18, 155nn25–26, 156n28, 156nn30–31, 157nn37–38, 159n49, 160n54. *See also* Britain; France; Germany; Poland; Portugal; Scandinavia; Spain
euro forming, 69, 146, 159n49

evolution: biological, 18, 26, 34, 107; cultural, 21, 29, 64, 74–75, 77, 79, 81, 126, 159n49

Foucault, Michel, 13, 22n10
Four Winds American Indian Council (4Winds), 2, 136–43, 148, 154n21, 157nn34–36, 158n40, 160n55
France, 46, 69, 78, 105–7
Franciscans, 61, 69, 81

General Allotment Act. *See* Dawes General Allotment Act
genocide: biological, 43, 45; Christian complicity, 26, 30, 53, 63, 67, 71, 83, 93, 118, 120, 128, 143–48; colonial project, part of, 26–27, 37, 51–54, 56, 63, 65, 80, 83, 93, 126, 134, 150; cultural, 30, 43–47, 49–51, 53, 63, 68, 73–74, 82, 89, 93, 119–21, 124, 134, 150; definition of, 42–43, 45–50, 52, 66, 80, 94, 119, 133, 159n46; denial of, 30–33, 43–45, 48–50, 66; Jews, of, 41, 43–44, 47–48; massacres, 1–2, 27, 128–29; physical, 41, 43–44, 47–50, 53, 68, 70, 73, 80, 82, 89, 93, 121, 126, 129, 150; Poles and Slavic, of, 43; Serbs, of, 48–49; studies, 46, 53
Genocide Convention, 45–47, 49
Germany, 44–45, 105
God, Christian, 14–15, 20, 28–29, 56, 59, 63, 66, 88–92, 95, 100, 103–7, 109–12, 114–15, 123, 130, 151, 152n2, 156n30
God is Red, 38, 88, 130
gospel, 5–6, 8–20, 21n6, 22n11, 63–64, 88, 117–18, 121–23, 125–28, 130–33, 135, 137–38, 142, 144–47
Greek language, 42, 104, 108, 136–38, 151n2
Greco-Roman, 12–16, 22n11, 42, 64, 103–5, 108
Greenland, 105, 109
Guatemala, 72, 74–75

Hanblecea, 138, 155n28
Hatuey, 81–82, 84
Hinduism, 108
Hollywood, 47, 110, 152n7
Hopi, 33, 154n21
human identity, 7, 8, 10, 14, 16, 26, 29, 36–37, 51, 67, 73, 78–79, 81, 83–84, 88, 98, 109, 119, 122, 135, 137, 139, 153n9

Iceland, 109
Idealized Cognitive Models (ICM), 55–56, 58–63, 65–66, 69–70
Iliff School of Theology, x, 2, 135–36, 153n15, 154nn18–19
Incas (Inkas), 64–65
India, 8, 19, 108, 127
Indian, American: ceremonies, 26, 34, 52, 87–88, 90–91, 95–96, 110–11, 128, 135–44, 149–50, 154n20, 154n22, 155n26, 155n28, 156n29, 157n35, 158nn40–41, 160n55; conversion to Christianity, 19, 21, 29–30, 50, 56, 61–65, 67, 69–70, 74–75, 81, 93, 97–98, 105–7, 109, 111, 118, 127–28, 130, 133, 139–50, 155–56, 159n45; enslavement of, 19, 26, 56, 61, 66, 119; heathen and devil-worshippers, as, 20, 57, 63–64, 73, 81, 106–7, 120, 122–23, 125, 132, 150, 156n29; identity, 10, 14, 26, 36, 51, 67, 73, 78–79, 88, 98, 106, 109, 122, 135, 139; language(s), 7–8, 12, 18, 37, 39n2, 51, 90–104, 117–28, 130, 134–36, 139–42, 144, 146, 155n27, 156n28, 156n30; poverty, 2, 35–36, 94, 108, 117–18, 131, 144; savage and inhuman, as, 6–7, 17–21, 21n2, 22n17, 27–33, 48, 62–63, 67–68, 71, 73–78, 78, 84, 109–10, 122, 126, 146, 148–50, 152n7; sovereignty, 1, 32, 35–37, 46, 59, 64, 152n8; spirit(s), 7, 27, 31, 38, 99, 106, 110–14, 115, 130; violence toward, 1, 3, 5, 8–9, 11–12, 14–15, 27, 36, 49, 55–56, 61–63, 65–66, 70, 78–79, 88, 104–5, 109, 119–21, 124, 128, 131, 139, 145; worldview, 5, 7–11, 13–19, 25, 34, 56, 58, 60, 77–78, 89–91, 96–97, 99–101, 114, 122–23, 126, 128–31, 135, 137–42, 147–50, 155n24, 156n30, 157n37. *See also* Andean people; Anishinaabe; Apache; Aztecs; Cherokee; Cheyenne; Cree; Dakota; Diné; Hopi; Incas; Iroquois; Lakota; Latin American; Lenape; Maya; Muskogee; Nakota; Nishnaabeg; Osage; Shawnee; Sioux; Taíno; Tupian
Indian Citizenship Act, 128
Indian Reorganization Act, 150, 158n42
individualism, 78, 141, 143–48, 150, 159n45
indigenismo, 80–82, 84
International Criminal Court (ICC), 49
Iroquois, 58, 69, 111, 113, 146
Islam, 105, 107
Israel, 47, 53

Jackson, Andrew, 107
Jackson, Robert H., 44–45
Jesuits, 62–63, 69, 107, 138, 155n26
Jesus Christ, 12–15, 60–61, 63, 88, 95, 106, 110, 112, 117–18, 120, 123, 127–28, 131, 137–42, 144–47, 150–51, 151n2
Johnson v. M'Intosh, 132–33, 137, 145, 151n1, 153n9, 160n59
Judaism, 14, 41, 43, 47–48, 104, 113, 123
just war, 56–57, 68

King, Martin Luther, 50
Ku Klux Klan (KKK), 134, 152n3

Lake Mohonk conferences, 77–78, 82, 145–47, 149, 156n31, 159n45, 159n47, 159n52

Lakota, 1, 26, 53, 113–14, 128–30, 135, 138–40, 153n16, 154n19, 155nn26–27, 158n40
land: abuse of, 27, 68; allotment of, 1, 78, 147, 149, 159n52, 160n53; colonization and/or Christianization through, 16, 25, 30, 51, 61, 66, 69, 77, 91, 98, 107, 117, 146–49, 158n38; commodification of, 30, 36, 70, 76, 78, 126, 146–47; promised to others, 59, 68, 123; relationship to Indians, 37, 58, 68–69, 73, 75–76, 78, 88, 91, 117, 129, 147–49, 160n55; removal of inhabitants, 42, 66, 120, 126–27, 149; returning of, 141–42, 157nn35–37, 158n40, 160n55; rights to/of, 1, 17, 30, 68, 74, 146–49; spatiality of, 27–28, 31–32, 38, 58, 88, 91, 94, 114, 140, 142; stolen, 1, 32, 36, 42–43, 59, 66, 69–70, 76, 78, 84, 104, 106–7, 117–19, 126, 131, 133–34, 144, 147–49, 158n38
Latin American Indians, 63–65, 72–76, 78–85
Latin language, 42, 59, 93, 104, 108, 119
Latinx, ix, x, 64
Lemkin, Raphaël, 41–46, 50–51, 53, 119–20
Lenape, 50, 55, 67, 117, 122, 153n9
Leon, Luis D., x, 55, 65, 70
Levinas, Emmanuel, 11
l'homme sauvage, 67, 73–78, 84
Liberation Theology, 72, 117–18
Linnaeus, Carl, 18, 23n17
Longsword, William, 106, 111–12
Luther, Martin, 16, 143
Lutheranism, 16, 87, 130, 134–36, 141–43, 148, 152n3, 153n14, 157nn34–35, 157n37, 158n40, 160n55

machismo, 81–82
Malcolm X, 49

Manifest Destiny, 31, 66, 107
Mann, Barbara Alice, 28, 31, 34, 38, 39n1, 55, 58, 65, 69–70, 155n23, 159n49
Marshall, John, 133–34, 137, 145, 149, 153n9, 155n23
Martí, José, 71–85
Marx, Karl, 22n10, 23n20, 31
Maxentius, Emperor, 13
Maya, 54
mestizo, 61, 79–81
Mexico, 54, 71, 74
Miles, Nelson, 77
Missionary Conquest, ix, 25, 49–50, 52, 67, 71, 88, 131, 137, 143, 145, 154n19, 156n28, 159n48, 159n51
Mozambique, 6
Muskogee, 54

Nakota, 50
Native American Theological Association (NATA), 136, 154n18, 154n20
natural law, 16, 36, 56–57
nazi, 41–45, 47–48
Nehiyaw. *See* Cree
Newcomb, Steven, 55, 58–60, 66, 68–70, 105, 153n9, 157n37
New Zealand, 118, 158n39
Nicholas V, Pope, 119
Nishnaabeg, 58, 133, 136
noble savage. *See l'homme sauvage*
Norse. *See* Odinism
Nuremberg trials, 44–45, 49

Obama, Barack, 32
Oceania, 118
Odawa. *See* Anishinaabe
Odin. *See* Odinism
Odinism, 105–15
Odyssey, 32
Oglala. *See* Lakota
Ojibwe. *See* Anishinaabe
oral history, 64, 121

Osage, 1–3, 26, 30, 38, 42, 55, 71, 117, 135–36, 144, 153nn12–13, 153n16, 154n19, 155n28, 156n30
Osage Allotment Act of 1906, 1
Osage Reservation, 1, 135–36, 144, 153n16
Ottoman Empire, 105, 108

Paraguay, 61, 72, 126
Paul, the apostle, 16, 123
Peace of Westphalia, 37
Persia, 104
Peru, 63–64, 109
Pine Ridge Lakota Reservation, 1–2, 128, 135, 155n27
pipe, 138, 144, 155n26
Pocahontas, 67
Poland, 41, 43
Portugal, 6–7, 60, 119
Potowattamie. *See* Anishinaabe
Pratt, Richard Henry, 82
Protestantism, 66–69, 70, 121, 129, 141, 146, 153nn14–15, 154n18, 157n34, 157nn35–37, 158n40, 159n50

Quechua, 60–61

Red Cloud Mission, 138, 155n26
Requerimiento, 56–57, 70, 70n1
reservation system, 1–2, 74, 76, 78, 94, 128, 135–36, 139, 140, 144, 149–50, 152n3, 153n16, 154n20, 155n27, 156n16, 158n41
Rhodesia, Southern, 7
Rollo, 106, 111–12
Roman Empire, 12–14, 16, 22n11, 48–49, 64, 104–6
Rosebud Lakota Reservation, 135, 140, 153n16, 154n20
Rousseau, Jacques, 73–74

Sand Creek, 27
Sartre, Jean-Paul, 51, 53
Scalia, Antonin, 41, 46, 49, 53
Scandinavia, 105–15, 135

science, 23n17, 26–33, 38, 43, 60, 64, 72
Sen, Amartya, 108
Seneca. *See* Iroquois
Serra, Junípero, 124
Shawnee, 55, 113, 117, 158n40
Sicangu Reservation, 153n16
Sioux, 58, 128–30
slavery, 25–26, 37, 56, 61, 66, 80–82, 107, 119, 147, 152n8
Spain, 56–57, 60–65, 70n1, 71–76, 78–85, 105, 107, 118
Spider Woman, 33, 35
Spirit and Resistance, 36, 52
spirit(s): animal, 7; Christian, 29; earth, 38, 112, 115; human, 26–27, 84, 110, 114; Indian, 27, 31, 38, 99, 106, 110–14, 115, 130; sky, 38, 115

Taíno, 73, 80–81, 83–84
Tammenend, King, 68
Thomas, Robert, 51–52
Thor, 110, 112
Tinker, George E. (Tink), ix, 1–3, 25–38, 39n1, 41, 49–55, 58–60, 66–67, 69–71, 73–74, 87–90, 93, 100, 107, 117–18, 120, 123–24, 127, 130–33, 135, 139, 145, 146n19, 154n47
Tinker, Sylvester, 3, 135, 153n11
Tupian, 63

United Nations (UN), 30, 43–45, 49, 159n46
United States: Central Intelligence Agency (CIA), 127; churches, 2, 20, 25–26, 93, 95, 98, 120, 123, 129, 134, 136–41, 143–44, 146–47, 151n2, 153nn14–15, 155nn26–27, 157nn35–37, 158nn40–41, 159n44; citizenship, 68, 78, 109, 128, 130, 146, 152n8; Civil War, 77; colonies, as, 66–68; Denver, 2, 52, 136, 140–41, 154n20, 157n37, 158n40, 160n54; empire, as, 71, 81–82, 84, 127; Florida, 107; Illinois,

110; Kansas, 144; Massachusetts, 68, 159n50; Michigan, x, 93–94; Minnesota, 93–94, 134, 152n3; Mississippi River, 109, 114; New England, 66–70, 146–47, 159n50; New York, 72, 76, 145, 152n7; Ohio, 110, 114; Oklahoma, 1, 136, 144; settler state, as, 2, 25–27, 30, 32–33, 36, 38, 47, 49–50, 52–54, 59, 67, 76–77, 108, 129–32, 135–36, 146, 158n39; South, the, 68; South Dakota, 129–30, 138, 152; Supreme Court, 41, 44, 132, 149; Virginia, 67; Washington, D.C., 158; Washington State, 127; Wisconsin, 93–94; World War II, in, 41, 44–45
Uruguay, 72

Vasconcelos, José, 79
Velázquez, Diego, 81

Venezuela, 126
Victoria, Francisco, 57
Viking. *See* Odinism

wanagi world, 140, 142, 150–51, 155n28, 156n30
wazhazhe, 55, 143, 153n16
Whipple, Henry Benjamin, 124, 145, 149n48
White Earth Reservation, 152n3
White Hat, Albert, 139, 155n27, 156n29
Whitehead, Alfred North, 26
William the Conqueror, 106
World Court, 49
Wounded Knee, 1–2, 128–29

Yugoslavia, 48–49

Zimbabwe, 6–7

About the Contributors

Loring Abeyta is John Wesley Iliff Senior Adjunct of Religion and Society at the Iliff School of Theology. A Templeton course award winner, she has taught graduate courses in security and environment, U.S. foreign policy, and critical race theory. She holds degrees in anthropology, theology, international relations, and elementary education. Her current research interests examine the connections of worldview differences and sustainability.

Edward P. Antonio is chief diversity officer and professor of humanities at Concordia College Moorhead in Minnesota. Originally from Zimbabwe, his areas of research include European continental philosophy, systematic and philosophical theology, conflict studies, postcolonial theory, social theory, and African studies. He has published numerous articles and book chapters.

Ward Churchill is an activist/scholar who served for over thirty years on the leadership council of the Colorado Chapter of the American Indian Movement. A former professor of American Indian studies and chair of the Department of Ethnic Studies at the University of Colorado, he has published more than twenty books and one hundred articles on American Indian history and the suppression of political dissent in the United States.

Mark D. Freeland is assistant professor of American Indian studies at South Dakota State University and the coordinator of the American Indian studies program. He is a citizen of the Bahweting Anishinaabe Nation (Sault Ste. Marie Tribe of Chippewa Indians). He is a father of five children, husband, uncle, and relative to many.

About the Contributors

Roger K. Green is a senior lecturer in the Department of English at Metropolitan State University of Denver.

Barbara Alice Mann is professor of humanities in the Jesup Scott Honors College of the University of Toledo, in Toledo, Ohio. She has published more than four hundred articles and chapters, along with fifteen books, the latest two of which are *President by Massacre: Indian-Killing for Political Gain* (2019) and *Spirits of Blood, Spirits of Breath: The Twinned Cosmos of Indigenous America* (2016). Dr. Mann regularly speaks at conferences, nationally and internationally. An Ohio Bear Clan Seneca, community recognition, she lives in her Ohio homeland.

Steven T. Newcomb (Shawnee, Lenape) is the author of *Pagans in the Promised Land: Decoding the Doctrine of Christian Discovery* (Fulcrum, 2008), and co-producer of a documentary movie *The Doctrine of Discovery: Unmasking the Domination Code*, directed by Sheldon Wolfchild (Dakota), which is based on *Pagans*. Newcomb is one of the world's foremost authorities regarding the patterns of domination and dehumanization in the Vatican papal bulls of the fifteenth century and their connection to U.S. federal Indian law and policy.

Natsu Taylor Saito is a distinguished university professor and professor of law at Georgia State University's College of Law in Atlanta, Georgia, where she teaches courses on international human rights, race, and Indigenous rights. She has published several dozen law review articles and three books, most recently *Settler Colonialism, Race, and the Law: Why Structural Racism Persists* (2020).

Miguel A. De La Torre is professor of social ethics and Latinx studies at the Iliff School of Theology in Denver. He has published over forty books (five of which won national awards). A Fulbright scholar, he served as the 2012 president of the *Society of Christian Ethics* and was the co-founder/first executive director of the *Society of Race, Ethnicity, and Religion*.

www.ingramcontent.com/pod-product-compliance
Lightning Source LLC
Chambersburg PA
CBHW050907300426
44111CB00010B/1411